The Method R Guide to
MASTERING ORACLE TRACE DATA

The Method R Guide to
MASTERING ORACLE TRACE DATA

Cary Millsap

Method R Corporation · Southlake, Texas USA

Cary Millsap has been a member of the Oracle community since 1989. He is the founder and president of Method R Corporation. He is widely known in the Oracle community as a speaker, educator, consultant, and writer. He is an Oracle ACE Director and a Founding Partner of the Oak Table Network. He wrote *Optimizing Oracle Performance* with Jeff Holt (for which they were named *Oracle Magazine Authors of the Year* in 2004), he is a co-author of *Oracle Insights: Tales of the Oak Table*, and he is published in *Communications of the ACM* and *ACM Queue*. Cary is also an architect of the Method R software tools that help professionals around the world manage Oracle performance. He blogs at *carymillsap.blogspot.com* and tweets at *@CaryMillsap*.

Method R Corporation, Southlake, Texas 76092-9017
http://method-r.com
© 2011 by Cary Millsap
All rights reserved.

Revised 11 September 2013.

ISBN-13: 978-1491267134
ISBN-10: 1491267135

This book was prepared with the following software versions:

Method R Profiler version 5.2.8
Method R Tools version 3.0.2

Method R, Method R Profiler, Method R Tools, Method R Trace, and their respective logos are trademarks of Method R Corporation.

Oracle and Java are registered trademarks of Oracle and/or its affiliates. Other names may be trademarks of their respective owners. Method R Corporation is independent of Oracle Corporation.

The author has made his best efforts to prepare this material to be accurate and complete. The content is based upon final release software whenever possible; however portions of the material may be based upon pre-release versions supplied by software manufacturers. Method R Corporation makes no representation or warranties of any kind about the completeness or accuracy of the contents herein and accept no liability of any kind including but not limited to performance, merchantability, fitness for any particular purpose, or any losses or damages of any kind caused or alleged to be caused directly or indirectly from this material.

Contents

Preface   i

Acknowledgments   iii

Method R Corporation   v
Courses   v
Software   vi
Consulting   vi

1 Thinking Clearly about Performance   1
An Axiomatic Approach   1
What is Performance?   2
Response Time vs. Throughput   3
Percentile Specifications   4
Problem Diagnosis   6
The Sequence Diagram   7
The Profile   9
The Bottleneck   10
Amdahl's Law   11
Skew   13
Minimizing Risk   14
Efficiency   14
Load   15
Deterministic and Random Arrivals   16
Queueing Delay   16
Queueing Theory   17
Coherency Delay   18
Managing Load   19
Capacity Planning   21
Parallelism   21
Performance Testing   23
Measuring   24
Performance is a Feature   24

2 Making Friends with the Oracle Database   27
Making Friends Begins with a Common Language   27
Where Software Speed Comes In   28
Feedback   29
Interpreting Your Trace File   29
Trace File Guided Tour   30
Optimizing the Query Program   32
Optimizing Begins with Measuring   35
On Specification Legitimacy   36

Trace File Guided Tour #2   36
Optimizing the Insert Program   38
Measuring is Vital   41
Summary   42
Trace File: Slow Query   43
Trace File: Improved Query   44
Trace File: Slow Insert   44
Trace File: Improved Insert   45

3 Oracle Extended SQL Trace   47

Performance and Tracing   47
Why You Should Trace   47
What Happens When You Trace   48
Controlling the Trace   49
Session Tracing   49
End-to-End Tracing   51
End-to-End Prerequisites   52
Finding Your Trace File   53
Performance Intrusion   53
Tracing in Multiplexed Architectures   54
Tracing While You Develop   55
Trace File Guided Tour   56
Trace File Alphabet   58
Trace File Alphabet: Database Calls   58
Trace File Alphabet: System Calls   59
Trace File Flow   60
Trace File Arithmetic: Part 1   60
Trace File Arithmetic: Part 2   61
Trace File Arithmetic: Part 3   62
Tracing Traps   62
Commercial Trace File Tools   63
Trace File: Hello World   63

4 Oracle Database Timed Event Reference   67

Where to Begin   67
Responding to Commonly Occurring Timed Events   67
Oracle Timed Event Instrumentation   69
Tracing Oracle Kernel System Calls   70
Some Tricks   73
Oracle Timed Event Example   73
SQL*Net message from client   74
The Bug with SQL*Net message to client   75

5 Cases in Oracle Trace Data Analysis   77

Importance of Careful Time Scoping   77
Java-Based Report   84
Order Entry Batch Job   89
Payroll Batch Job   94
Purchasing Batch Job   96
Book Order, with Connection Pooling   101
Oracle Exadata   105

Reference Tables   109
Units of Duration   109
Performance Instrumentation   109

Glossary   111

Bibliography   115

Index   117

Preface

There are many options these days for measuring and monitoring Oracle Database application performance. This book is about the first one that ever made sense to me, and it's the one that endures in my mind to this day as the best foundation there is for understanding Oracle performance: the Oracle extended SQL trace feature.

In 1999, Jeff Holt and I embarked upon creating a method with a single starting point, so that no matter what your performance problem might be, you would always be able to solve it using a single, step-by-step method, with no need for guessing anywhere along the way. We studied many different ways of doing it. We embarked upon two projects in parallel: one to use Oracle fixed views (the ones whose names begin with v$ and x$), and one to use Oracle extended SQL trace data. I chose the fixed view approach, because I knew that one was going to win, and I was the boss.

I was wrong. The limitations of using the fixed views were so numerous and so profound that after about a half a year's worth of dedicated effort, I abandoned the project and gave over to the side of the trace data. Trace files have two huge advantages:

- They are far easier to understand than the fixed views. Fixed views seem simple at first, but their omissions and inconsistencies soon make understanding what's in the fixed views themselves more difficult than solving the problem you're trying to diagnose. Trace files, on the other hand, look complicated at first, but their completeness and consistency pays off in the end. Trace files simply show the sequence of database calls and system calls that made up your response time; that's it. Everything the Oracle Database does is laid out in the order that your calls have finished, complete with timing data. Once you know how to read a trace file, and especially *to process them with tools*, you're in a whole new world.

- They are easier to make available to the most important people in the performance formula: the developers who write the applications. Granting access upon the right Oracle fixed views to application developers is complicated, but it's nowhere near as complicated as trying to explain to a developer why a column called *seconds_in_wait* really isn't the number of seconds that a syscall has been waiting, that the value is updated every three seconds by the LGWR process regardless of whether the call being measured is complete, and ...oh, never mind. Developers need to be thinking about developing software, not worrying about all the details of how the Oracle Database management system works, and the idiosyncrasies of how they're measured. Handing a trace file to a developer—or better yet, a *profile*, literally an invoice of response time—and saying, "Here's what is holding our code back today,..." It's a far better way to work.

This is not a book about discarding your Oracle fixed views or your monitoring tools that poll them. It's merely a book about how to look at Oracle performance another way, a way that has worked extraordinarily well for many of us. It's about new ways of thinking about performance using new tools for understanding aspects of your applications that you've never understood before.

Thank you for your interest in this book. I hope you enjoy the experience.

Cary Millsap
November 2011

Acknowledgments

Every day when I go home, I'm grateful for the extraordinary people who live with me. The bulk of what I accomplish as a human being is through the love and grace of my wife and children: Mindy, Alexander, Nikolas, and Cathryne.

Every day I go to work, I'm grateful for the extraordinary people who surround me. The bulk of what I accomplish as a professional is through the leverage granted to me by having access to people at Method R Corporation like Jeff Holt, Ron Crisco, Ken Ferlita, Harold Palacio, and Karen Morton. As with the *Optimizing Oracle Performance* project with O'Reilly, Jeff Holt has been an especially significant contributor. Jeff's influence on my work is tremendously important to me.

That's just the beginning. The customers and colleagues we work with, who push us forward, are vital to our work. Some of the people who have been especially helpful in preparing this book are: Alex Gorbachev, Andrew Zitelli, Andy Rivenes, Robyn Sands, Tanel Põder, James Morle, Tom Kyte, Jonathan Lewis, Mark Farnham, Mogens Nørgaard, Dominic Delmolino, Jared Still, Alain Caron, Dave Ensor, Anjo Kolk, Chris Antognini, Michael Thomas, Jimmy Harkey, Baron Schwartz, Neil Gunther, Mark Sweeney, Laura Nogaj, and the members of the Oak Table Network.

Method R Corporation

Companies hire Method R Corporation to make their high-speed software applications run faster and more efficiently. We can teach your application developers and database administrators how to make faster software, or we can write it for you. We make software tools that help you understand exactly how your Oracle-based applications are spending your time. Method R Corporation was founded in 2008 by Cary Millsap.

Courses

Method R Corporation offers courses taught by instructors including Cary Millsap, Ron Crisco, and C. J. Date. Subject matter includes general principles of software performance, diagnosing and fixing Oracle application performance problems, Oracle SQL and PL/SQL programming, and relational database design.

The book you are holding is the official course book of the "Mastering Oracle Trace Data" course designed and taught by Cary Millsap. In class, students learn how to use Method R Trace and Method R Tools software, included with each enrollment. Students may also include Method R Profiler at a discounted price. For information about this course and others, visit *method-r.com*.

The *Mastering Oracle Trace Data* class of London 2011-09-08.

Method R Corporation

SOFTWARE

The Method R software tools featured in this book are available for purchase at the *method-r.com* online store:

Method R Trace is our zero-click trace file collector for users of the Oracle SQL Developer integrated development environment.

Method R Tools is a flexible and versatile utility suite that includes a trace file data mining tool, utilities for adjusting trace files, and more.

Method R Profiler shows exactly how your programs spend your time, using color and structure to guide your analysis.

CONSULTING

Method R Corporation consultants help businesses of all sizes optimize systems that use Oracle software. Their capabilities include:

- Helping you optimize your software products
- Designing and writing high-performance applications that scale to outrageous user volumes
- Assessing performance of applications before go-live
- Helping developers write better code through education and coaching
- Fixing performance problems on production systems
- Advising department leaders on policies, procedures, or procurement decisions

For more information about Method R consulting services, visit *method-r.com*.

1 Thinking Clearly about Performance

Creating "high performance" as an attribute of complex software is extremely difficult business for developers, technology administrators, architects, system analysts, and project managers. However, by understanding some fundamental principles, performance problem solving and prevention can be made far simpler and more reliable. This chapter describes those principles, linking them together in a coherent journey covering the goals, the terms, the tools, and the decisions that you need to maximize your application's chance of having a long, productive, high-performance life. Examples in this chapter touch upon Oracle experiences, but the scope of the chapter is not restricted to Oracle products.

An Axiomatic Approach

When I joined Oracle Corporation in 1989, performance—what everyone called "Oracle tuning"—was difficult. Only a few people claimed they could do it very well, and those people commanded nice, high consulting rates. When circumstances thrust me into the "Oracle tuning" arena, I was quite unprepared. Recently, I've been introduced into the world of "MySQL tuning," and the situation seems very similar to what I saw in Oracle over twenty years ago.

It reminds me a lot of how difficult I would have told you that beginning algebra was, if you had asked me when I was about 13 years old. At that age, I had to appeal heavily to my "mathematical instincts" to solve equations like $3x + 4 = 13$. The problem with needing to appeal to one's mathematical instincts is this: what if you don't *have* mathematical instincts? Does that mean that mathematics will be forever beyond your reach?

I can remember looking at a problem like "$3x + 4 = 13$; find x" and stumbling upon the answer $x = 3$ using trial and error. But what about a tougher problem like "$7/x - 6 = 20$; find x"? Then what?

The trial-and-error method of feeling my way through algebra problems worked—albeit sometimes slowly and uncomfortably—for easy equations, but it didn't scale as the problems got tougher. My problem was that I wasn't thinking clearly enough yet about algebra. I didn't understand yet how algebra worked and *why* it worked that way. My introduction at age fifteen to Mr. James R. Harkey put me on the road to solving that problem.

Mr. Harkey taught us what he called an *axiomatic approach* to solving algebra problems. He showed us a set of steps that worked every time (and he gave us plenty of homework to practice on).[1] In addition to working every time, by executing those steps, he made us *document* our thinking as we worked. Not only were we thinking clearly, using a reliable and repeatable sequence of steps, we were *proving* to anyone who read our work that we were thinking clearly. As a parent now who checks his children's homework several times

---

[1] Cary Millsap, "An axiomatic approach to algebra and other aspects of life" at *http://carymillsap.blogspot.com/2011/01/axiomatic-approach-to-algebra-and-other.html*.

Chapter 1. Thinking Clearly about Performance

a week, I wish more teachers taught better show-your-work habits. It's easier to debug my kids' thinking when their debug logging is switched on.

1.	$\frac{7}{x} - 6 = 20$	Given
2.	$\left(\frac{7}{x} - 6\right) + 6 = (20) + 6$	Addition property of equality
3.	$\frac{7}{x} + (-6 + 6) = 26$	Associative property of addition
4.	$\frac{7}{x} + (0) = 26$	Additive inverse property
5.	$\frac{7}{x} = 26$	Additive identity element
6.	$\left(\frac{7}{x}\right)x = 26x$	Multiplication property of equality
7.	$7\left(\frac{x}{x}\right) = 26x$	Associative property of multiplication
8.	$7(1) = 26x$	Multiplicative inverse property
9.	$7 = 26x$	Multiplicative identity element
10.	$\frac{7}{26} = \frac{26x}{26}$	Division property of equality
11.	$\frac{7}{26} = \frac{26}{26}x$	Associative property of multiplication
12.	$\frac{7}{26} = (1)x$	Multiplicative inverse property
13.	$\frac{7}{26} = x$	Multiplicative identity element
14.	$x = \frac{7}{26}$	Symmetrical property of equality

> This is what homework and tests for Mr. Harkey looked like. He made us show each step, because Mr. Harkey cared more about the code path in our heads than what our final answer was. In essence, he required us to execute our work with debug logging switched on so that he could help us debug our thinking.

This was Mr. Harkey's axiomatic approach to algebra, geometry, trigonometry, and calculus: one small, logical, provable, easy-to-audit step at a time. Working this way for a few weeks earned me my first-ever feeling of confidence toward mathematics.

Naturally, I didn't realize it at the time, but of course *proving* was a skill that would be vital for my success in the world after school. In life, I've found that, of course, knowing things matters. But proving those things—to other people—matters more. Without good proving skills, it's difficult to be a good consultant, a good leader, or even a good employee.

My goal since the mid-1990s has been to create a similarly rigorous approach to Oracle performance optimization. Lately, I have expanded the scope of that goal beyond Oracle, to creation of an axiomatic approach to computer software performance optimization. My aim is to help you think clearly about how to optimize the performance of your computer software; ...to help you really understand it.

What is Performance?

If you google for the word *performance*, you get over a half a billion hits on concepts ranging from bicycle racing to the dreaded employee review process that many companies these days are learning to avoid. When I googled for *performance*, most of the top hits related to the subject of this chapter: the time it takes for computer software to perform whatever task you ask it to do.

And that's a great place to begin: the task. A **task** is a business-oriented unit of work. Tasks can nest: "Print Invoices" is a task; "Print One Invoice"—a sub-task—is also a task. When a computer user talks about performance he usually means the time it takes for the system to execute some task. An individual execution of a task can result in a personal *experience* with that task. So, while a *task* corresponds to lines of code in your application and has a name like "Book Order," an *experience* corresponds to a single execution of a task. Each task implemented in a software application will typically be executed many times, resulting in many experiences. For example, the code to implement a "Book Order" task might be executed (and experienced) a million times per month.

Response time is the duration of an experience. For example, *google.com* reported that my search for the word *performance* had a response time of 0.24 seconds. The Google web page rendered that measurement right in my browser. This is evidence that Google values my perception of Google application performance. **Throughput** is the count of experiences that complete within a specified time interval. For example, "300 'Book Order' clicks per second" is an expression of *throughput* for the "Book Order" task.

RESPONSE TIME VS. THROUGHPUT

Average throughput and average response time have a generally reciprocal type of relationship, but not exactly. The real relationship is more complex.

> *Example:* Imagine that you have measured your throughput at 10 executions per second for some benchmark. What, then, is your users' average response time? Is your average response time 1/10 = .1 seconds per execution?
>
> Imagine that your system processing this throughput had 10 parallel, independent, homogeneous service channels inside it (that is, it's a system with 10 independent, equally competent service providers inside it, each awaiting your request for service). Imagine further that each service channel is capable of processing a request for service in exactly 1 second. Then if 10 requests for service arrive simultaneously into the system, exactly 1 second later, 10 task executions will complete, each with a response time of exactly 1 second.

The relationship between average response time R and average throughput X is

$$R = \frac{N}{X} - Z,$$

where Z is the average duration between request arrivals into the system (called **think time**), and N is the number of service channels in the hardware configuration.[2]

Likewise, if you know your average response time R for a given task in your unit testing environment, you know how many service channels N you have, and you know your average think time Z, then you can predict your average throughput X as

$$X = \frac{N}{R + Z}.$$

Capacity planners use formulas like these to determine average throughput and response times,[3] but from models like these, you will not learn operational details about individual user experiences. You might learn from a model that your average "Book Order" throughput is 500 orders per second, but you won't learn that your actual "Book Order" throughput was only 117 orders per second between 2:00 P.M. and 3:00 P.M. last Wednesday. You might learn from a model that your average response time is .742 seconds per order, but you won't learn that Nancy had "Book Order" response times as high as 42.895 seconds from Golden, Colorado last Friday morning around 10:00 A.M. Models and formulas can inform you about average behavior, but many times understanding average behavior isn't enough. To manage performance well, you need to know actual throughput behavior and

---

[2] Raj Jain, *The Art of Computer Systems Performance Analysis*, New York: John Wiley, 563.

[3] See, for example, the works of Jain, Menascé, Smith & Williams, and Gunther.

Chapter 1. Thinking Clearly about Performance

actual response time behavior, *as actual people experience them*. To know them both, you have to measure them both.

So, which is more important: response time, or throughput? In general, group managers care more about throughput than solo contributors do. For example, a sales clerk cares whether the response time of an afternoon report execution will require him to stay late after work, whereas the sales department manager cares additionally about whether the system can process all the orders that all her clerks will need to book today.

In many circumstances, both response time and throughput are vital constraints to which you need to manage. For example, a system owner may have a business requirement that response time must be 1.0 seconds or less for a given task in 99% or more of executions (experiences), and the system must support a sustained throughput of 1,000 executions of the task within any arbitrary 10-minute interval.

PERCENTILE SPECIFICATIONS

In the prior section, I used the phrase "in 99% or more of executions" to qualify a response time expectation. Many people are more accustomed to statements like, "average response time must be *r* seconds or less." The percentile way of stating requirements maps better to the human experience.

> ***Example:*** Imagine that your response time tolerance is 1 second for some task that you execute on your computer every day. Further imagine that the lists of numbers shown below represent the measured response times of ten typical executions of that task. The average response time for each list is 1.000 seconds. Which one do you think you'd like better?

	List A	List B
1	.924	.796
2	.928	.798
3	.954	.802
4	.957	.823
5	.961	.919
6	.965	.977
7	.972	1.076
8	.979	1.216
9	.987	1.273
10	1.373	1.320
$\bar{x}$	1.000	1.000

> The average response time for each of these lists of response times is 1.000 seconds, yet the two lists depict clearly different user experiences.

Although the two lists have the same average response time, the lists represent significantly different experiences. In List A, 90% of response times were 1 second or less. In List B, only 60% of response times were 1 second or less. Stated in the opposite way, List B represents a set of user experiences of which 40% were unsatisfactory, but List A (having the same average response time as List B) represents only a 10% dissatisfaction rate.

In List A, the 90th percentile response time is .987 seconds. In List B, the 90th percentile response time is 1.273 seconds. These statements about percentiles are more informative than merely saying that each list represents an average response time of 1.000 seconds.

Percentile-based response time goals are more compelling requirement specifications because they match what people really care about. Users feel the variance, not the mean.[4]

Users feel the variance, not the mean.

A specification like, "Average response time for 'Book Order' must be less than .5 seconds" is not enough. You need something like, "The 90th percentile response time for 'Book Order' must be less than 1.0 seconds." An "average response time" specification is roughly the same as a 50th percentile specification. You probably need for your percentile to be in at least the 90s and possibly 99, or 99.9, or even more.

A percentile specification like this does a better job of measuring the variance that users feel, but it's still not quite enough.

Example: Continuing the previous example, with your 1-second response time tolerance, compare the familiar List A with the new List C shown here.

	List A	List C
1	.924	.091
2	.928	.109
3	.954	.134
4	.957	.136
5	.961	.159
6	.965	.172
7	.972	.185
8	.979	.191
9	.987	.207
10	1.373	8.616
$\bar{x}$	1.000	1.000

Both lists yield the same success rate with respect to the specification, "90th percentile response time is less than 1 second," yet the two lists depict clearly different user experiences.

Again, these two lists depict identical average response times, and List C depicts a superior 90th percentile response time of .207 seconds (versus .987 seconds in List A). Yet, you might argue that, if users really do feel the variance and not the mean, then List C represents a worse response time experience, because the worst response time (8.616 seconds) is over *six times worse* than the worst response time in List A (1.373 seconds).

Here are depictions of two clearly different experiences, yet a simple 90th percentile specification wasn't enough to describe the distinction. A two-tier specification like the following resolves the problem:

"The 90th percentile response time for 'Book Order' must be less than 1.0 seconds, *and* the 99th percentile response time must be less than 2.0 seconds."

Stated in a way that perhaps more users can relate to:

Weak specification: "'Book Order' average response time must be less than 1.0 seconds."

Better specification: "'Book Order' must respond in less than 1.0 seconds in at least 90% of executions."

---

[4] General Electric Company, "What Is Six Sigma? The roadmap to customer impact" at *http://www.ge.com/sixsigma/SixSigma.pdf*.

Chapter 1. Thinking Clearly about Performance

Best specification: "'Book Order' must respond in less than 1.0 seconds in at least 90% of executions, and in less than 2.0 seconds in at least 99% of executions."

Problem Diagnosis

The barrier to performance improvement is often the lack of a clear and useful problem statement. A good performance problem statement has two parts:

- *Current state*: a quantitative description of the way the system behaves now, expressed in terms of response time or throughput of one or more tasks.

- *Goal state*: a quantitative description of the way you want the system to behave, expressed in the same terms as the current state, and a quantitative description of the investment you're willing to make for the system to behave that way.

Bad problem statements typically match one of the following patterns:

- *Bad*: It doesn't name the task whose execution you're looking to improve. For instance, "Our whole [adjectives redacted] system is so slow we can't use it." This statement provides no ability to focus; it gives you nowhere to begin, and it gives you no quantitative way to measure your progress.[5]

- *Bad*: It presumes the cause of the problem before the cause has been proven. Imagine stating your goal as "to upgrade to a higher-throughput storage device." Now imagine that your project successfully completes the upgrade, but the upgrade doesn't improve the performance of a key task that the business was hoping the upgrade would fix. In this case, the project is successful relative to its stated goal, but the real problem remains, because the real goal was not correctly identified.

- *Bad*: It does use the terms "response time" or "throughput," but only to quantify technical details about tasks instead of the tasks themselves. For instance, don't describe the throughput of disk I/O performance associated with a "Book Order" execution; talk about the throughput of the whole "Book Order" task itself.

- *Bad*: It is expressed indirectly in technical terms of "utilization," "latency," or "miss rate" instead of direct language that describes business results. Once I asked a CIO what his real performance goals were. He said, "I'd like the CPU utilization on my database server not to exceed 80% during our peak business hours." I told him that we could accomplish that goal by replacing his fast, high-end storage subsystems with really old, slow ones.[6] His real goal wasn't reduction of CPU utilization; it was to make his business task executions run faster. He figured that having leftover CPU capacity would ensure his real goal, but it's not necessarily so.

Say your real goal. Sometimes it takes a little work to figure out what your real goal really is. A good problem statement is expressed in non-technical language that *users* of systems use in their everyday work lives.

There's a problem, though, with trying to learn the current and goal states of a system's performance. What you want is something like this:

"Response time of 'Book Order' is more than 20 seconds in many cases. We'll be happy when response time is 1 second or less in at least 95% of executions."

---

[5] Cary Millsap, "My whole system is slow. Now what?" at *http://carymillsap.blogspot.com/2009/12/my-whole-system-is-slow-now-what.html*.

[6] To degrade I/O response times would cause processes to spend more time awaiting the results of read or write calls. When a process awaits a synchronous read or write call, it doesn't use CPU. Each I/O-consuming process would thus spend more time waiting for I/O calls to complete, causing many of its previously used CPU cycles in a given time interval to remain unused (while it waits for I/O). The net effect would be reduced CPU utilization.

That sounds good in theory, but what if your user doesn't have a specific quantitative goal like "1 second or less in at least 95% of executions?" There are two quantities right there (1 and 95); what if your user doesn't know either one of them? Worse yet, what if your user *does* have specific ideas about his expectations, but those expectations are impossible to meet? How would you know what "possible" or "impossible" even is?

Let's work our way up to answering those questions. First, I want to introduce a couple of tools.

The Sequence Diagram

A **sequence diagram** is a type of graph specified in the Unified Modeling Language (UML), used to show the interactions between objects in the sequential order that those interactions occur. The sequence diagram is an exceptionally useful tool for visualizing response time. Here is a standard UML sequence diagram for a simple application system composed of a browser, an application server, a database, and its host operating system:

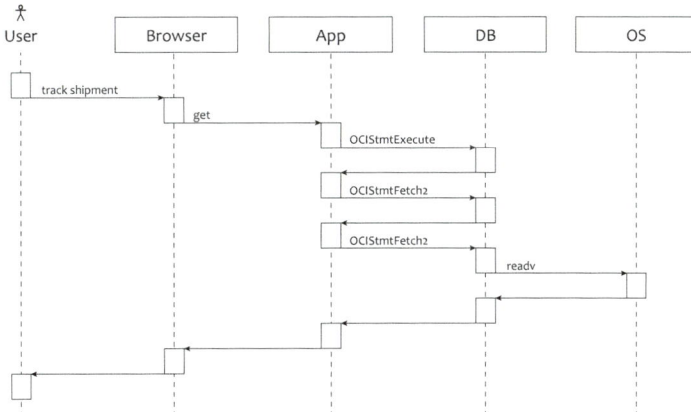

This UML sequence diagram shows the interactions among a user, a browser, an application server, a database, and the database's host operating system.

Imagine now drawing the sequence diagram to scale, so that the distance between each "request" arrow coming in and its corresponding "response" arrow going out is proportional to the duration spent servicing the request, as follows:

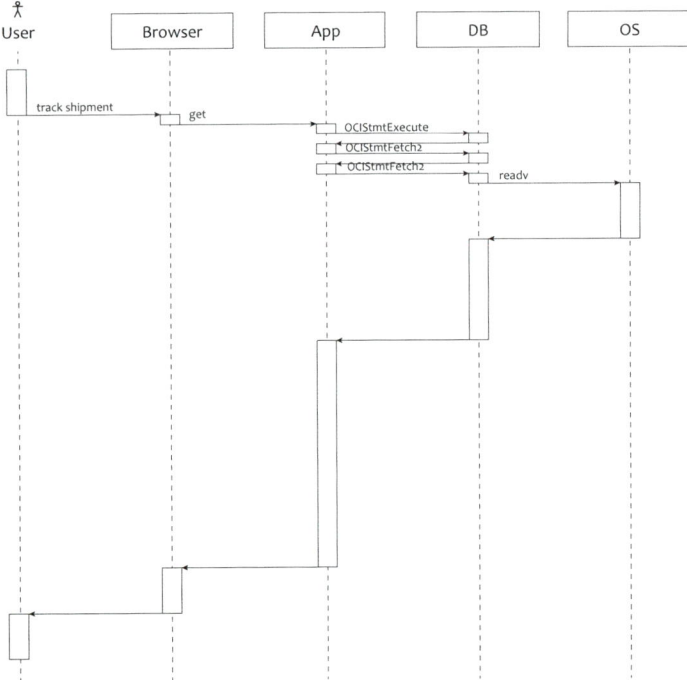

A UML sequence diagram drawn so that vertical distance in the diagram is proportional to the response time consumed.

With a sequence diagram like this, you have a good graphical representation of how the components represented in your diagram are spending your user's time. You can "feel" the relative contribution to response time by looking at the picture.

Sequence diagrams are just right for helping people conceptualize how their response is consumed on a given system, as one tier hands control of the task to the next. Sequence diagrams also work well to show how simultaneous threads of processing work in parallel. Sequence diagrams are good tools for analyzing performance outside of the information technology business, too.[7]

But there's a problem with sequence diagrams. Imagine that the task you're supposed to fix has a response time of 77,148 seconds (that's 21 hours 25 minutes 48 seconds). In that roughly 21.4 hours, running that task causes your application server to execute over

---

[7] Cary Millsap, "Performance optimization with Global Entry. Or not?" at *http://carymillsap. blogspot.com/2009/11/performance-optimization-with-global.html*.

10,000 database calls, and your database to execute over 10,000,000 operating system calls. Here is what your sequence diagram for that task would look like:

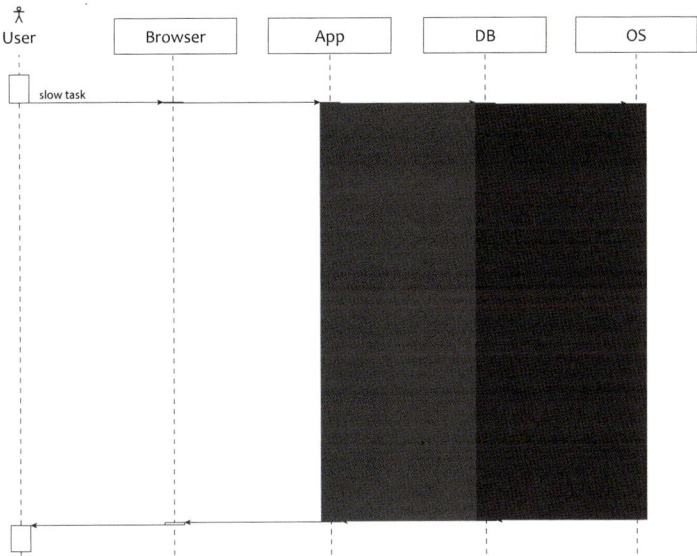

A UML sequence diagram is incapable of showing what we need to see for an experience during which the application server executed over 10,000 database calls, and the database server executed over 10,000,000 operating system calls.

There are so many request and response arrows between the application and database tiers that you can't see any of the detail. Such a diagram would be nearly useless. Printing the sequence diagram on a very long scroll isn't a useful solution, because the resulting visual inspection would be just too difficult. The sequence diagram is a good tool for conceptualizing flow of control, but to think clearly about response time, you need something else.

THE PROFILE

The sequence diagram doesn't scale well. To deal with tasks that have huge call counts, you need a convenient aggregation of the sequence diagram so that you can understand the most important patterns in how your time has been spent. A **profile** is a tabular decomposition of response time, typically listed in descending order of component response time contribution. Here is a profile that matches the sequence diagram shown previously:

```
 1  CALL-NAME                                              DURATION       %       CALLS        MEAN       MIN        MAX
 2  -------------------------------------------------  -------------   ------  ----------   --------   --------   ---------
 3  db file sequential read                             59,081.406102   76.6%  10,013,394   0.005900   0.000010   15.853019
 4  log buffer space                                     6,308.758563    8.2%       9,476   0.665762   0.000004    1.010092
 5  free buffer waits                                    4,688.730190    6.1%     200,198   0.023420   0.000004    1.021281
 6  EXEC                                                 4,214.190000    5.5%      36,987   0.113937   0.000000    5.400000
 7  log file switch completion                           1,552.471890    2.0%       1,853   0.837815   0.000006    1.013093
 8  db file parallel read                                  464.976815    0.6%       7,641   0.060853   0.000030    8.964706
 9  log file switch (checkpoint incomplete)                316.968886    0.4%         351   0.903045   0.000003    1.014777
10  rdbms ipc reply                                        244.937910    0.3%       2,737   0.089491   0.000001    2.010042
11  undo segment extension                                 140.267429    0.2%       1,411   0.099410   0.000001    0.108950
12  log file switch (private strand flush incomplete)      112.680587    0.1%         134   0.840900   0.002781    1.000239
13  17 others                                               23.367228    0.0%      58,126   0.000402   0.000000    5.045291
14  -------------------------------------------------  -------------   ------  ----------   --------   --------   ---------
15  TOTAL (27)                                          77,148.755600  100.0%  10,332,308   0.007467   0.000000   15.853019
```

A profile is a tabular decomposition of response time.

The two defining characteristics of a profile are:

- The bottom-line duration (77,148.755600 seconds here) must match the user response time experience that you're trying to diagnose.

- The durations in the table must sum to exactly this value; no more (that is, no overlaps) and no less (that is, no gaps).

If your profile meets these two criteria, then you have an unambiguous account of exactly the response time you want to analyze. From the data shown in this profile, you know that 76.6% of your user's response time is consumed by 10,013,394 *db file sequential read* calls.

A profile shows you where your code has spent your time and—sometimes even more importantly—where it has *not*. There is tremendous value in not having to guess about these things. With a profile, you can begin to formulate the answer to the question, "How long *should* this task run?" ...Which, by now, you know is an important question in the first step of the problem diagnosis process.

A profile shows where your code has spent its time and can answer the question, "How long *should* this task run?"

THE BOTTLENECK

The resource that dominates the response time for a task execution is that execution's **bottleneck**. The bottleneck for an execution (for an experience) thus is simply the resource listed in the top line of that execution's profile.

> **Example:** Consider the following profile, which describes a 1,957.470000-second experience running a payroll application batch job. Which resource is the bottleneck?

```
16  CALL-NAME                       DURATION       %      CALLS      MEAN       MIN       MAX
17  -----------------------------  -----------  ------  --------  --------  --------  --------
18  SQL*Net message from client     984.010000   50.3%    95,161  0.010340  0.000000  0.310000
19  SQL*Net more data from client   418.820000   21.4%     3,345  0.125208  0.000000  0.270000
20  db file sequential read         279.340000   14.3%    45,084  0.006196  0.000000  0.050000
21  EXEC                            136.880000    7.0%    67,888  0.002016  0.000000  1.320000
22  PARSE                            74.490000    3.8%    10,098  0.007377  0.000000  0.090000
23  FETCH                            37.320000    1.9%    57,217  0.000652  0.000000  0.130000
24  latch free                       23.690000    1.2%    34,695  0.000683  0.000000  0.080000
25  log file sync                     1.090000    0.1%       506  0.002154  0.000000  0.050000
26  SQL*Net more data to client       0.830000    0.0%    15,982  0.000052  0.000000  0.020000
27  log file switch completion        0.280000    0.0%         3  0.093333  0.080000  0.110000
28  enqueue                           0.250000    0.0%       106  0.002358  0.000000  0.020000
29  SQL*Net message to client         0.240000    0.0%    95,161  0.000003  0.000000  0.010000
30  buffer busy waits                 0.220000    0.0%        67  0.003284  0.000000  0.020000
31  db file scattered read            0.010000    0.0%         2  0.005000  0.000000  0.010000
32  SQL*Net break/reset to client     0.000000    0.0%         2  0.000000  0.000000  0.000000
33  -----------------------------  -----------  ------  --------  --------  --------  --------
34  TOTAL (15)                     1,957.470000  100.0%   425,317  0.004602  0.000000  1.320000
```

> The bottleneck for this experience is *SQL*Net message from client*.

It is important to define *bottleneck* in terms of an individual task execution. Many people regard the *bottleneck* as an attribute of another entity. It is especially common for people to ask, for example, "What is the system's bottleneck?" The answer is that different task executions on a given system often have different bottlenecks, so to identify one of those experiences' bottlenecks as the *system*'s bottleneck is often confounding.

> **Example:** During the 1,957.470000-second payroll batch job experience profiled in the prior example, a system monitoring tool had reported that, while this job was running, the "system's bottleneck" was overwhelmingly the *latch free* resource. This diagnosis led an IT department to work for months toward reducing *latch free* calls on this system, with the top priority of improving this payroll job's performance. However, no amount of *latch free* reduction on this system was ever going to make an appreciable improvement to the response time of this payroll job. This is abundantly evident from the job's profile, where you can see that *latch free* calls have contributed only 1.2% of the job's total response time.

In this example, *latch free* might have been the aggregate bottleneck among all the task executions on the system, but this top-priority payroll job was experiencing a different bottleneck entirely. The very notion that the *bottleneck* is an attribute of a whole system helped to prevent this system's managers from seeing their real network configuration problem.

AMDAHL'S LAW

Profiling helps you think clearly about performance. Even if Gene Amdahl hadn't done the work that he did back in 1967, you'd have probably come up with the gist of Amdahl's famous law yourself after the first few profiles you looked at. Amdahl's law implies that a task execution's performance improvement is proportional to how much that execution uses the thing you improved.

> Performance improvement is proportional to how much a program uses the thing you improved.

For example, if the thing you're trying to improve contributes only 5% to your task's total response time, then the maximum impact you'll be able to make is 5% of your total response time. This means that the closer to the top of a profile that you work (assuming that the profile is sorted in descending response time order), the bigger the benefit potential you'll have for your overall response time.

This doesn't mean that you always work a profile in top-down order, though, because you also need to consider the cost of the remedies you'll be executing.[8]

Example: Consider the following profile. Here you can see, for each row in the profile, how much time you think you can save by implementing the best remedy and how much you think each remedy will cost to implement.

	Response time (seconds)		Expected potential R improvement %	Expected relative cost of remedy
1	1,748.229	70.8%	34.5%	1,000,000
2	338.470	13.7%	12.3%	1
3	152.654	6.2%		+∞
4	97.855	4.0%	4.0%	10
5	58.147	2.4%	0.1%	1,000
6	48.274	2.0%	1.6%	1
7	23.481	1.0%		+∞
8	0.890	0.0%		+∞
Total	2,468.000	100.0%	52.5%	

This profile shows the potential for improvement and the corresponding cost (difficulty) of improvement for each line item.

What remedy action would you implement first? Amdahl's law says that implementing the repair that will reduce response time by 34.5% (of 2,468 seconds) has the greatest potential benefit. But if that remedy is truly 1,000,000 times more expensive than the remedy reducing response time by 12.3%, then focusing on the second remedy may yield better net benefit.

The key to your response is to have both parts of the two-part problem statement that I described in "Problem Diagnosis" on page 6: you need to know your current state, *and* you need to know the goal state. The current state here is easy: the response time

---

[8] Cary Millsap, "On the importance of diagnosing before resolving" at *http://carymillsap.blogspot.com/2009/09/on-importance-of-diagnosing-before.html*.

is 2,468.000 seconds for the experience we're looking at. But the goal state? I've given you no clue. Here's why it matters...

Case 1: Imagine that your biggest customer will fire you—causing your entire business to end forever—if you don't make this 2,468-second task execute in at least 15% less time. What do you do? It's easy: you attack the "dirt cheap" remedies, which will yield a 12.3% + 4.0% + 1.6% = 17.9% response time improvement. That's enough to satisfy your customer, and you did it without spending very much.

Case 2: Imagine that your biggest customer will fire you—causing your entire business to end forever—if you don't make this 2,468-second task execute in at least 35% less time. What do you do? You should assign the easy work on line 2 to an assistant, and then, in parallel—*immediately*—get cracking on the expensive remedy action on line 1 of the profile. You simply cannot reach the 35%-better goal without accomplishing at least part of the highest-cost (1,000,000) improvement.

Which remedy action should you implement first? The deciding factor is your goal state. To make wise investment decisions, you have to know what you need, and you need to know how much you're willing to pay for it.

A tremendous value of the profile is that you can learn exactly how much improvement you should expect for a proposed investment. It opens the door to making better decisions about what remedies to implement first. Your predictions give you a yardstick for measuring your own performance as an analyst. And finally, it gives you a chance to showcase your cleverness and intimacy with your technology as you find more efficient remedies for better-than-expected response time reductions, at lower-than-expected costs.

What remedy action you implement first really boils down to how much you trust your cost estimates. Do your cost estimates really take into account the risks that the proposed improvement may inflict upon the system? For example, it may seem inexpensive to change that parameter or drop that index, but does that change potentially disrupt the good performance behavior of something out there that you're not even considering right now? Reliable cost estimation is another area in which your technological skills pay off.

Another factor worth considering is the political capital that you can earn by creating small victories. Maybe cheap, low-risk improvements won't amount to much overall response time improvement, but there's value in establishing a track record of small improvements that exactly fulfill your predictions about how much response time you'll save for the slow task. A track record of prediction and fulfillment ultimately—especially in the area of software performance, where myth and superstition have reigned at many locations for decades—gives you the credibility you need to influence your colleagues (your peers, your managers, your customers, ...) to let you perform increasingly expensive remedies that may produce bigger payoffs for the business.

A word of caution, however: don't get careless as you propose bigger, costlier, riskier remedies. Credibility is fragile. It takes a lot of work to build it up but only one careless mistake to bring it down.

SKEW

When you work with profiles, you will encounter problems like this one:

Example: Here is the profile you saw earlier in "The Profile" on page 9:

```
 1  CALL-NAME                                              DURATION       %      CALLS      MEAN      MIN        MAX
 2  ---------------------------------------------     --------------  ------  ----------  --------  --------  ---------
 3  db file sequential read                           59,081.406102   76.6%  10,013,394   0.005900  0.000010  15.853019
 4  log buffer space                                   6,308.758563    8.2%       9,476   0.665762  0.000004   1.010092
 5  free buffer waits                                  4,688.730190    6.1%     200,198   0.023420  0.000004   1.021281
 6  EXEC                                               4,214.190000    5.5%      36,987   0.113937  0.000000   5.400000
 7  log file switch completion                         1,552.471890    2.0%       1,853   0.837815  0.000006   1.013093
 8  db file parallel read                                464.976815    0.6%       7,641   0.060853  0.000030   8.964706
 9  log file switch (checkpoint incomplete)              316.968886    0.4%         351   0.903045  0.000003   1.014777
10  rdbms ipc reply                                      244.937910    0.3%       2,737   0.089491  0.000001   2.010042
11  undo segment extension                               140.267429    0.2%       1,411   0.099410  0.000001   0.108950
12  log file switch (private strand flush incomplete)    112.680587    0.1%         134   0.840900  0.002781   1.000239
13  17 others                                             23.367228    0.0%      58,126   0.000402  0.000000   5.045291
14  ---------------------------------------------     --------------  ------  ----------  --------  --------  ---------
15  TOTAL (27)                                        77,148.755600  100.0%  10,332,308   0.007467  0.000000  15.853019
```

This profile shows that 10,013,394 read calls had consumed 59,081 seconds of response time. How much response time would you eliminate if you could eliminate half of those *db file sequential read* calls? If you eliminate half of those calls, then won't you eliminate half of the time consumed by those calls?

The answer is, *not necessarily*. The response time you'll save is not always proportional to the number of calls you eliminate. Consider this simpler example for a moment:

Example: Four calls to a subroutine consumed four seconds. How much unwanted response time would you eliminate if you could eliminate half of those calls?

The answer depends upon the response times of the individual calls that you could eliminate. You might have assumed that each of the call durations was the average (4 seconds)/(4 calls) = 1 second/call. But nowhere in the problem statement did I tell you that the call durations were uniform.

Imagine the following two possibilities, where each list represents the response times of the four subroutine calls:

$A = \{1, 1, 1, 1\}$
$B = \{3.7, .1, .1, .1\}$

In list A, the response times are uniform, so no matter which half (two) of the calls you eliminate, you'll reduce total response time to 2 seconds. However, in list B, it makes a tremendous difference which two calls you eliminate. If you eliminate the first two calls, then the total response time will drop to .2 seconds (a 95% reduction). However, if you eliminate the final two calls, then the total response time will drop to 3.8 seconds (only a 5% reduction), which is probably not enough of an improvement for a user to notice.

Skew is a non-uniformity in a list of values. The possibility of skew is what prohibits you from providing a precise answer to the question about eliminating half of your *db file sequential read* calls. Let's look again:

Example: How much time will you conserve if you eliminate half of the 10,013,394 *db file sequential read* calls?

```
16  CALL-NAME                                              DURATION       %      CALLS      MEAN      MIN        MAX
17  ---------------------------------------------     --------------  ------  ----------  --------  --------  ---------
18  db file sequential read                           59,081.406102   76.6%  10,013,394   0.005900  0.000010  15.853019
19  log buffer space                                   6,308.758563    8.2%       9,476   0.665762  0.000004   1.010092
20  free buffer waits                                  4,688.730190    6.1%     200,198   0.023420  0.000004   1.021281
21  EXEC                                               4,214.190000    5.5%      36,987   0.113937  0.000000   5.400000
22  log file switch completion                         1,552.471890    2.0%       1,853   0.837815  0.000006   1.013093
23  db file parallel read                                464.976815    0.6%       7,641   0.060853  0.000030   8.964706
24  log file switch (checkpoint incomplete)              316.968886    0.4%         351   0.903045  0.000003   1.014777
25  rdbms ipc reply                                      244.937910    0.3%       2,737   0.089491  0.000001   2.010042
26  undo segment extension                               140.267429    0.2%       1,411   0.099410  0.000001   0.108950
27  log file switch (private strand flush incomplete)    112.680587    0.1%         134   0.840900  0.002781   1.000239
28  17 others                                             23.367228    0.0%      58,126   0.000402  0.000000   5.045291
29  ---------------------------------------------     --------------  ------  ----------  --------  --------  ---------
30  TOTAL (27)                                        77,148.755600  100.0%  10,332,308   0.007467  0.000000  15.853019
```

Without knowing anything about skew, the only answer you can provide is, "Somewhere between 0 and 59,081.406102 seconds." That is the most precise correct answer you can return. Imagine, however, that you had some additional information that shows a histogram of the call durations, like this:

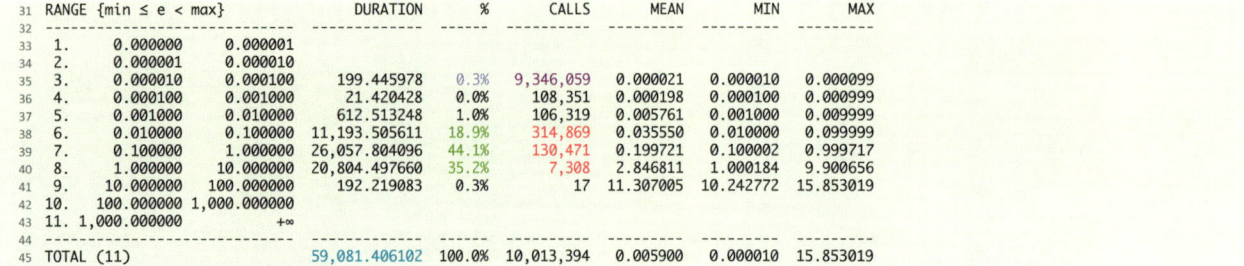

Then you could formulate much more precise best-case and worst-case estimates. Specifically, if you had information like this, then you'd know how important it is to target the highest-latency calls and leave the low-latency ones alone. Eliminating the wrong 93% of the calls will eliminate only 0.3% of your response time, but eliminating the right 5% of your calls will eliminate 98.5% of your response time.

The ability to find skew gives you the precious ability to *target* your efforts to maximize your efficiency as an optimizer.

Minimizing Risk

A couple of sections back, I mentioned the risk that repairing the performance of one task can damage the performance of another. It reminds me of something that happened to me once in Denmark. It's a quick story:

> SCENE: A kitchen table in Måløv, Denmark. A dozen people sat around the table, working on their laptop computers and conducting various conversations.
>
> CARY: Guys, I'm burning up. Would you mind if I opened the window for a little bit to let some cold air in?
>
> CAREL-JAN: Why don't you just take off your sweater?
>
> THE END.

There's a general principle at work here that people who optimize know. When everyone is happy except for you, make sure you're locally efficient before you go messing around with the global stuff that affects everyone else, too. In other words:

> Match the scope of your solution to the scope of your problem.

This principle is why I flinch whenever someone proposes to change a system's Oracle SQL*Net packet size, when the problem is really a couple of badly-written Java programs that make too many database calls (and hence too many network I/O calls). If everybody is getting along fine except for the user of one or two programs, then the safest solution to the problem is a change whose scope is localized to just those one or two programs.

Efficiency

One of the most difficult problems that a performance analyst can face is the dreaded "everything is slow" dilemma. If everyone on the entire system is suffering, then what should you focus on first? The task that is most constricting the business is the one you should focus on first.[9] The way to begin is to ensure that the program is working as efficiently as it can. **Efficiency** is the inverse of how much of a task execution's total service time can be eliminated without adding capacity, and without sacrificing required business function.

In other words, efficiency is an inverse measure of waste. Here are some examples of waste that commonly occur in the database application world:

Example: A middle tier program creates a distinct SQL statement for every row it inserts into the database. It executes 10,000 database prepare calls when it could have accomplished the job with one prepare call.

Example: A middle tier program makes 100 database fetch calls (and thus 100 network I/O calls) to fetch 994 rows. It could have fetched 994 rows in 10 fetch calls (and thus 90 fewer network I/O calls).

Example: A SQL statement[10] touches the database buffer cache 7,428,322 times to return a 698-row result set. An extra filter predicate could have returned the 7 rows that the user really wanted to see, with only 52 touches upon the database buffer cache.

Certainly, if a system has some global problem that creates inefficiency for broad groups of tasks across the system (e.g., missing index, badly set parameter, poorly configured hardware), then you should fix it. But don't tune a system to accommodate programs that are inefficient.[11] There is a lot more leverage in curing the program inefficiencies themselves. Even if the programs are commercial, off-the-shelf applications, it will benefit you better in the long run to work with your software vendor to make your programs efficient, than it will to try to optimize your system to be as efficient as it can with inherently inefficient workload.

Improvements that make your program more efficient can produce tremendous benefits for everyone on the system. It's easy to see how top-line reduction of waste helps the response time of the task being repaired. What many people don't understand as well is that making one program more efficient creates a side-effect of performance improvement for other programs on the system that have no apparent relation to the program being repaired. It happens because of the influence of *load* upon the system.

LOAD

Load is competition for a resource induced by concurrent task executions. Load is the reason that the performance testing done by software developers doesn't catch all the performance problems that show up later in production.

One measure of load is *utilization*. **Utilization** is resource usage divided by resource capacity for a specified time interval. As utilization for a resource goes up, so does the response time a user will experience when requesting service from that resource. Anyone who has ridden in an automobile in a big city during rush hour has experienced this phenomenon. When the traffic is heavily congested, it takes longer to get where you're going. There are two reasons that systems get slower as load increases: queueing delay, and coherency delay.

---

[9] Eliyahu M. Goldratt and Jeff Cox, *The Goal: a Process of Ongoing Improvement.*

[10] My choice of article adjective here is a dead giveaway that I was introduced to SQL through the Oracle community.

[11] Admittedly, sometimes you need a tourniquet to keep from bleeding to death. But don't use a stopgap measure as a permanent solution. Address the inefficiency.

DETERMINISTIC AND RANDOM ARRIVALS

The process through which requests arrive into a system influences how that system will perform. Such an arrival process is said to be **deterministic** if and only if the timing of its arrivals can be predicted with certainty. An arrival process that cannot be predicted with certainty are said to be **random**.

> *Example:* Several years' worth of data suggest that the arrival rate of customers to your favorite restaurant at lunchtime is 542 customers per hour. Although you have confidence in predicting how many customers will arrive at lunchtime tomorrow, you do not know exactly when each customer will arrive; thus, the arrival process into the restaurant is *random*.

> *Example:* A busy superhighway has a traffic signal on its on-ramp that allows exactly one car to enter the highway every 5 seconds. During peak times, drivers queue behind the traffic signal in an unpredictable way, but the rate at which cars are allowed onto the highway is completely predictable; thus, the arrival process onto the highway is *deterministic*.

Determinism makes systems easier to manage. If you can control exactly when your next service request is coming, then you can plan your activity so that none of your capacity goes wasted and yet your system will never get hit with more workload than it can handle. However, on a system with *random* arrivals, the arrivals tend to clump up, which makes managing your capacity much more difficult. There will be periods when no requests enter the system, and then there will be periods when dozens of requests all arrive, inconveniently, at the same time. During the lulls, capacity will go unused—wasted—but during the spikes, users will have to wait for resources that are busy serving other requests.

QUEUEING DELAY

When you are on an unloaded system, where there's nobody else to wait on, each response time will consist exclusively of *service time*. **Service time** is the duration that a task execution spends consuming a given resource, measured in time per execution (e.g., seconds per click). Service times usually fluctuate. You can describe service times using averages and percentiles ("Percentile Specifications" on page 4).

> *Example:* It usually takes 3 minutes to cook a hamburger, but sometimes it takes 2.7 minutes, sometimes 3.4 minutes. If the mean time it takes to cook a hamburger is 3 minutes, then perhaps the 95th percentile cook time is 3.71 minutes. You can find out by measuring and recording all your hamburger cook times.

When you are on an unloaded system, your response time is all service time. However, as others join you on the system, your response times will begin to include not just service times, but also the time you'll spend waiting in line behind other requests. **Queueing delay** is the duration that a request spends enqueued at a given resource, awaiting its opportunity to consume that resource.

Like service time, queueing delay is measured in time per task execution. Queueing delay varies with load.

> *Example:* Imagine that you and one friend are the only users on a typical computer with one single-core CPU. Each of you will execute a request requiring 2 seconds of CPU time. You make your request first, and she makes hers 1 second later, while yours is running. For the first second, you'll get the CPU's full attention, but once you friend's request arrives, the operating system will begin time-slicing CPU time between the two of you, probably in .01-second increments (most schedulers use a CPU quantum of 1/100th of a second). While you are using the CPU for .01 seconds, your friend will wait in the CPU run queue. While she uses the CPU for the next .01 seconds, you'll wait. The scheduler will switch the two of you back and forth until your request is finished, and then, with your request out of the way, she'll get the CPU's full attention for her final second of processing. (The operating system scheduler code would continue to run every .01 seconds, but since there would be nobody in the run queue, your friend's process would never get preempted.) After all this, your response time would

be 3 seconds: 2 seconds of service time, and 1 second of queueing delay, as shown in the figure below (the blue thread on the sequence diagram). And so would hers (the red thread).

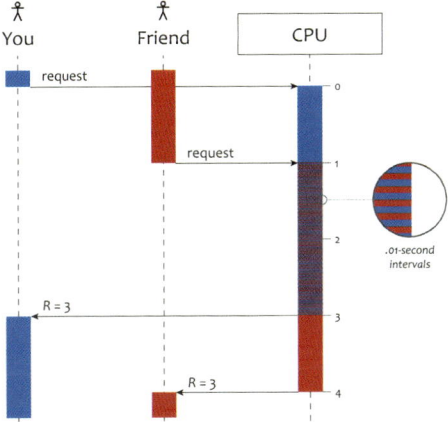

Two people competing for CPU capacity on a preemptive multitasking system. Waiting each 1/100th of a second while your friend gets her time slice degrades your response time.

While service time fluctuations for a given unit of work are usually small, load-induced fluctuations in queueing delay can be huge, dwarfing service times by an order of magnitude or more. It is thus important to know how much you can expect queueing delays to change as load changes. This is where mathematical models enter the conversation.

Queueing Theory

In the early 1900s, the Danish mathematician Agner Erlang developed models to determine how many circuits the Copenhagen Telephone Company would need to provide acceptable telephone service.[12] Erlang's "M/M/m" model (also called "M/M/c") also helps predict how modern computing systems will perform. Most systems you use won't be exactly M/M/m, but nevertheless, most systems behave in a manner that the model helps to explain.

The lowercase m in "M/M/m" is the number of *service channels* in the system.[13] A **service channel** is a resource that shares a single queue with other such resources, like a clerk at a multi-clerk airport ticket counter or a CPU in a symmetric multiprocessor computer. M/M/m models only those systems whose service channels are homogeneous, parallel, and independent. Specifically, the service channel independence assumption omits *coherency delays* from the model. M/M/m represents response time (R) as consisting of just the two components, *service time* (S) and *queueing delay* (Q):

$R = S + Q.$

For most real-life Oracle-based applications, M/M/m will not be able to give you high-precision response time predictions. But it will be able to help you understand—and explain— why your performance behaves as it does as your loads change.

Example: The following graph explains how it feels to use an 8-channel M/M/m system under different load conditions (think of an 8-lane highway or an 8-CPU computer). At low utilization values, your response times are so nice that it feels like nobody else is on the

---

[12] See *http://en.wikipedia.org/wiki/Agner_Krarup_Erlang*.

[13] See *http://en.wikipedia.org/wiki/Kendall%27s_notation*; or Cary Millsap and Jeff Holt, *Optimizing Oracle Performance*,

Chapter 1. Thinking Clearly about Performance

system. As load ramps up, you sense a slight, gradual degradation in response time. That gradual degradation doesn't hurt much, but as load continues to ramp up, response time begins to degrade in a manner that is neither slight nor gradual. Ultimately, the degradation becomes quite unpleasant and, in fact, hyperbolic.

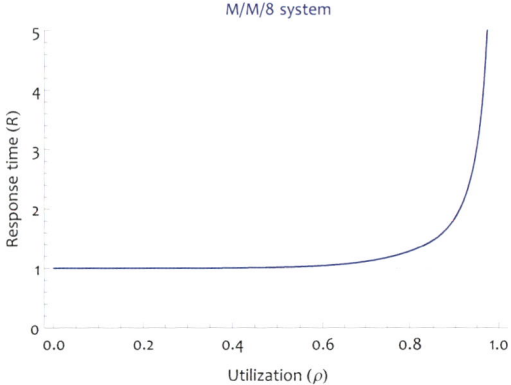

This curve shows response time as a function of utilization for an M/M/m system with 8 service channels.

COHERENCY DELAY

It's a reasonably safe bet that no matter what computer application system you're thinking of right now, it does *not* meet the M/M/m "service channels are independent" assumption. *Coherency delay* is a measure of the service channel interdependencies. **Coherency delay** is the duration that a task spends communicating and coordinating access to a shared resource. Like response time, service time, and queueing delay, coherency delay is measured in time per task execution.

I won't describe here a mathematical model for predicting coherency delay,[14] but if you profile your software task executions, you'll see it when it occurs. In Oracle, timed events like the following are examples of coherency delay:

> *enqueue*
> *log file sync*
> *buffer busy waits*
> *latch free*

You can't model coherency delays like these with M/M/m, because M/M/m assumes that all *m* of your service channels are parallel, homogeneous, and independent. The model assumes that after your request waits politely in a FIFO queue for long enough that all the requests that arrived ahead of it have exited the queue for service, it'll be your turn to be serviced. However, coherency delays don't work like that.

Example: Imagine an HTML data entry form in which one button labeled "Update" executes a SQL *update* statement, and another button labeled "Save" executes a SQL *commit* statement. An application built like this would almost guarantee abysmal performance. That's because the design makes it possible—quite likely, actually—for a user to click Update, look at his calendar, realize uh-oh he's late for lunch, and then go to lunch for two hours before clicking Save later that afternoon.

The impact to other tasks on this system that wanted to update the same row would be devastating. Each task would necessarily wait for a lock on the row (or, on some systems, worse: a lock on the row's page) until the locking user decided to go ahead and click Save. ...Or until

---

[14] Neil Gunther, "Universal law of computational scalability" at *http://en.wikipedia.org/wiki/Neil_J._Gunther#Universal_Law_of_Computational_Scalability*.

a database administrator killed the user's session, which of course would have unsavory side effects to the person who had thought he had updated a row.

In the example, the amount of time a task would wait on the lock to be released has nothing to do with how busy the system is. It would be dependent upon random factors that exist outside of the system's various resource utilizations. That's why you can't model this kind of thing in M/M/m. It is also why you can never assume that a performance test executed in a unit testing type of environment is sufficient for a making a go/no-go decision about insertion of new code into a production system.

Managing Load

The goal of having a big system is to get lots of work done. But, if you crank the load up too much, the response time degradation will make everyone on the system unhappy. So, then, how much load is too much? At what utilization value is the optimal load? This question is relevant for every resource on your system that is affected by load. When you say "utilization," most people first think of CPU, but, for example, disk and network I/O performance also suffers under loads that are too strenuous, so you need to understand the optimal loads for these resources as well.

On resources with deterministic arrivals, your optimal resource utilization is 100%. That is, if you can *completely* plan your load, then you can fill every cycle of capacity that you have. ...But don't overfill, or of course you'll create queueing problems. On resources with random arrivals, it's more difficult. You would love to run at 100% utilization, but you need to leave some headroom for spikes in utilization caused by the randomness in your request arrivals. So another way to ask the optimal load question is, "How much headroom should I leave?" If you leave too much, then you're wasting expensive capacity, but if you leave too little, then performance will suffer. So, what's the right amount?

In the past, I have written that the values in the following table are good starting points for defining an operational utilization ceiling for a given resource:

Service channel count (m)	M/M/m knee utilization
1	50%
2	57%
4	67%
8	74%
16	81%
32	86%
64	89%
128	92%

M/M/m knee values for common values of m.

These values represent the **knee** in an M/M/m queueing system defined as the utilization value at which response time divided by throughput is at its minimum.[15] The knee defined this way is a starting point for defining an operational utilization ceiling for each resource on your system. If a given system met all of the M/M/m qualifications, then limiting your sustained utilization to the knee utilization would yield response times with small

---

[15] Mary Vernon, "CS 547: Computer system modeling fundamentals" at *http://www.cs.wisc.edu/~vernon/cs547/01/assighments/s5.pdf*.

Chapter 1. Thinking Clearly about Performance

queueing delays. Systems running at less than the M/M/m knee utilization tend to feel like unloaded systems, as you can see in the following graph:

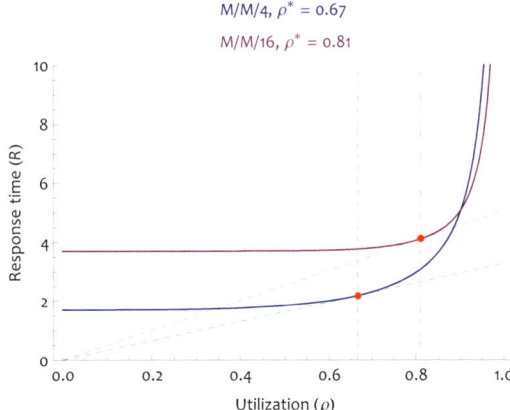

Operating to the left of the knee utilization on these two M/M/m systems would result in response times that are very similar to unloaded response times.

However, the M/M/m knee utilization is not necessarily your best utilization ceiling:

- The M/M/m knee utilization value might be too big. Your system probably isn't a perfect M/M/m system. It probably has scalability defects like *coherency delays*, which the model doesn't take into account. If these imperfections cause your system to perform more poorly than the model predicts, then you'll want a utilization ceiling that is *smaller* than the knee value.

- The M/M/m knee utilization value might be too small. Perhaps your users' response time tolerances are forgiving enough that you could run your system above your M/M/m knee utilization value without anyone perceiving a performance compromise. In this case, you might want a utilization ceiling that is *larger* than the knee value.

    Example: A system owner who is willing to tolerate mean response times of $R \leq 1$ seconds per execution of a given task should be able to run his system at higher sustained utilizations than the owner of an identical system who is willing to tolerate mean response times of no more than $R \leq 0.1$ seconds per execution of the same task.

Any useful utilization ceiling must be derived from inquiries about response time requirements, not solely from mathematical observations about your system.[16]

Keeping your utilization below some ceiling is not a goal in and of itself, it's something you do because you want to meet the real goal of providing consistent performance experiences to your system's users. Those experiences are the most important things to measure ("Percentile Specifications" on page 4). To that end, you should define your operational utilization ceiling for a given resource (CPU, disk drive, network interface, etc.) as follows:

1. Use the resource's knee value in the table on page 19 as a starting point. Your best operational utilization ceiling value may be larger or smaller than this number.

2. If your response times fail to meet your requirements, then adjust your utilization ceiling downward.[17] If your response times contain no queueing delays, yet they

---

[16] Neil Gunther, "Mind your knees and queues" at *http://www.cmg.org/measureit/issues/mit62/m_62_15.html*.

[17] How? By scheduling jobs intelligently, by eliminating workload inefficiencies, by refusing to admit load onto your system that exceeds your system's ability to meet your required service levels, or by upgrading to a more powerful system.

still violate your response time requirements, then you'll need to renegotiate your requirements, optimize your software, or increase your system capacity.

3. If your response times are consistently better than your requirements, then you may adjust your utilization ceiling upward.

Example: Imagine that your system has a single quad-core CPU, and that your business requires for 95% of task executions to respond faster than your users' tolerances for the tasks they run on the system. A single quad-core CPU system is not exactly M/M/4, but you can begin with a utilization ceiling value of 67% (choosing the m = 4 entry from the knee utilization table). If more than 95% of your response time experiences are better than your users' tolerances, then you may adjust your ceiling upward from 67%.

If fewer than 95% of your users' response time experiences meet their tolerances, then you must adjust your ceiling downward from 67%. If running your system at ever lower utilizations (by removing or deferring load) doesn't fix the problem, then your problem is not load induced. You'll need either to improve the efficiency of the tasks that are not performing satisfactorily or upgrade your hardware.

It's one thing to claim that you have a utilization ceiling value. It's another thing entirely to enforce it.

Example: It's easy to say that your utilization ceiling is 80%, but it's much more difficult to refuse to run a new financial report during a busy period when your CPU utilization is standing at 79.8%. The owner of the system may point at the spare 20.2% of capacity and demand that you run the report. If you have a record of historical response times (see "Performance Instrumentation" on page 109) and the utilization values that correspond to those response times, you'll be able to make a much better informed decision about it.

Utilization is a *surrogate* metric. We care about it only because we think it's related to something else (user experiences) that we care about more. It is okay to measure utilization in addition to response times. Measuring utilization *instead of* response times will lead you to mistakes.

Capacity Planning

Using utilization ceilings can simplify your capacity planning process. It works like this:

1. If you keep your utilizations less than your ceilings, your system will behave roughly linearly: no big hyperbolic surprises.

2. Your goal capacity for a given resource is thus the amount at which you can comfortably run your tasks at peak times without driving utilization beyond your ceiling.

3. However, if you're letting your system run any of its resources beyond their ceiling utilizations, then you have performance problems (whether you're aware of them or not).

4. If you have performance problems, then you don't need to be spending your time with mathematical models; you need to be spending your time fixing those problems by either rescheduling load, eliminating load, or increasing capacity.

That's how capacity planning fits into the performance management process.

Parallelism

What can you do when you can't make a task run fast enough? One option is to *parallelize* it. The Oracle Database, for example, makes it relatively easy to convert a long-running process into a whole fleet of processes that all work on different pieces of a problem at the same time. Parallelism works like this:

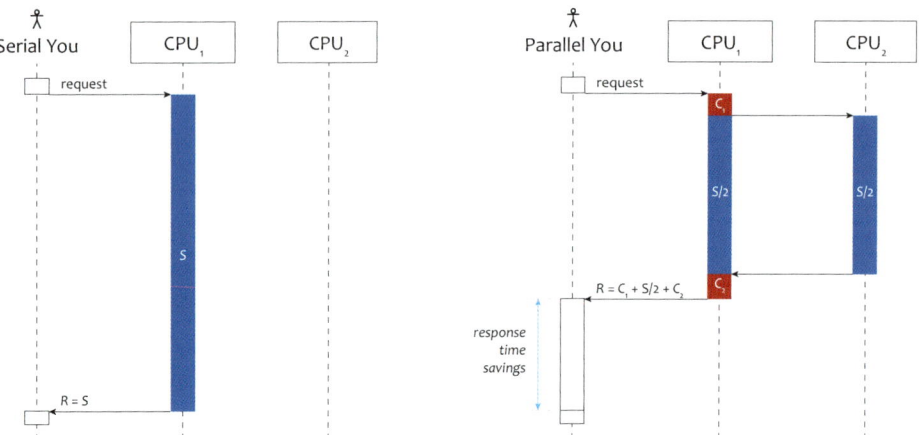

The system on the left shows serial execution of a task; on the right, a 2-way parallel execution of the same task. In the parallel execution, there is some extra coordination overhead shown in red. Here, there are the same number of blue pixels in both cases; this is the best-case scenario.

The point of parallelizing a task is to reduce that task's response time by exploiting unused capacity. It doesn't work very well if there is no unused capacity to parallelize into.

Example: A task, executed serially, runs in 30 minutes on an unloaded computer with two quad-core CPUs. Using 8 parallel processes, it runs in 7 minutes on an unloaded computer. Running the task in parallel will save 23 minutes of response time when there's no other load on the system.

However, if the system is already busy running other load, then adding the parallelized task—which, on Oracle, can add up to 8 × 2 + 1 = 17 new processes—may overwhelm the system for the duration of the task's execution, which, because of queueing delays induced by the overwhelming load, may be far more than the 7 minutes you might have expected.

Parallelism helps only if you have spare capacity available to parallelize into.

When you don't have any spare capacity available to parallelize into, then using parallel execution features is just an easy way to add load to your system, which, as you've seen, can quickly lead to catastrophic (literally hyperbolic) performance consequences.

Parallel operations can reduce response time, but they doesn't reduce load. Parallelization in fact puts *more* load on a system than a corresponding serial execution. There are two reasons for this:

- There is extra effort required to partition the workload among the parallel processes and then harvest the work done by those processes, and
- The code path executed by parallel processes is often less efficient than the code path executed by a serial process.

    Example: A parallel execution on an Oracle system typically uses a different, higher load execution plan than a serial execution of the same SQL statement.

Parallelism *redistributes* work horizontally in the sequence diagram, across more resources. Parallelization thus increases concurrency on a system while the parallel work is executing. This directly increases the *load* on a system, by cramming more total work into less total time. Parallelism can be a fine, response time reducing idea on big systems with few users. It tends to be a worse idea on busy systems. Even system with small user counts get busy really quickly if each user is allowed to parallelize his work.

PERFORMANCE TESTING

Understanding the impact of load—how it leads to queueing delays and coherency delays—leads to a very difficult question. How can you be confident that unforeseen performance problems won't wreck your production implementation? You can model. You can test. However, nothing you do will assure you that you'll avoid every performance problem. It is extremely difficult to create models and tests in which you'll foresee *all* your production problems in advance of actually encountering those problems in production.[18]

Some people allow the apparent futility of this observation to justify not testing at all. Don't get trapped in that mentality. The following points are certain:

- You'll catch a lot more problems if you try to catch them prior to production than if you don't even try. As Boehm has argued, it is absolutely worth considerable effort to catch problems early in the software development life cycle.

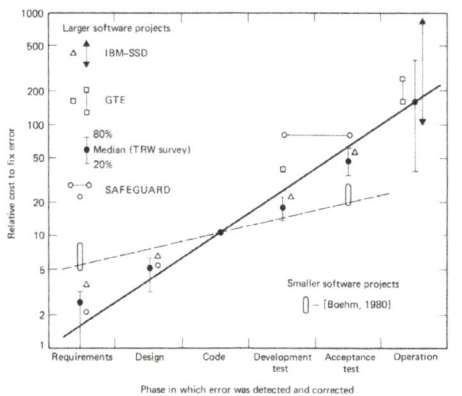 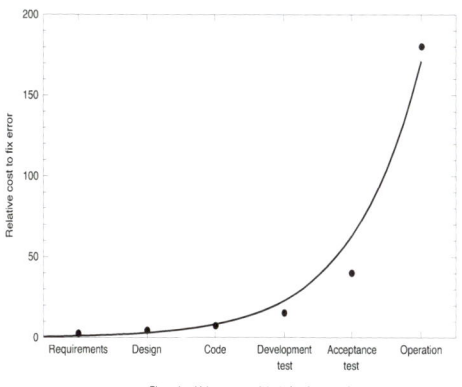

Boehm's famous graphic showing how the cost to fix software errors increases exponentially throughout the software life cycle.[19] The plot at right shows Boehm's data on a linear vertical scale, which emphasizes the data's exponential nature.

- You'll never catch all your problems in pre-production testing. That's why you need a reliable and efficient method for solving the problems that leak through your pre-production testing processes.

Somewhere in the middle between "no testing" and "complete production emulation" is the right amount of testing. The right amount of testing for aircraft manufacturers is probably more than the right amount of testing for companies that sell baseball caps. But don't skip performance testing altogether. At the very least, your performance test plan will make you a more competent diagnostician (and clearer thinker) when it comes time to fix the performance problems that will inevitably occur during production operation.

---

[18] The Computer Measurement Group (*http://www.cmg.org*) is a network of professionals who study these problems.

[19] Barry Boehm, *Software Engineering Economics*, 40.

MEASURING

People feel throughput, and they feel response time. Throughput is often easy to measure, because all you have to do is count results over a specific time interval. Measuring response time is usually much more difficult. It may not be difficult to time an end-user action with a stopwatch, but it might be very difficult to get what you really need, which is the ability to drill down into the details of why a given response time is as large as it is.

Unfortunately, people tend to measure what's easy to measure, which is not necessarily what they *should* be measuring. It's a bug. When it's not easy to measure what we need to measure, we tend to turn our attention to measurements that are easy to get. Measures that aren't what you need, but that are easy enough to obtain and seem related to what you need are called **surrogate measures**. Examples of surrogate measures include subroutine call counts and samples of subroutine call execution durations.

I'm ashamed that I don't have greater command over my native language than to say it this way, but here is a catchy, modern way to express what I think about surrogate measures:

> Surrogate measures suck.

Here, unfortunately, "suck" doesn't mean "never work." It would actually be better if surrogate measures never worked. Then nobody would use them. The problem is that surrogate measures work *sometimes*. This inspires people's confidence that the measures they're using should work all the time, and then they don't. Surrogate measures have two big problems. They can tell you your system's ok when it's not. That's what statisticians call *type I error*, the false positive. And they can tell you that something is a problem when it's not. That's what statisticians call *type II error*, the false negative. I've seen each type of error waste years of people's time.

When it comes time to assess the specifics of a real system, your success is at the mercy of how good the measurements are that your system allows you to obtain. I've been fortunate to work in the Oracle market segment, where the software vendor at the center of our universe participates actively in making it possible to measure systems the right way. Getting application software developers to use the tools that Oracle offers is another story, but at least the capabilities are there in the product.

PERFORMANCE IS A FEATURE

Performance is a software application feature, just like when my bug tracking system automatically converts strings like "case 1234" into hyperlinks.[20] Performance, like any other feature, doesn't just "happen"; it has to be designed and built. To do performance well, you have to think about it, study it, design it, write extra code for it, test it, and support it.

However, like many other features, you can't know exactly how performance is going to work out while it's still early in the project when you're writing, studying, designing, and creating the application. For many applications (arguably, for the vast majority), performance is *completely unknown* until the production phase of the software development life cycle. What this leaves you with is this:

> Since you can't know how your application is going to perform in production, you need to write your application so that it's easy to fix performance in production.

---

[20] FogBugz (*http://www.fogcreek.com/fogbugz/*), which is software that I enjoy using, does this.

As David Garvin has taught us, it's much easier to manage something that's easy to measure.[21] Writing an application that's easy to fix in production begins with an application that's easy to measure in production.

Most times, when I mention the concept of production performance measurement, people drift into a state of worry about the measurement intrusion effect of performance instrumentation. They immediately enter a mode of data collection compromise, leaving only surrogate measures on the table. Won't software with extra code path to measure timings be slower than the same software without that extra code path?

I like an answer that Tom Kyte gave once in response to this question.[22] He estimated that the measurement intrusion effect of Oracle's extensive performance instrumentation is *negative* 10% or less, where *or less* means *or better*, as in −20% or −30%. He went on to explain to a now-vexed questioner that the Oracle Database product is at least 10% faster now because of the knowledge that Oracle Corporation has gained from its performance instrumentation code, more than making up for any "overhead" the instrumentation might have caused.

I think that vendors tend to spend too much time worrying about how to make their measurement code path efficient without figuring out how first to make it effective. It lands squarely upon the idea that Knuth wrote about in 1974 when he wrote that "premature optimization is the root of all evil."[23] The software designer who integrates performance measurement into his product is much more likely to create a fast application and—more importantly—an application that will become faster over time.

---

[21] David Garvin, "Building a learning organization" in *Harvard Business Review*, Jul. 1993.

[22] Tom Kyte, "A couple of links and an advert…" at *http://tkyte.blogspot.com/2009/02/couple-of-links-and-advert.html*.

[23] Donald Knuth, "Structured programming with Go To statements" in ACM Journal *Computing Surveys*, Vol. 6, No. 4, Dec. 1974, p268.

2 Making Friends with the Oracle Database

To many application developers, a database is just a "data store" with an API that they call when they need to persist an object. It's an abstraction that makes sense from one perspective: in a world where you're expected to write dozens of new features every day in Java, PHP, or C#, who has the time or the inclination to dive into what's going on deep inside the Oracle Database? As a result of this abstraction, though, developers sometimes inflict unintended performance horrors upon their customers. The good news is that you can avoid most of these horrors simply by better understanding a bit more about what's going on inside the Oracle kernel. The trick is knowing which details you need to study, and which you can safely learn later. This presentation describes, from a developer's perspective, some of the most important code paths inside the Oracle kernel that can make the difference between an application that breaks down under load and one that can scale to thousands of users.

MAKING FRIENDS BEGINS WITH A COMMON LANGUAGE

Since the early 1990s, my professional focus has been software performance. By that I mean speed. I'm a developer, too. In my career, I've written a lot of C code. These days, I write a lot of Perl. My aim in this paper is to give you a better understanding about what goes on inside the Oracle Database in response to the code you write. I'm going to show you examples of code written in Java, but what you'll see applies equally regardless of whether your code is PHP, C#, Ruby, Python, Perl, C, or something else.

My goal is simple. If I can get you to understand a little more clearly what's going on inside the Oracle Database kernel, you'll write better, faster code. Although developers are often "taught" that they shouldn't concern themselves with what goes on inside the database, that's really not true. Not if you want to build big applications that run fast, anyway.

So my job is to help you make friends with Oracle. When we're done, you'll write faster code, and you'll probably write less code, too, and it'll be easier to maintain. I'll show you an example. I think that once you get to know your database a little better, you'll be impressed with some of the things it does for you.

Making friends with new software is not altogether different from making a new human friend. The best way to get started is to learn your new friend's language.

Now, you're probably already at least a little bit familiar with the SQL language, which enables you to read and write data to the Oracle Database. Teaching you SQL is not my aim here. My aim is to teach you how to communicate about the performance of the application code you write. There are lots of tools that let you assess the performance of the client code you write. In this chapter, I'll acquaint you with a tool that Oracle Corporation provides, which will help you measure how efficiently the code you write uses the Oracle Database.

Chapter 2. Making Friends with the Oracle Database

WHERE SOFTWARE SPEED COMES IN

Let's take a look at how an application that uses Oracle might work. The following rough sequence diagram shows how a business task that fetches rows from an Oracle database:

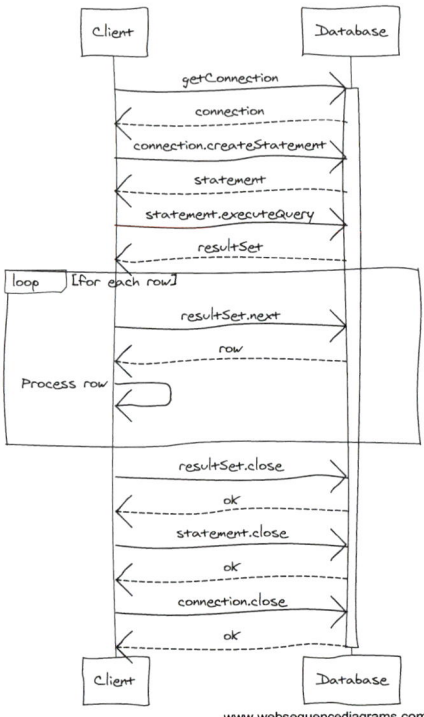

Sequence diagram for a multi-row database query.

It's a simple model. First, the application does what it has to do to connect to Oracle and prepare a SQL statement for fetching the data. Then it fetches a row at a time, processing each row in turn. It does this until it has processed all the data that it needs. Then it cleans up after itself.

Mission accomplished, right? It's certainly a thrill the first time you make something like this happen: making data go from this complex and expensive "black box" into your application, then perhaps into an HTML page where anyone on the Internet can see it.

But what about the performance of the application? Maybe on your development system, the code you wrote is lightning fast. There are two questions you need to be able to answer:

1. Is your code as fast as it *should* be?

2. Will your code *scale*?

When I say "scale," I mean it in the mathematical sense that means the rate at which a user's response times will change as some other factor in the system changes. For example, for a system "not to scale well to large user counts" means that it slows down more aggressively than you want as more users log into the system. If it doesn't scale well to large data volumes, then that means it will slow down more aggressively than you want as people insert rows into your database.

The point of this chapter is to give you some insight into how you can measure how efficiently your application is written, so that you can know whether your code is as fast as it should be and whether it will scale.

> Why guess? ...when you can know.

FEEDBACK

Probably the most important tool you need to make learning happen more efficiently is feedback. A little girl reaches for the hot stove. Mommy yells, "No!" That's feedback. The little boy standing close by wants to see what all the fuss is about, so he decides to touch the stove anyway. POW! More feedback. Feedback from the stove is even more memorable than the feedback from Mommy. Feedback that is close in time to the behavior it measures is more valuable than feedback that happens much later than the behavior it measures.

Example: Imagine what would happen if, when the little boy touched the hot stove, it didn't hurt until three months later. Without immediate feedback, the boy might leave his hand on the stove. Three months later, none of the good choices would be available anymore.

Example: Imagine if there were a ten-second delay on what you could see through your car's windshield.

Example: See the story of the chemical element radium for an important historical example.[1]

Deferred feedback can be deadly. So, how can you shorten the feedback loop about the performance of the application you are writing today? With a feature that comes standard with every release and edition of the Oracle Database since version 7. The feature is called "extended SQL trace." I've written about its history in *Oracle Insights: Tales of the Oak Table*.[2]

In this chapter, I'm going to show you the kinds of things you'll find in a trace file that will help you write better code. In the next chapter, I'll show you more details, like how to generate and find your own trace files.

INTERPRETING YOUR TRACE FILE

Trace files can be intimidating, especially when they contain hundreds of thousands of lines. But even the most complicated trace files are rooted in a surprisingly small number of fundamental principles, which I'll cover here.

Oracle trace files record only two basic categories of useful information about where your time has gone. These two categories are sufficient to explain your entire response time experience. They're ultimately all you need to create a response time *profile*.

Database calls
  Each line that begins with the token PARSE, EXEC, or FETCH represents a single, completed database call executed by the Oracle kernel. A database call line tells you, with its *e* value, how many microseconds of elapsed time the call consumed. Its *c* value tells you approximately[3] how many microseconds of CPU time the call consumed.

---

[1] Wikipedia: "Radium" at *http://en.wikipedia.org/wiki/Radium*.

[2] Mogens Nørgaard et al. *Oracle Insights: Tales of the Oak Table*, 155–182.

[3] The *c* statistic in Oracle trace data is only as accurate as the *getrusage* or *times* OS function that the Oracle Database calls to acquire its CPU timing statistics; thus, a *c* statistic is accurate to only ±10,000 µs. For more details, see Cary Millsap and Jeff Holt, *Optimizing Oracle Performance*, chapter 7

Chapter 2. Making Friends with the Oracle Database

Operating system calls (OS calls)

Each line that begins with the token WAIT represents a single, completed OS call executed by the Oracle kernel.[4] An OS call line tells you, with its *ela* value, how many microseconds of elapsed time the call consumed.

The trick to understanding Oracle trace data is to learn what the various database calls and OS calls mean. Once you figure this out, you'll be able to read for yourself an irrefutable play-by-play account of exactly what your code has spent its time doing, measured from the Oracle Database's perspective.

TRACE FILE GUIDED TOUR

Now let's take a look at the guts of an Oracle trace file. When we discuss Oracle trace file contents, you need to remember that it's the Oracle kernel process that writes to the trace file. The play-by-play you'll see in the Oracle trace data stream is the story told from the perspective of an Oracle server process like the one shown in the following sequence diagram:

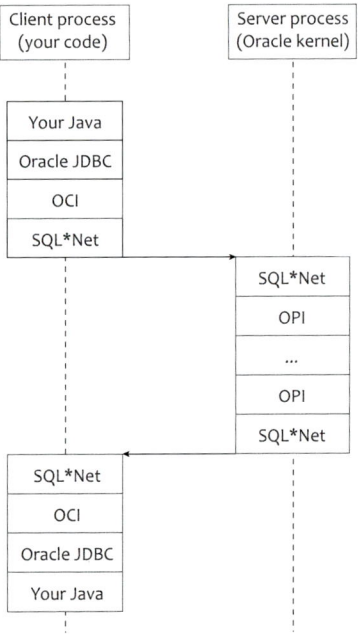

The Oracle two-tier, client-server architecture; the Oracle kernel process is the one that writes the trace data you'll be reading.

On the client process is your Java code, which makes calls to the Oracle Java Database Connectivity API (the Oracle JDBC),[5] which calls the Oracle Call Interface (OCI),[6] which calls the SQL*Net interface to communicate with the server process. On the server process is the SQL*Net communication interface which allows the OCI calls from the client to run

---

[4] It's a little more complicated than that, because sometimes the Oracle kernel calls more than one OS call in the context of a single WAIT line. But it usually doesn't matter if you don't know this.

[5] For a description of the *oracle.jdbc* package, see *http://download.oracle.com/docs/cd/ E18283_01/appdev.112/e13995/oracle/jdbc/package-summary.html*.

[6] Oracle Corporation, 2008: "Oracle Call Interface Programmer's Guide" at *http://download. oracle.com/docs/cd/B28359_01/appdev.111/b28395/toc.htm*.

Oracle Program Interface (OPI) functions, which are responsible for the bulk of the work on the Oracle Database.

The following paragraphs contain a play-by-play analysis of an Oracle trace file produced by a Java program that consumed about 23 seconds of response time querying 142,517 rows from an Oracle database. You can see more details from that trace file in "Trace File: Slow Query" on page 43. The action within the trace file that we're interested in begins on line 24:

```
24 =====================
25 PARSING IN CURSOR #1 len=21 dep=0 uid=55 oct=3 lid=55 tim=1198860497738418 hv=3808180571 ad='2d45e9d0'
26 select * from sla_run
27 END OF STMT
```

These lines reveal what future references to cursor #1 will mean: they'll be references to an Oracle Database cursor associated with the SQL statement "select * from sla_run". References to cursor #1 will refer to that SQL statement until cursor #1 is redefined with another PARSING IN CURSOR #1.[7]

```
28 PARSE #1:c=0,e=251,p=0,cr=0,cu=0,mis=0,r=0,dep=0,og=1,tim=1198860497738414
```

Line 28 is where the recording of time consumption begins. This line reveals that the Oracle kernel process executed an OPI parse function upon the *select* statement shown on line 26. The OPI parse function is the server-side companion of the *OCIStmtPrepare* call, which the Oracle JDBC executed within our client process. This parse function consumed 251 μs (that is, 251 microseconds, or 0.000251 seconds) of response time.

```
29 BINDS #1:
```

There were no placeholders in the SQL statement to which values were to be bound; otherwise, we would have seen more information (more lines of trace data) here.

```
30 EXEC #1:c=0,e=84,p=0,cr=0,cu=0,mis=0,r=0,dep=0,og=1,tim=1198860497738645
31 WAIT #1: nam='SQL*Net message to client' ela= 2 driver id=1952673792 #bytes=1 p3=0 obj#=-1 tim=1198860497738727
```

The Oracle kernel executed an OPI execute function (companion of *OCIStmtExecute*) upon the cursor described in the PARSING IN CURSOR #1 section. The function consumed 84 μs of response time. Then the Oracle kernel wrote some information back to its caller (the Java program) through its SQL*Net interface. The 2-μs duration reported here is not the duration of an OS *write* call, although you have a right to expect that it would be. It is actually only the duration of an OS timer call executed before the *write*. It's an Oracle bug, but not a very important one.[8]

```
32 WAIT #1: nam='SQL*Net message from client' ela= 25227 driver id=1952673792 #bytes=1 p3=0 obj#=-1 tim=1198860497764024
```

Then the Oracle kernel blocked upon an OS *read* call (the same way a *read* of your keyboard will block until you press the Enter key), passing 25,227 μs of end-user response time. This is actually the duration of the whole network round-trip from the Oracle kernel process to the client and back. It also includes all the time spent executing code on the client, including time the client spends waiting on user input.

```
33 WAIT #1: nam='SQL*Net message to client' ela= 24 driver id=1952673792 #bytes=1 p3=0 obj#=-1 tim=1198860497764438
34 FETCH #1:c=0,e=355,p=0,cr=4,cu=0,mis=0,r=10,dep=0,og=1,tim=1198860497764514
35 WAIT #1: nam='SQL*Net message from client' ela= 7851 driver id=1952673792 #bytes=1 p3=0 obj#=-1 tim=1198860497772417
```

The kernel executed an OPI fetch function (the Oracle Database kernel's companion function to the *OCIStmtFetch* call that a client program can make) upon the cursor executed in line 30. The fetch returned 10 rows in one network round-trip, consuming 355 μs. The *SQL*Net message to client* call is a tiny little sequence of code path executed within the context of the fetch, which consumed 24 μs. After the fetch, the kernel blocked upon an OS read call for another 7,851 μs awaiting the next call from the client.

```
36 WAIT #1: nam='SQL*Net message to client' ela= 2 driver id=1952673792 #bytes=1 p3=0 obj#=-1 tim=1198860497772500
37 FETCH #1:c=0,e=84,p=0,cr=1,cu=0,mis=0,r=10,dep=0,og=1,tim=1198860497772568
```

---

[7] Starting in Oracle Database version 11.2.0.2, the cursor numbers are no longer small integers like 1, 2, or 3. Now, they're cursor handle ids, which look like 47112802701552, and which are considerably more difficult for human brains to parse.

[8] See "The Bug with SQL*Net message to client" on page 75 for details.

Chapter 2. Making Friends with the Oracle Database

```
38 WAIT #1: nam='SQL*Net message from client' ela= 1306 driver id=1952673792 #bytes=1 p3=0 obj#=-1 tim=1198860497773924
39 WAIT #1: nam='SQL*Net message to client' ela= 2 driver id=1952673792 #bytes=1 p3=0 obj#=-1 tim=1198860497773985
40 FETCH #1:c=0,e=81,p=0,cr=1,cu=0,mis=0,r=10,dep=0,og=1,tim=1198860497774051
41 WAIT #1: nam='SQL*Net message from client' ela= 1282 driver id=1952673792 #bytes=1 p3=0 obj#=-1 tim=1198860497775378
...
42788 WAIT #1: nam='SQL*Net message to client' ela= 2 driver id=1952673792 #bytes=1 p3=0 obj#=-1 tim=1198860521138223
42789 FETCH #1:c=0,e=86,p=0,cr=1,cu=0,mis=0,r=7,dep=0,og=1,tim=1198860521138298
42790 WAIT #1: nam='SQL*Net message from client' ela= 2141 driver id=1952673792 #bytes=1 p3=0 obj#=-1 tim=1198860521140722
```

Here, the same three-line pattern repeats thousands of times. The kernel returns 10 rows per network round-trip to the client until finally there are only 7 rows returned in the final attempted ten-row fetch, at which point the client code path can detect that it has fetched all the rows that the kernel had to offer, and the query is finished.

Understanding an individual line of trace data is usually not difficult. Another layer of difficulty unfolds when you want to summarize the information presented by a block of trace file lines. The job is more complicated than you might have guessed by now, because there are gaps and overlaps in how the Oracle kernel emits its own timing data.

You can often get a good general sense of what's going on in a trace file simply by aggregating c or e values for database calls and *ela* values for OS calls. I summarize trace data with a software tool that I helped design and develop, called the Method R Profiler.[9] You could summarize with the *mrskew* tool, as well. The two tools will give slightly different answers, for reasons I'll explain in chapter 5.

Summarizing the elapsed time consumed by database calls and OS calls yields the information shown here:

Call	Response time (seconds)	
SQL*Net message from client	20.070	85.8%
fetch	1.652	7.1%
all other	1.683	7.2%
Total response time	23.405	100.0%

Response time profile of our 23-second query program execution.

The code spends 85.8% of its user's time moving rows across the network[10] and only 7.1% fetching rows out of the database. That's a pattern I want you to recognize when you see it, this issue of response time being dominated by network I/O. It is an important performance antipattern.[11]

OPTIMIZING THE QUERY PROGRAM

Whenever network I/O time dominates the response time of a program you've written, it's probably an easy opportunity for you to optimize your code. It's usually not hard to perform the optimization. The step that most people miss is to look at response time decomposed this way to begin with. Once you see the problem, you can focus your energy on fixing it. So, here we go…

Did you flinch at all when you saw line 34 of the trace data that I showed you earlier?

```
34 FETCH #1:c=0,e=355,p=0,cr=4,cu=0,mis=0,r=10,dep=0,og=1,tim=1198860497764514
```

---

[9] Method R Profiler at *http://method-r.com/software/profiler*.

[10] Some of the 20.070 seconds of *SQL*Net message from client* time is spent by client Java code path. If I wanted to test exactly how much time the client program is spending, I would profile the client-side Java code.

[11] Many Oracle authors teach that you should ignore all *SQL*Net message from client* calls. But that's an absolutely awful idea; you will misdiagnose performance problems if you do that.

Notice that the fetch call returned not just one row to the application, but 10. Whenever your Java code asks the JDBC for *rowSource.next*, the JDBC cleverly grabs and buffers rows for you in batches of ten. The default array size is 10. Had the array size been set to 1 instead, can you guess what our response time would have looked like?

The answer is that the program's response time would have been about ten times worse. We tried it:

Array fetch size	Response time (seconds)
1	240.297
10	23.405

Our performance was ten times worse when we used an array fetch size of 1 instead of the default value of 10.

It's easy to understand why, once you've seen the trace data. If our program had fetched one row at a time instead of ten, it would have made ten times more network round-trips to fetch all the data. Thus, instead of the 23 seconds of response time you saw in the profile on the prior page, you should expect over 200 seconds of network I/O time. ...Which is exactly what did happen.

At this point, I hope you've begun to wonder about the following questions:

1. What if you were to make the array fetch size bigger than 10? Would it improve response time?

2. Is there a point of diminishing returns, beyond which the array fetch size can be too big?

3. How do you manipulate the array fetch size?

The answer to the first question is that yes, absolutely, increasing the array fetch size improves response time for our program. We tried several array fetch sizes, and you can see from the shape of the curve here that manipulating the array fetch size had a profound impact upon performance:

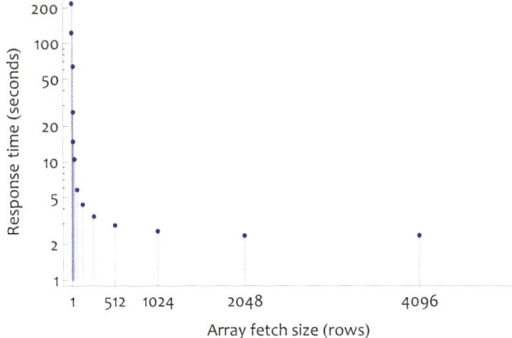

Our array fetch size had a profound impact upon our query's performance.

In our program testing, we tried lots of array fetch sizes, and we found that the sweet spot for us (given our row sizes, our TCP/IP packet sizes, etc.) was roughly 2,048. That's where our response times settled in at about 2.4 seconds. That array fetch size yields about a 90% reduction in response time compared to the default setting of 10.

Array sizes larger than 2,048 didn't produce a performance benefit for us, in spite of consuming a lot more memory. For array fetch sizes larger than 4,096, response times actually degraded a bit. When we tried an array fetch size setting of 16,384, our Java program

Chapter 2. Making Friends with the Oracle Database

promptly died of an out-of-memory error.[12] Bigger is better to a point, at which too big becomes bad.

So how can you manipulate your array fetch size? If you use the Oracle JDBC, it's easy. You execute the *setFetchSize* method upon the statement object, like this:

```
1  statement.setFetchSize(size);              // Set the array fetch size.
2  resultSet = statement.executeQuery(query);
3  while (resultSet.next()) {
4      // do your business upon resultSet
5  }
```

Here is how the program that used the array fetch size of 2,048 spent our 2.4 seconds:

Call	Response time (seconds)	
SQL*Net message from client	0.890	37.1%
SQL*Net more data to client	0.823	34.3%
fetch	0.745	31.0%
all other	−0.058	−2.4%
Total response time	2.400	100.0%

Response time profile of our improved 2.4-second query program execution.

Don't feel too unsettled by the negative number shown in the *all other* category of this table. It is an artifact of the ±10,000-µs accuracy on the CPU statistic, which I mentioned earlier. Sometimes, the c statistic over-accounts for elapsed duration. For example, a database call with $c=10000, e=8000$ would indicate:

Call	Response time (microseconds)	
some dbcall	10,000	125.0%
all other	−2,000	−25.0%
Total response time	8,000	100.0%

Response time profile that shows the negative unaccounted-for time effect of a single database call with $c=100000, e=8000$.

The point is that by manipulating our array fetch size, we reduced the total time we spent waiting for network I/O calls from 20.070 seconds to a much more bearable .890 + .823 = 1.713 seconds. We even reduced the amount of CPU time we spent in fetch calls, presumably because we're not making nearly as many fetch calls with the larger array fetch size.

The overall performance improvement is spectacular (from 23.405 seconds to 2.400 seconds) because we targeted the exact reason that the program spent so much of our time. Such is the principal beauty of profiling: it focuses our attention where it belongs, and it safely allows us to ignore everything that doesn't matter.

In "Trace File: Improved Query" on page 44, you can see some of the raw trace data for the improved program. Here's a brief walk-through of how that program progressed. The interesting action begins, again, on line 24:

```
24 =====================
25 PARSING IN CURSOR #1 len=21 dep=0 uid=55 oct=3 lid=55 tim=1200121349671182 hv=3808180571 ad='2d7dd08c'
26 select * from sla_run
27 END OF STMT
28 PARSE #1:c=1000,e=121,p=0,cr=0,cu=0,mis=0,r=0,dep=0,og=1,tim=1200121349671176
29 BINDS #1:
30 EXEC #1:c=0,e=57,p=0,cr=0,cu=0,mis=0,r=0,dep=0,og=1,tim=1200121349671305
31 WAIT #1: nam='SQL*Net message to client' ela= 3 driver id=1952673792 #bytes=1 p3=0 obj#=-1 tim=1200121349671351
32 WAIT #1: nam='SQL*Net message from client' ela= 5960 driver id=1952673792 #bytes=1 p3=0 obj#=-1 tim=1200121349677368
```

---

[12] We used a maximum Java heap size of 64 MB by specifying `java -Xms 2m -Xmx 64m`.

This is the same pattern as you saw previously in the slow code. However, what comes next is very different:

```
33 WAIT #1: nam='SQL*Net message to client' ela= 6 driver id=1952673792 #bytes=1 p3=0 obj#=-1 tim=1200121349677583
34 WAIT #1: nam='SQL*Net more data to client' ela= 149 driver id=1952673792 #bytes=2001 p3=0 obj#=-1 tim=1200121349677942
35 WAIT #1: nam='SQL*Net more data to client' ela= 7 driver id=1952673792 #bytes=2002 p3=0 obj#=-1 tim=1200121349678167
36 WAIT #1: nam='SQL*Net more data to client' ela= 9 driver id=1952673792 #bytes=2000 p3=0 obj#=-1 tim=1200121349678404
...
68 WAIT #1: nam='SQL*Net more data to client' ela= 10 driver id=1952673792 #bytes=1997 p3=0 obj#=-1 tim=1200121349699464
69 FETCH #1:c=11998,e=22206,p=0,cr=16,cu=0,mis=0,r=2048,dep=0,og=1,tim=1200121349699630
```

Here, the Oracle kernel makes a *SQL*Net message to client* call to ship results back to the client, but the result set is so big that it won't fit into a single network packet. So the kernel makes a number of *SQL*Net more data to client* calls to fulfill the passage of data that it owes to the client. Finally, the kernel completes the fetch call, which you can see returned 2,048 rows in 22,206 µs, after consuming approximately 11,998 µs of CPU time.

The pattern repeats until the end of the trace file:

```
2928 WAIT #1: nam='SQL*Net more data to client' ela= 8 driver id=1952673792 #bytes=1999 p3=0 obj#=-1 tim=1200121352050874
2929 FETCH #1:c=6999,e=6837,p=0,cr=16,cu=0,mis=0,r=1205,dep=0,og=1,tim=1200121352051111
2930 WAIT #1: nam='SQL*Net message from client' ela= 18557 driver id=1952673792 #bytes=1 p3=0 obj#=-1 tim=1200121352069816
```

...where the last 6,837-µs fetch returns the final 1,205 rows. It makes sense, this final fetch size. Earlier, I mentioned that this query returns 142,517 rows. Note that 142,517 % 2,048 = 1,205 (using '%' as the modulus operator), so 1,205 is exactly the number of rows you should expect to be left, after several 2,048-row fetches, for the final fetch to grab.

OPTIMIZING BEGINS WITH MEASURING

Here's a quick quiz. What have you learned so far?

a. Your optimal Oracle array fetch size is 2,048.

b. You should always check to make sure that you've optimized your array fetch size.

c. You should always check to see where your response time is going before you optimize anything.

Choice (a) is a really poor one, because the optimal Oracle array fetch size for the next program you write is probably going to be different than the optimal array fetch size for the program we just analyzed. Your optimal array fetch size is a function of several factors, including at least these:

How big are the rows you're returning?

How big are your network packets?

I can easily imagine, for example, that if our rows had been 100 times larger than they were, then our optimal array fetch size might have been 100 times smaller. However, I've learned enough over the years to believe that any kind of a mathematical model is useful only as a starting point, and that you should base your optimizations upon real operational data.

Choice (b) is therefore superior to choice (a). The problem with choice (b), though, is that instead of an array fetch size example, I could have chosen an example to highlight any of thousands of other problems that code *can* have. Are you supposed to check those thousands of other things, too? You can't do it. And you shouldn't try to.

Choice (c) is therefore superior to choice (b). Not every program you write will have response time dominated by network I/O. There are thousands of different ways your program can spend your user's time. Why use a checklist to attack everything that might possibly be slowing your code down when you have a tool at your disposal—the Oracle extended SQL trace data—to show you exactly how your code is spending its time? Why guess? ...when you can know.

Chapter 2. Making Friends with the Oracle Database

Oracle's trace files give you a language for understanding the performance of the code you write.

ON SPECIFICATION LEGITIMACY

I've just described a process of analyzing and improving performance for a query that returns 142,517 rows. I didn't tell you anything about how the Java program fetching those rows was going to use those rows. I left that to your imagination. I merely hoped you would tacitly assume that someone needed all those rows. Developers can tend to do that.

I, of course, chose such an example because it's easier to showcase the problem of "too much network I/O" when you illustrate with a query that returns a lot of rows. However, in real life, it's fair to ask the question, "Why do you need 142,517 rows?" Or even, "Do you really want all those rows?"

Dan Tow and I once had a dinner conversation in which we agreed on the following postulate:

> No human ever wants to see more than ten rows (Tow-Millsap law).

Our idea was that once you're presented with more than ten rows to look at, all in one picture, you'd really rather see some kind of aggregation (count, sum, mean, …whatever) of the data instead.[13]

So, the next time you're asked to improve the performance of a query that returns a jillion rows, at least ask the question whether the user using your program really, really wants to see a jillion rows in the first place. It's easier, cheaper, and more effective to give a user less data—if that's what he really wants—than to make your program faster at returning stuff that people didn't really want to begin with.

TRACE FILE GUIDED TOUR #2

Let's look at another example of some trace data that reveals another performance antipattern you should know about. In "Trace File: Slow Insert" on page 44, you can see an excerpt of an Oracle trace file for a sequence of 10,000 inserts, which consumed 32.706 seconds—about 33 seconds—of end-user response time.

First, before you look at the trace data, let me ask you this: Is 33 seconds a good response time for a program that inserts 10,000 rows into a table? Or is it a bad response time?

People's first response when I ask a question like that is usually either eyes-averted silence or a question like, "What kind of machine did it run on?" The truth is, unless you've recently encountered an application that did something similar to what this program did, you probably don't have any idea. There's nothing wrong with that. In a few minutes, you'll know the answer anyway.

So, let's walk through the lines and see what's going on. The interesting action begins on line 24:

```
24 ====================
25 PARSING IN CURSOR #2 len=40 dep=0 uid=55 oct=2 lid=55 tim=1198862067286178 hv=223277221 ad='30d87524'
26 insert into JAVA_TEST_TABLE values ('0')
27 END OF STMT
```

These lines indicate that cursor #2 refers to the SQL statement that inserts a row into *java_test_table*.

---

[13] Our corollary, of course, was, "Auditors are not human."

```
28  PARSE #2:c=0,e=678,p=0,cr=0,cu=0,mis=1,r=0,dep=0,og=1,tim=1198862067286173
29  BINDS #2:
```

These lines indicate that an OPI parse call has consumed 678 μs of response time, and that there were no values bound to placeholders in the statement. (That makes sense, because there aren't any placeholders in the statement.)

```
30  EXEC #2:c=2000,e=1245,p=0,cr=0,cu=4,mis=0,r=1,dep=0,og=1,tim=1198862067287560
```

The Oracle kernel executed an OPI exec function, which consumed 1,245 μs of response time to insert one row.

```
31  XCTEND rlbk=0, rd_only=0
```

The kernel executed an OPI commit function (the server-side companion of *OCITransCommit*), which committed everything this session has done thus far to the database.

```
32  WAIT #2: nam='SQL*Net message to client' ela= 2 driver id=1952673792 #bytes=1 p3=0 obj#=-1 tim=1198862067288169
33  WAIT #2: nam='SQL*Net message from client' ela= 1154 driver id=1952673792 #bytes=1 p3=0 obj#=-1 tim=1198862067289370
```

A network round-trip consumed 1,156 μs (2 μs + 1,154 μs) of response time.

And then, in the following lines, you see the same pattern over and over…

```
34  =====================
35  PARSING IN CURSOR #2 len=40 dep=0 uid=55 oct=2 lid=55 tim=1198862067289787 hv=1228865179 ad='2d6c3ea4'
36  insert into JAVA_TEST_TABLE values ('1')
37  END OF STMT
38  PARSE #2:c=0,e=302,p=0,cr=0,cu=0,mis=1,r=0,dep=0,og=1,tim=1198862067289781
39  BINDS #2:
40  EXEC #2:c=0,e=202,p=0,cr=1,cu=4,mis=0,r=1,dep=0,og=1,tim=1198862067290111
41  XCTEND rlbk=0, rd_only=0
42  WAIT #2: nam='log file sync' ela= 113 buffer#=737 p2=0 p3=0 obj#=-1 tim=1198862067290479
43  WAIT #2: nam='SQL*Net message to client' ela= 2 driver id=1952673792 #bytes=1 p3=0 obj#=-1 tim=1198862067290546
44  WAIT #2: nam='SQL*Net message from client' ela= 1918 driver id=1952673792 #bytes=1 p3=0 obj#=-1 tim=1198862067292503
45  =====================
46  PARSING IN CURSOR #2 len=40 dep=0 uid=55 oct=2 lid=55 tim=1198862067292826 hv=2978669578 ad='2d75ac84'
47  insert into JAVA_TEST_TABLE values ('2')
48  END OF STMT
49  PARSE #2:c=0,e=232,p=0,cr=0,cu=0,mis=1,r=0,dep=0,og=1,tim=1198862067292821
50  BINDS #2:
51  EXEC #2:c=0,e=146,p=0,cr=1,cu=4,mis=0,r=1,dep=0,og=1,tim=1198862067293093
52  XCTEND rlbk=0, rd_only=0
53  WAIT #2: nam='log file sync' ela= 107 buffer#=739 p2=0 p3=0 obj#=-1 tim=1198862067293425
54  WAIT #2: nam='SQL*Net message to client' ela= 2 driver id=1952673792 #bytes=1 p3=0 obj#=-1 tim=1198862067293477
55  WAIT #2: nam='SQL*Net message from client' ela= 2050 driver id=1952673792 #bytes=1 p3=0 obj#=-1 tim=1198862067295563
       ...
106360  =====================
106361  PARSING IN CURSOR #2 len=43 dep=0 uid=55 oct=2 lid=55 tim=1198862099985077 hv=3863691391 ad='2d494c40'
106362  insert into JAVA_TEST_TABLE values ('9999')
106363  END OF STMT
106364  PARSE #2:c=2000,e=1518,p=0,cr=0,cu=0,mis=1,r=0,dep=0,og=1,tim=1198862099985071
106365  BINDS #2:
106366  EXEC #2:c=0,e=84,p=0,cr=1,cu=5,mis=0,r=1,dep=0,og=1,tim=1198862099985234
106367  XCTEND rlbk=0, rd_only=0
106368  WAIT #2: nam='SQL*Net message to client' ela= 3 driver id=1952673792 #bytes=1 p3=0 obj#=-1 tim=1198862099985576
106369  WAIT #2: nam='SQL*Net message from client' ela= 2227 driver id=1952673792 #bytes=1 p3=0 obj#=-1 tim=1198862099987834
106370  XCTEND rlbk=0, rd_only=1
```

However, you can see, on lines 42 and 53, a kind of OS call that I haven't shown you yet. The Oracle name *log file sync* refers to a synchronization event that takes place between the Oracle kernel process inserting the rows and a "background" Oracle process called the "log writer." The two *log file sync* calls shown here consumed 113 μs and then 107 μs of response time.

Summarizing the elapsed time consumed by database calls and OS calls (aggregating the *e* and *ela* values for the individual call types) yields the information shown here:

Call	Response time (seconds)	
SQL*Net message from client	14.637	44.8%
log file sync	6.389	19.5%
parse	4.901	15.0%
exec	0.943	2.9%
all other	5.836	17.8%
Total response time	32.706	100.0%

Response time profile of our 33-second insert program execution.

OPTIMIZING THE INSERT PROGRAM

Now let's revisit the question, "Is 33 seconds a good response time for this program?" The profile gives enough data to prove that the answer is a resounding no. Here's why…

The whole point of our program is to insert 10,000 rows into a table. The Oracle function that does that work is represented in the trace data by the EXEC lines. This program spent only 2.9% of its time—less than a second!—actually putting rows into the database; yet I had to wait more than half a minute for the program to complete. The remainder of the time was spent (wasted?) doing other things.

Again, you can see in the profile, the dominant response time contributor fits the "excessive network I/O" antipattern. The trace file actually shows one network round-trip for every single row that's inserted into the database. The next step should be obvious to you by now: we need to find a way to insert more than one row per network round-trip.

Here's how the original Java code was written:

```
 6  import java.sql.Connection;
 7  import java.sql.PreparedStatement;
 8  import java.sql.SQLException;
 9  import java.sql.Statement;
10
11  for (Integer i : ilist) {
12      String sql = String.format("insert into t values ('%d')", i);   // Create a SQL text string with the inserted value built in.
13      Statement st = conn.createStatement();                           // Create a statement from the text string.
14      st.executeUpdate(sql);                                            // Execute the statement.
15  }
```

This code performs the extraordinarily nasty act of creating 10,000 (the size of *ilist*) distinct SQL statements within the Oracle Database. Yes, your database administrator might tell you not to worry, that he has a database parameter called *cursor_sharing* that will take care of the problem.

But it won't.

…Because your problem isn't so much the 4.901 seconds of parse work that's being done on the Oracle Database server as it is the 14.637 seconds of work moving data across the network from your client code to your server code. Manipulating your Oracle Database's *cursor_sharing* parameter may make your database administrator happy (some of the red lights on his dashboard will turn green), but it's not going to make your users happy, because their response times will still be intolerable.[14]

---

[14] The Oracle *cursor_sharing* parameter lets your database administrator instruct the Oracle Database kernel to translate your SQL statements into what those statements might have looked like if you had used placeholders instead of literal values. It's a clever plan, but there are two big problems with it. First, it puts even *more* workload onto your database server.

People can argue all they want about whether to make adjustments to the network or the database, but a good application developer can stop all the discussion by writing the code a different way. I'll show you how we re-wrote it shortly. Before I get into the code changes, let me show you the performance improvement we were able to achieve, which you can see in the next profile. That should serve as some motivation for you to move forward.

Call	Response time (seconds)	
SQL*Net message from client	0.083	55.0%
log file sync	0.040	26.4%
exec	0.029	19.2%
all other	−0.001	−0.5%
Total response time	0.151	100.0%

Response time profile of our rewritten 0.151-second insert program execution, for the program that previously required 32.706 seconds.

That's a 99.5% performance improvement, from 32.706 seconds to 0.151 seconds. More importantly, that's an improvement from "get up from your desk while this finishes" slow to "click-done" fast. And it frees up over 32 seconds' worth of capacity on your system that allows other work to take place without having to compete against your program for resources.

The changes we made to the code are all in response to what the profile on page 38 showed us. A simple top-down walk of that profile led us to ask the following questions:

- Do we really need to spend 14.637 seconds doing network communications?

- Do we really need to spend 6.389 seconds executing log file sync calls?

- Do we really need to spend 4.901 seconds preparing SQL?

Now let's answer those questions.

We've already seen the "excessive network I/O" antipattern in the query example I worked through for you earlier. It is related to the excessive amount of time we've spent preparing SQL (those *parse* calls that showed up in our raw trace data).

The answer here is, once again, to figure out how to process more than one row per database call. The general strategy we want to employ is to prepare our SQL statement only once, bind values into that statement to represent all our rows to be inserted, and then make sure we're bundling bunches of row insertions into each database call our code motivates.

You can do that with the Oracle JDBC. Here's the code we used to produce our 0.151-second example:

```
16  import java.sql.Connection;
17  import java.sql.PreparedStatement;
18  import java.sql.SQLException;
19  import java.sql.Statement;
20  import oracle.jdbc.OracleConnection;          // Need this to use setDefaultExecuteBatch method.
21
22  ((OracleConnection)conn).setDefaultExecuteBatch(1000);   // Set array execute size.
23  conn.setAutoCommit(false);                    // Do not commit every row.
24  String sql = String.format("insert into t values (?)");  // SQL uses '?' placeholder that will be bound to a value later.
25  PreparedStatement pst = conn.prepareStatement(sql);
26  for (Integer i : ilist) {
27      pst.setInt(1, i);                         // Bind the value of i into the 1st '?' placeholder slot.
28      pst.executeUpdate();                      // Execute the statement with the bound value.
29  }
30  conn.commit();                                // Commit once at the end.
```

More importantly, it does nothing to reduce the quantity of network I/O that is our example's dominant problem.

Chapter 2. Making Friends with the Oracle Database

We used the *setDefaultExecuteBatch* method to set the array execute size to 1,000. Now, instead of preparing thousands of distinct SQL statements inside the loop, we've prepared a single SQL statement outside the loop, which uses the '?' character as a placeholder for the values that will be inserted. Using (and reusing) a *PreparedStatement* will eliminate 9,999 of the OPI parse calls that plagued the original 32-second program.

Inside the loop, we now have a *setInt* call that binds the value of *i* to the first (and only) '?' placeholder in the SQL statement, and then an *executeUpdate* call does the insertion. Since the default execute batch size is now set to 1,000, this code will only make a real Oracle database call (and the associated network round-trip) once for every 1,000 calls.

So, with this code, we've saved thousands of network I/Os and reduced the amount of time the program spends parsing inside the database to practically zero. Magic.

But there's more. The *log file sync* time represents another important performance improvement opportunity.[15] The repeated appearance of either *log file sync* calls or XCTEND lines in a trace file (in our case, we had both) is an indication of repeated database *commit* processing. Excessive *commit* processing can create a performance problem that accelerates as the amount of concurrent workload increases (so it's a scalability problem, too), and it even creates a functional problem as well.

Let's talk about the functional problem first. Imagine that you're responsible for running this 10,000-row insert once a day. Imagine that it clicks along just fine for weeks on end, but then one day, part-way into the program's execution, your system housing the Oracle database crashes. It happens.

So when someone gets the Oracle database restarted, one of the things you're going to have to do is figure out how many of the rows made it into the database before it crashed. In fact, you're going to have to figure out exactly *which* rows made it into the database before it crashed, because you're going to need to make sure that either you delete those rows so you can run your program again, or you're going to need to insert the ones that didn't make it in, so that all 10,000 will be in the database when you're done. When you're finished with the recovery, you'll need to ensure that no rows are missing, and none are duplicated.

If you're like most application developers, you're only going to want to do this job once. It's not going to be a lot of fun figuring out which rows made it and which rows didn't. If you're lucky, there will be some kind of batch id or date field that will allow you to pinpoint exactly which rows made it in. Maybe you'll be tempted to write some kind of clean-up functions to go with your application so that this kind of scenario will be easier for you (or your customers) to deal with if it ever happens again.

If you use Oracle differently, however, you won't have to do that.

If, instead of committing every single row to the database as your application inserts it, you waited until the end of all 10,000 insertions and then committed the whole transaction, your life would be much simpler. Then, if the Oracle system ever failed in the midst of your job, you'd know: either there are 10,000 new rows in the database (if your commit call succeeded) or there are 0 new rows in the database (if your *commit* call failed).

Plus, you'll save a lot of unnecessary work that consumes a lot of unnecessary time. Implementing the single-commit idea reduced our time spent waiting for *log file sync* events from 6.389 seconds (page 38) to 0.040 seconds (page 39). That's huge. And we eliminated over six seconds of resource consumption that other processes on the system had to wait behind, which makes the whole system faster for everyone.

The decision of how often to commit is an important one. I've shown here why committing after every row can be bad. However, committing only once at the end of a multi-million-row insert may be bad, too, because of the stress upon the Oracle Database undo manage-

---

[15] I'll cover what these event names mean in chapter 4.

ment subsystem, and because maybe you don't want to have to restart a whole multi-million-row transaction after an instance failure. Maybe it would be better to commit in batches of 10,000 rows, or maybe even 10 rows. Part of your application design responsibility is to manage this tradeoff, which should include the task of using measurements instead of guesses about the costs of *commit* processing.

In "Trace File: Improved Insert" on page 45, you can see some of the trace data for an execution of the new program. Notice that each EXEC line now processes 1,000 rows (r=1000) instead of just one. And notice that there is only one *log file sync* call now, right at the end of the trace file. This is because the new code uses *setAutoCommit* to disable automatic *commit* processing after each row insertion and then commits the whole batch in one call at the end.

Measuring is Vital

So, what have you learned from this chapter? It's easy to start thinking in absolutes about "best practices." I'm suspicious about most so-called best practices because I believe in Clarke's fourth law:[16]

> For every expert, there is an equal and opposite expert.

There is one "best practice," though, in which I do believe deeply:

> You should always measure your application's performance and target your optimization efforts at places where your code will benefit from it most.

This was Knuth's point in his famous statement about premature optimization being the root of all evil:[17]

> There is no doubt that the grail of efficiency leads to abuse. Programmers waste enormous amounts of time thinking about, or worrying about, the speed of noncritical parts of their programs, and these attempts at efficiency actually have a strong negative impact when debugging and maintenance are considered. We should forget about small efficiencies, say about 97% of the time: premature optimization is the root of all evil.
>
> Yet we should not pass up our opportunities in that critical 3%. A good programmer will not be lulled into complacency by such reasoning, he will be wise to look carefully at the critical code; but only *after* that code has been identified. It is often a mistake to make a priori judgments about what parts of a program are really critical, since the universal experience of programmers who have been using measurement tools has been that their intuitive guesses fail. After working with such tools for seven years, I've become convinced that all compilers written from now on should be designed to provide all programmers with feedback indicating what parts of their programs are costing the most; indeed, this feedback should be supplied automatically unless it has been specifically turned off.

As you now understand, the way I implement this practice in the Oracle world today is with the extended SQL trace feature. There are other ways to peek into what the Oracle kernel is doing,[18] but no other way gives you such a simple sequential listing of exactly

---

[16] Wikipedia: "Clarke's three laws" at *http://en.wikipedia.org/wiki/Clarke%27s_three_laws*.

[17] Donald Knuth, "Structured programming with Go To statements" in ACM Journal *Computing Surveys*, 268.

[18] Oracle's Active Session History (ASH) is one name you might recognize.

where all of the time has gone for just the code path that you're interested in. If you learn how to use the extended SQL trace feature, you'll learn a lot more about Oracle, and you'll learn exactly what you need to know, right when you need to learn it.

I think one of the nicest things about Oracle tracing (and profiling in general) is that it focuses your attention where it needs to be right now. It doesn't leave you feeling like you have to know everything about Oracle all at once. It's also a feature that's available in development, testing, and production environments, so it's truly a single tool that you can use throughout your entire software life cycle.

As a developer, you can make it really easy to trace your code. My team have tried to make it easy for developers to instrument code the right way by publishing a free, open source instrumentation library for Oracle called ILO.[19] ILO consists of a couple of Oracle PL/SQL packages with functions you can call from Java, PHP, or whatever language you're writing in. If you're curious about how good instrumentation works, studying the PL/SQL within ILO is a good place to start.

SUMMARY

Speed is a vital feature of good software. Speed doesn't just happen by accident. It is a feature that you have to design into good programs. Designing good performance into your code is extremely difficult to do without good feedback about the speed of your code as you're writing it.

Many Oracle application developers work under the assumption that the Oracle Database kernel is a "black box" that they shouldn't bother to understand. But writing code within the abstraction model that the Oracle Database is merely a "persistent data store" almost assures that you will write code that is slower and that wastes far more precious computing resources than it should.

The Oracle extended SQL trace mechanism provides the feedback that you need to write fast, efficient code for Oracle-based systems. Extended SQL tracing reveals where your time is being spent inside the Oracle Database kernel, all the way down to the individual database or operating system subroutine call.

With this chapter, I hope I have illuminated the following key points for you:

- Oracle extended SQL trace data shows you exactly where your code spends your user's time.

- With trace data, you can determine whether your code is efficient.

- If your code can run faster, tracing shows you why and by how much. It allows you to predict the performance impact of changing your code, without so much trial and error.

- Tracing prevents you from wasting time "tuning" aspects of your program that won't result in appreciable response time benefits.

- Tracing prevents the feeling that you have to know "everything about Oracle" before you can write fast, provably efficient code.

- You can use performance feedback in your programs to create self-adjusting applications that adapt to your software's true operational constraints.

- Not every perceived requirement is a legitimate requirement. Tracing allows you to measure objectively the performance cost of a feature, which in turn helps the business make better decisions about which software features it truly requires.

---

[19] Method R Corporation, 2008: "Instrumentation library for Oracle (ILO)" at *http://method-r.com/software/ilo*.

- Knowing how to measure performance, and knowing how to determine whether the performance you have observed is optimal are more important than your being able to remember lists of software performance "best practices."
- You can make your application easier to tune and debug by incorporating extended SQL tracing into your code. Ideally, you should regard the ability to measure performance at run-time as an important functional specification.

I hope this chapter encourages you to instrument your code, gain access to your Oracle trace data, and study it for some of your own applications that mean something to you and that need to be fast.

I haven't covered everything you need to know yet, of course. For example, I haven't discussed how connection management code paths prevent your application from scaling. I haven't told you any details about why excessive parse calls and excessive visits to the database buffer cache cause an application not to scale. But I have shown you enough to get you started upon a much more informed path toward writing scalable, high-performance Oracle-based applications. In chapter 3, I'll show you more details about trace data, including how to turn the tracing facility on and off, and how to interpret the data you'll find in a trace file. In chapter 4, I'll explain the call names that you'll encounter frequently as you look through trace files.

TRACE FILE: SLOW QUERY

The following trace file excerpt shows trace data for the 23.405-second query program.

```
 1  /usr/lib/oracle/xe/app/oracle/admin/XE/udump/xe_ora_9024_METHODR_TESTING_.trc
 2  Oracle Database 10g Express Edition Release 10.2.0.1.0 - Production
 3  ORACLE_HOME = /usr/lib/oracle/xe/app/oracle/product/10.2.0/server
 4  System name:    Linux
 5  Node name:      oracle01.dev.method-r.com
 6  Release:        2.6.25.6-27.fc8
 7  Version:        #1 SMP Fri Jun 13 16:38:52 EDT 2008
 8  Machine:        i686
 9  Instance name: XE
10  Redo thread mounted by this instance: 1
11  Oracle process number: 18
12  Unix process pid: 9024, image: oracleXE@oracle01.dev.method-r.com
13
14  *** SERVICE NAME:(SYS$USERS) 2008-11-25 11:12:29.682
15  *** SESSION ID:(26.22686) 2008-11-25 11:12:29.682
16  =====================
17  PARSING IN CURSOR #2 len=69 dep=0 uid=55 oct=42 lid=55 tim=1198860497736569 hv=3164292706 ad='30e088a4'
18  alter session set events '10046 trace name context forever, level 12'
19  END OF STMT
20  EXEC #2:c=1000,e=91,p=0,cr=0,cu=0,mis=0,r=0,dep=0,og=1,tim=1198860497736561
21  XCTEND rlbk=0, rd_only=1
22  WAIT #2: nam='SQL*Net message to client' ela= 2 driver id=1952673792 #bytes=1 p3=0 obj#=-1 tim=1198860497737042
23  WAIT #2: nam='SQL*Net message from client' ela= 985 driver id=1952673792 #bytes=1 p3=0 obj#=-1 tim=1198860497738097
24  =====================
25  PARSING IN CURSOR #1 len=21 dep=0 uid=55 oct=3 lid=55 tim=1198860497738418 hv=3808180571 ad='2d45e9d0'
26  select * from sla_run
27  END OF STMT
28  PARSE #1:c=0,e=251,p=0,cr=0,cu=0,mis=0,r=0,dep=0,og=1,tim=1198860497738414
29  BINDS #1:
30  EXEC #1:c=0,e=84,p=0,cr=0,cu=0,mis=0,r=0,dep=0,og=1,tim=1198860497738645
31  WAIT #1: nam='SQL*Net message to client' ela= 2 driver id=1952673792 #bytes=1 p3=0 obj#=-1 tim=1198860497738727
32  WAIT #1: nam='SQL*Net message from client' ela= 25227 driver id=1952673792 #bytes=1 p3=0 obj#=-1 tim=1198860497764024
33  WAIT #1: nam='SQL*Net message to client' ela= 24 driver id=1952673792 #bytes=1 p3=0 obj#=-1 tim=1198860497764438
34  FETCH #1:c=0,e=355,p=0,cr=4,cu=0,mis=0,r=10,dep=0,og=1,tim=1198860497764514
35  WAIT #1: nam='SQL*Net message from client' ela= 7851 driver id=1952673792 #bytes=1 p3=0 obj#=-1 tim=1198860497772417
36  WAIT #1: nam='SQL*Net message to client' ela= 2 driver id=1952673792 #bytes=1 p3=0 obj#=-1 tim=1198860497772500
37  FETCH #1:c=0,e=84,p=0,cr=1,cu=0,mis=0,r=10,dep=0,og=1,tim=1198860497772568
38  WAIT #1: nam='SQL*Net message from client' ela= 1306 driver id=1952673792 #bytes=1 p3=0 obj#=-1 tim=1198860497773924
39  WAIT #1: nam='SQL*Net message to client' ela= 2 driver id=1952673792 #bytes=1 p3=0 obj#=-1 tim=1198860497773985
40  FETCH #1:c=0,e=81,p=0,cr=1,cu=0,mis=0,r=10,dep=0,og=1,tim=1198860497774051
41  WAIT #1: nam='SQL*Net message from client' ela= 1282 driver id=1952673792 #bytes=1 p3=0 obj#=-1 tim=1198860497775378
    ...
42788  WAIT #1: nam='SQL*Net message to client' ela= 2 driver id=1952673792 #bytes=1 p3=0 obj#=-1 tim=1198860521138223
42789  FETCH #1:c=0,e=86,p=0,cr=1,cu=0,mis=0,r=7,dep=0,og=1,tim=1198860521138298
42790  WAIT #1: nam='SQL*Net message from client' ela= 2141 driver id=1952673792 #bytes=1 p3=0 obj#=-1 tim=1198860521140722
```

Chapter 2. Making Friends with the Oracle Database

TRACE FILE: IMPROVED QUERY

The following trace file excerpt shows trace data for the improved 2.400-second insert program:

```
1  /usr/lib/oracle/xe/app/oracle/admin/XE/udump/xe_ora_28638_QUERY_2048.trc
2  Oracle Database 10g Express Edition Release 10.2.0.1.0 - Production
3  ORACLE_HOME = /usr/lib/oracle/xe/app/oracle/product/10.2.0/server
4  System name:    Linux
5  Node name:      oracle01.dev.method-r.com
6  Release:        2.6.25.6-27.fc8
7  Version:        #1 SMP Fri Jun 13 16:38:52 EDT 2008
8  Machine:        i686
9  Instance name: XE
10 Redo thread mounted by this instance: 1
11 Oracle process number: 18
12 Unix process pid: 28638, image: oracleXE@oracle01.dev.method-r.com
13
14 *** SERVICE NAME:(SYS$USERS) 2008-12-10 09:51:02.061
15 *** SESSION ID:(26.27749) 2008-12-10 09:51:02.061
16 =====================
17 PARSING IN CURSOR #2 len=69 dep=0 uid=55 oct=42 lid=55 tim=1200121349669845 hv=3164292706 ad='30d22bc0'
18 alter session set events '10046 trace name context forever, level 12'
19 END OF STMT
20 EXEC #2:c=0,e=59,p=0,cr=0,cu=0,mis=0,r=0,dep=0,og=1,tim=1200121349669837
21 XCTEND rlbk=0, rd_only=1
22 WAIT #2: nam='SQL*Net message to client' ela= 1 driver id=1952673792 #bytes=1 p3=0 obj#=-1 tim=1200121349670096
23 WAIT #2: nam='SQL*Net message from client' ela= 869 driver id=1952673792 #bytes=1 p3=0 obj#=-1 tim=1200121349671014
24 =====================
25 PARSING IN CURSOR #1 len=21 dep=0 uid=55 oct=3 lid=55 tim=1200121349671182 hv=3808180571 ad='2d7dd08c'
26 select * from sla_run
27 END OF STMT
28 PARSE #1:c=1000,e=121,p=0,cr=0,cu=0,mis=0,r=0,dep=0,og=1,tim=1200121349671176
29 BINDS #1:
30 EXEC #1:c=0,e=57,p=0,cr=0,cu=0,mis=0,r=0,dep=0,og=1,tim=1200121349671305
31 WAIT #1: nam='SQL*Net message to client' ela= 3 driver id=1952673792 #bytes=1 p3=0 obj#=-1 tim=1200121349671351
32 WAIT #1: nam='SQL*Net message from client' ela= 5960 driver id=1952673792 #bytes=1 p3=0 obj#=-1 tim=1200121349677368
33 WAIT #1: nam='SQL*Net message to client' ela= 6 driver id=1952673792 #bytes=1 p3=0 obj#=-1 tim=1200121349677583
34 WAIT #1: nam='SQL*Net more data to client' ela= 149 driver id=1952673792 #bytes=2001 p3=0 obj#=-1 tim=1200121349677942
35 WAIT #1: nam='SQL*Net more data to client' ela= 7 driver id=1952673792 #bytes=2002 p3=0 obj#=-1 tim=1200121349678167
36 WAIT #1: nam='SQL*Net more data to client' ela= 9 driver id=1952673792 #bytes=2000 p3=0 obj#=-1 tim=1200121349678404
37 WAIT #1: nam='SQL*Net more data to client' ela= 7 driver id=1952673792 #bytes=2006 p3=0 obj#=-1 tim=1200121349678670
38 WAIT #1: nam='SQL*Net more data to client' ela= 8 driver id=1952673792 #bytes=1998 p3=0 obj#=-1 tim=1200121349678893
39 WAIT #1: nam='SQL*Net more data to client' ela= 10 driver id=1952673792 #bytes=2000 p3=0 obj#=-1 tim=1200121349679321
40 WAIT #1: nam='SQL*Net more data to client' ela= 7 driver id=1952673792 #bytes=2000 p3=0 obj#=-1 tim=1200121349679641
41 WAIT #1: nam='SQL*Net more data to client' ela= 3402 driver id=1952673792 #bytes=2002 p3=0 obj#=-1 tim=1200121349683312
42 WAIT #1: nam='SQL*Net more data to client' ela= 132 driver id=1952673792 #bytes=2000 p3=0 obj#=-1 tim=1200121349683800
43 WAIT #1: nam='SQL*Net more data to client' ela= 121 driver id=1952673792 #bytes=2002 p3=0 obj#=-1 tim=1200121349684161
44 WAIT #1: nam='SQL*Net more data to client' ela= 8 driver id=1952673792 #bytes=2001 p3=0 obj#=-1 tim=1200121349684409
45 WAIT #1: nam='SQL*Net more data to client' ela= 10 driver id=1952673792 #bytes=2000 p3=0 obj#=-1 tim=1200121349684666
46 WAIT #1: nam='SQL*Net more data to client' ela= 6 driver id=1952673792 #bytes=2002 p3=0 obj#=-1 tim=1200121349684920
47 WAIT #1: nam='SQL*Net more data to client' ela= 828 driver id=1952673792 #bytes=2000 p3=0 obj#=-1 tim=1200121349685966
48 WAIT #1: nam='SQL*Net more data to client' ela= 123 driver id=1952673792 #bytes=2002 p3=0 obj#=-1 tim=1200121349686428
49 WAIT #1: nam='SQL*Net more data to client' ela= 68 driver id=1952673792 #bytes=2000 p3=0 obj#=-1 tim=1200121349686696
50 WAIT #1: nam='SQL*Net more data to client' ela= 7 driver id=1952673792 #bytes=2001 p3=0 obj#=-1 tim=1200121349686943
51 WAIT #1: nam='SQL*Net more data to client' ela= 8 driver id=1952673792 #bytes=2003 p3=0 obj#=-1 tim=1200121349687223
52 WAIT #1: nam='SQL*Net more data to client' ela= 6 driver id=1952673792 #bytes=1999 p3=0 obj#=-1 tim=1200121349687468
53 WAIT #1: nam='SQL*Net more data to client' ela= 9 driver id=1952673792 #bytes=2002 p3=0 obj#=-1 tim=1200121349687736
54 WAIT #1: nam='SQL*Net more data to client' ela= 6 driver id=1952673792 #bytes=2002 p3=0 obj#=-1 tim=1200121349688054
55 WAIT #1: nam='SQL*Net more data to client' ela= 2047 driver id=1952673792 #bytes=2002 p3=0 obj#=-1 tim=1200121349690352
56 WAIT #1: nam='SQL*Net more data to client' ela= 11 driver id=1952673792 #bytes=2000 p3=0 obj#=-1 tim=1200121349690646
57 WAIT #1: nam='SQL*Net more data to client' ela= 7 driver id=1952673792 #bytes=2001 p3=0 obj#=-1 tim=1200121349690905
58 WAIT #1: nam='SQL*Net more data to client' ela= 7 driver id=1952673792 #bytes=2001 p3=0 obj#=-1 tim=1200121349691160
59 WAIT #1: nam='SQL*Net more data to client' ela= 8 driver id=1952673792 #bytes=2006 p3=0 obj#=-1 tim=1200121349691597
60 WAIT #1: nam='SQL*Net more data to client' ela= 8 driver id=1952673792 #bytes=1997 p3=0 obj#=-1 tim=1200121349691851
61 WAIT #1: nam='SQL*Net more data to client' ela= 7 driver id=1952673792 #bytes=2001 p3=0 obj#=-1 tim=1200121349692248
62 WAIT #1: nam='SQL*Net more data to client' ela= 7 driver id=1952673792 #bytes=2002 p3=0 obj#=-1 tim=1200121349692507
63 WAIT #1: nam='SQL*Net more data to client' ela= 5125 driver id=1952673792 #bytes=2003 p3=0 obj#=-1 tim=1200121349697850
64 WAIT #1: nam='SQL*Net more data to client' ela= 11 driver id=1952673792 #bytes=1997 p3=0 obj#=-1 tim=1200121349698254
65 WAIT #1: nam='SQL*Net more data to client' ela= 9 driver id=1952673792 #bytes=2005 p3=0 obj#=-1 tim=1200121349698541
66 WAIT #1: nam='SQL*Net more data to client' ela= 7 driver id=1952673792 #bytes=2003 p3=0 obj#=-1 tim=1200121349698782
67 WAIT #1: nam='SQL*Net more data to client' ela= 10 driver id=1952673792 #bytes=1999 p3=0 obj#=-1 tim=1200121349699020
68 WAIT #1: nam='SQL*Net more data to client' ela= 10 driver id=1952673792 #bytes=1997 p3=0 obj#=-1 tim=1200121349699464
69 FETCH #1:c=11998,e=22206,p=0,cr=16,cu=0,mis=0,r=2048,dep=0,og=1,tim=1200121349699630
   ...
2928 WAIT #1: nam='SQL*Net more data to client' ela= 8 driver id=1952673792 #bytes=1999 p3=0 obj#=-1 tim=1200121352050874
2929 FETCH #1:c=6999,e=6837,p=0,cr=16,cu=0,mis=0,r=1205,dep=0,og=1,tim=1200121352051111
2930 WAIT #1: nam='SQL*Net message from client' ela= 18557 driver id=1952673792 #bytes=1 p3=0 obj#=-1 tim=1200121352069816
```

TRACE FILE: SLOW INSERT

The following trace file excerpt shows trace data for the slow 32.706-second insert program:

```
1  /usr/lib/oracle/xe/app/oracle/admin/XE/udump/xe_ora_9835_METHODR_TESTING_.trc
2  Oracle Database 10g Express Edition Release 10.2.0.1.0 - Production
3  ORACLE_HOME = /usr/lib/oracle/xe/app/oracle/product/10.2.0/server
4  System name:    Linux
5  Node name:      oracle01.dev.method-r.com
6  Release:        2.6.25.6-27.fc8
7  Version:        #1 SMP Fri Jun 13 16:38:52 EDT 2008
8  Machine:        i686
```

```
   9  Instance name: XE
  10  Redo thread mounted by this instance: 1
  11  Oracle process number: 21
  12  Unix process pid: 9835, image: oracleXE@oracle01.dev.method-r.com
  13
  14  *** SERVICE NAME:(SYS$USERS) 2008-11-25 11:39:16.895
  15  *** SESSION ID:(24.25822) 2008-11-25 11:39:16.895
  16  =====================
  17  PARSING IN CURSOR #3 len=69 dep=0 uid=55 oct=42 lid=55 tim=1198862067281227 hv=3164292706 ad='30e088a4'
  18  alter session set events '10046 trace name context forever, level 12'
  19  END OF STMT
  20  EXEC #3:c=0,e=71,p=0,cr=0,cu=0,mis=1,r=0,dep=0,og=1,tim=1198862067281220
  21  XCTEND rlbk=0, rd_only=1
  22  WAIT #3: nam='SQL*Net message to client' ela= 2 driver id=1952673792 #bytes=1 p3=0 obj#=-1 tim=1198862067281755
  23  WAIT #3: nam='SQL*Net message from client' ela= 3633 driver id=1952673792 #bytes=1 p3=0 obj#=-1 tim=1198862067285447
  24  =====================
  25  PARSING IN CURSOR #2 len=40 dep=0 uid=55 oct=2 lid=55 tim=1198862067286178 hv=223277221 ad='30d87524'
  26  insert into JAVA_TEST_TABLE values ('0')
  27  END OF STMT
  28  PARSE #2:c=0,e=678,p=0,cr=0,cu=0,mis=1,r=0,dep=0,og=1,tim=1198862067286173
  29  BINDS #2:
  30  EXEC #2:c=2000,e=1245,p=0,cr=1,cu=4,mis=0,r=1,dep=0,og=1,tim=1198862067287560
  31  XCTEND rlbk=0, rd_only=0
  32  WAIT #2: nam='SQL*Net message to client' ela= 2 driver id=1952673792 #bytes=1 p3=0 obj#=-1 tim=1198862067288169
  33  WAIT #2: nam='SQL*Net message from client' ela= 1154 driver id=1952673792 #bytes=1 p3=0 obj#=-1 tim=1198862067289370
  34  =====================
  35  PARSING IN CURSOR #2 len=40 dep=0 uid=55 oct=2 lid=55 tim=1198862067289787 hv=1228865179 ad='2d6c3ea4'
  36  insert into JAVA_TEST_TABLE values ('1')
  37  END OF STMT
  38  PARSE #2:c=0,e=302,p=0,cr=0,cu=0,mis=1,r=0,dep=0,og=1,tim=1198862067289781
  39  BINDS #2:
  40  EXEC #2:c=0,e=202,p=0,cr=1,cu=4,mis=0,r=1,dep=0,og=1,tim=1198862067290111
  41  XCTEND rlbk=0, rd_only=0
  42  WAIT #2: nam='log file sync' ela= 113 buffer#=737 p2=0 p3=0 obj#=-1 tim=1198862067290479
  43  WAIT #2: nam='SQL*Net message to client' ela= 2 driver id=1952673792 #bytes=1 p3=0 obj#=-1 tim=1198862067290546
  44  WAIT #2: nam='SQL*Net message from client' ela= 1918 driver id=1952673792 #bytes=1 p3=0 obj#=-1 tim=1198862067292503
  45  =====================
  46  PARSING IN CURSOR #2 len=40 dep=0 uid=55 oct=2 lid=55 tim=1198862067292826 hv=2978669578 ad='2d75ac84'
  47  insert into JAVA_TEST_TABLE values ('2')
  48  END OF STMT
  49  PARSE #2:c=0,e=232,p=0,cr=0,cu=0,mis=1,r=0,dep=0,og=1,tim=1198862067292821
  50  BINDS #2:
  51  EXEC #2:c=0,e=146,p=0,cr=1,cu=4,mis=0,r=1,dep=0,og=1,tim=1198862067293093
  52  XCTEND rlbk=0, rd_only=0
  53  WAIT #2: nam='log file sync' ela= 107 buffer#=739 p2=0 p3=0 obj#=-1 tim=1198862067293425
  54  WAIT #2: nam='SQL*Net message to client' ela= 2 driver id=1952673792 #bytes=1 p3=0 obj#=-1 tim=1198862067293477
  55  WAIT #2: nam='SQL*Net message from client' ela= 2050 driver id=1952673792 #bytes=1 p3=0 obj#=-1 tim=1198862067295563
      ...
106360  =====================
106361  PARSING IN CURSOR #2 len=43 dep=0 uid=55 oct=2 lid=55 tim=1198862099985077 hv=3863691391 ad='2d494c40'
106362  insert into JAVA_TEST_TABLE values ('9999')
106363  END OF STMT
106364  PARSE #2:c=2000,e=1518,p=0,cr=0,cu=0,mis=0,r=0,dep=0,og=1,tim=1198862099985071
106365  BINDS #2:
106366  EXEC #2:c=0,e=84,p=0,cr=1,cu=5,mis=0,r=1,dep=0,og=1,tim=1198862099985234
106367  XCTEND rlbk=0, rd_only=0
106368  WAIT #2: nam='SQL*Net message to client' ela= 3 driver id=1952673792 #bytes=1 p3=0 obj#=-1 tim=1198862099985576
106369  WAIT #2: nam='SQL*Net message from client' ela= 2227 driver id=1952673792 #bytes=1 p3=0 obj#=-1 tim=1198862099987834
106370  XCTEND rlbk=0, rd_only=1
```

TRACE FILE: IMPROVED INSERT

The following trace file shows the complete trace data for the improved 0.154-second insert program:

```
   1  /usr/lib/oracle/xe/app/oracle/admin/XE/udump/xe_ora_3807_INSERT_TEST.trc
   2  Oracle Database 10g Express Edition Release 10.2.0.1.0 - Production
   3  ORACLE_HOME = /usr/lib/oracle/xe/app/oracle/product/10.2.0/server
   4  System name:    Linux
   5  Node name:      oracle01.dev.method-r.com
   6  Release:        2.6.25.6-27.fc8
   7  Version:        #1 SMP Fri Jun 13 16:38:52 EDT 2008
   8  Machine:        i686
   9  Instance name: XE
  10  Redo thread mounted by this instance: 1
  11  Oracle process number: 22
  12  Unix process pid: 3807, image: oracleXE@oracle01.dev.method-r.com
  13
  14  *** SERVICE NAME:(SYS$USERS) 2008-12-22 16:37:52.283
  15  *** SESSION ID:(24.34335) 2008-12-22 16:37:52.283
  16  =====================
  17  PARSING IN CURSOR #2 len=69 dep=0 uid=55 oct=42 lid=55 tim=1201157687776660 hv=3164292706 ad='28e47760'
  18  alter session set events '10046 trace name context forever, level 12'
  19  END OF STMT
  20  EXEC #2:c=0,e=53,p=0,cr=0,cu=0,mis=0,r=0,dep=0,og=1,tim=1201157687776652
  21  XCTEND rlbk=0, rd_only=1
  22  WAIT #2: nam='SQL*Net message to client' ela= 2 driver id=1952673792 #bytes=1 p3=0 obj#=-1 tim=1201157687776907
  23  WAIT #2: nam='SQL*Net message from client' ela= 60441 driver id=1952673792 #bytes=1 p3=0 obj#=-1 tim=1201157687837388
  24  =====================
  25  PARSING IN CURSOR #1 len=39 dep=0 uid=55 oct=2 lid=55 tim=1201157687837622 hv=2094431222 ad='28f82278'
  26  Insert into JAVA_TEST_TABLE values (:1)
  27  END OF STMT
  28  PARSE #1:c=0,e=160,p=0,cr=0,cu=0,mis=0,r=0,dep=0,og=1,tim=1201157687837613
  29  BINDS #1:
```

Chapter 2. Making Friends with the Oracle Database

```
 30 kkscoacd
 31  Bind#0
 32   oacdty=02 mxl=22(22) mxlc=00 mal=00 scl=00 pre=00
 33   oacflg=03 fl2=1000000 frm=01 csi=178 siz=24 off=0
 34   kxsbbbfp=b7f27e2c  bln=22  avl=01  flg=05
 35   value=0
 36 WAIT #1: nam='SQL*Net more data from client' ela= 27 driver id=1952673792 #bytes=3 p3=0 obj#=-1 tim=1201157687844067
 37 WAIT #1: nam='SQL*Net more data from client' ela= 11 driver id=1952673792 #bytes=1 p3=0 obj#=-1 tim=1201157687844425
 38 EXEC #1:c=7999,e=7941,p=0,cr=396,cu=499,mis=0,r=1000,dep=0,og=1,tim=1201157687845652
 39 WAIT #1: nam='SQL*Net message to client' ela= 3 driver id=1952673792 #bytes=1 p3=0 obj#=-1 tim=1201157687845745
 40 WAIT #1: nam='SQL*Net message from client' ela= 4885 driver id=1952673792 #bytes=1 p3=0 obj#=-1 tim=1201157687850661
 41 BINDS #1:
 42 kkscoacd
 43  Bind#0
 44   oacdty=02 mxl=22(22) mxlc=00 mal=00 scl=00 pre=00
 45   oacflg=03 fl2=1000000 frm=01 csi=178 siz=24 off=0
 46   kxsbbbfp=b7f27e2c  bln=22  avl=02  flg=05
 47   value=1000
 48 WAIT #1: nam='SQL*Net more data from client' ela= 17 driver id=1952673792 #bytes=1 p3=0 obj#=-1 tim=1201157687851385
 49 WAIT #1: nam='SQL*Net more data from client' ela= 14 driver id=1952673792 #bytes=1 p3=0 obj#=-1 tim=1201157687852578
 50 EXEC #1:c=1999,e=2057,p=0,cr=131,cu=169,mis=0,r=1000,dep=0,og=1,tim=1201157687852764
 51 WAIT #1: nam='SQL*Net message to client' ela= 2 driver id=1952673792 #bytes=1 p3=0 obj#=-1 tim=1201157687852809
 52 WAIT #1: nam='SQL*Net message from client' ela= 2455 driver id=1952673792 #bytes=1 p3=0 obj#=-1 tim=1201157687855292
    ...
137 BINDS #1:
138 kkscoacd
139  Bind#0
140   oacdty=02 mxl=22(22) mxlc=00 mal=00 scl=00 pre=00
141   oacflg=03 fl2=1000000 frm=01 csi=178 siz=24 off=0
142   kxsbbbfp=b7f27e2c  bln=22  avl=02  flg=05
143   value=9000
144 WAIT #1: nam='SQL*Net more data from client' ela= 17 driver id=1952673792 #bytes=1 p3=0 obj#=-1 tim=1201157687884646
145 WAIT #1: nam='SQL*Net more data from client' ela= 12 driver id=1952673792 #bytes=1 p3=0 obj#=-1 tim=1201157687885716
146 EXEC #1:c=1000,e=1539,p=0,cr=118,cu=153,mis=0,r=1000,dep=0,og=1,tim=1201157687885866
147 WAIT #1: nam='SQL*Net message to client' ela= 3 driver id=1952673792 #bytes=1 p3=0 obj#=-1 tim=1201157687885907
148 WAIT #1: nam='SQL*Net message from client' ela= 398 driver id=1952673792 #bytes=1 p3=0 obj#=-1 tim=1201157687886334
149 XCTEND rlbk=0, rd_only=0
150 WAIT #0: nam='log file sync' ela= 39869 buffer#=376 p2=0 p3=0 obj#=-1 tim=1201157687927436
151 WAIT #0: nam='SQL*Net message to client' ela= 4 driver id=1952673792 #bytes=1 p3=0 obj#=-1 tim=1201157687927533
152 WAIT #0: nam='SQL*Net message from client' ela= 1743 driver id=1952673792 #bytes=1 p3=0 obj#=-1 tim=1201157687929301
153 XCTEND rlbk=0, rd_only=1
```

3 Oracle Extended SQL Trace

Oracle's extended SQL trace data stream contains a linear sequential record of every database call and every operating system call that the Oracle Database kernel executes in response to the code in your application. The trace file contains timings that enable you to precisely measure how long your code takes to run and why. The detailed information about individual database calls and operating system calls is vital to building scalable applications (as well as troubleshooting them in production). The information in there is a gold mine, and some of it is available nowhere else.

Performance and Tracing

You click a button on a web form. It's a button that you click all the time. Normally, the system you're using responds to that click almost instantaneously, but now... Now, it's taking more than 5 seconds every time you do it, and sometimes it takes more than 10. The obvious and very simple question is: *why*?

The vast majority of people who experience a problem like this never find out the answer.

Think for a minute about what the answer ought to look like. If you're a IT professional, then you've probably seen so many reports that the simple answer doesn't even occur to you. Here's what I want: I want a report telling me where my time went.

I don't want to see how busy the whole system was when my click took 5 seconds; I don't want to see all the "bad" SQL that executed at or near the time when I had my problem; and I don't want to see all the different kinds of waiting that the system was doing when I clicked. I just want to see where *my* time went, untainted by information about anything not directly relevant to *my* response time.

With Oracle, you can have it. The feature that gives it to you is included with every release and every edition of the Oracle Database, including Oracle Exadata, Oracle Database Enterprise Edition, Oracle Database Standard Edition, and even Oracle's free Express Edition, since 1992. You don't have to buy an extra-price Option or a Pack to use it. It's called **extended SQL trace**.

Why You Should Trace

Oracle extended SQL trace helps you diagnose, it helps you learn, and it helps you debug:[1]

- System administrators, diagnosticians, and trouble-shooters will find it invaluable for solving problems with programs for which the source is not readily available (or not easily navigable) since they do not need to be recompiled in order to trace them.

- Students, hackers, and the overly-curious will find that a great deal can be learned about a system and its system calls by tracing even ordinary programs.

---

[1] Oracle extended SQL trace is useful for the same kinds of reasons that the Unix *strace* tool is useful. My description here is paraphrased from the *strace* manual page at *http://linuxcommand.org/man_pages/strace1.html*.

- And programmers will find trace data very useful for bug isolation, sanity checking, and performance optimization. Some problems cannot be solved without it.

What makes tracing so good compared to the other performance information you can get from Oracle is that with tracing, you get a linear sequential record of everything your Oracle kernel process does while it's trying to compute the answer you've asked for. You don't have to worry about gaps in your data (like with Oracle's Active Session History) or figuring out how to isolate your process's work in the huge picture of everything the system is doing right now (like with some of Oracle's v$ fixed views and all of the GUI tools that use them).

With trace data, you see every database call your application makes to the Oracle kernel, and you see every system call your kernel makes to its host operating system. And it's the perfect tool for developers, because you don't have to have loads of complicated permissions to use it. I believe you can learn more about Oracle performance with trace data in a day than you can learn studying v$ data for a month, because trace data so directly maps to the reality of how the user, the application code, and the database interact.

> Trace files can teach you more about Oracle performance than any other data source.

What Happens When You Trace

Tracing is an attribute of an Oracle session.[2] For each session with trace enabled, any Oracle kernel process[3] that executes instructions for that session writes trace data for that session to the process's currently open trace file. Some facts:

- Tracing is a session attribute.
- But Oracle kernel processes are what write your trace data.
- Since more than one process can execute instructions for a given Oracle session (for example, by using Oracle Parallel Execution features, or by enabling Oracle Shared Server), your trace data can appear in more than one file.
- The more exotic your architecture (for example, the more tiers you use, the more pooling features you use), the more difficult it may be to map your trace data to a specific user's request.

---

[2] An **Oracle session** is an entity with a unique *sid-serial#* combination within an Oracle instance, which you can see in *v$session*.

[3] An **Oracle kernel process** is an operating system process (which you can inspect with, for example, Linux commands like *ps*, *lsof*, or *strace*) that executes the instructions required by an Oracle session.

The following illustration shows a simple case in which a user traces an Oracle session connected through *sqlplus*, causing an Oracle kernel process to write trace data to a *.trc* file.

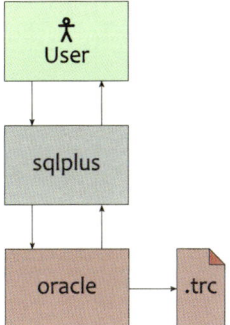

The Oracle kernel process, to which a user connects through some type of application like *sqlplus*, is the process that writes the trace file.

CONTROLLING THE TRACE

You can trace any Oracle session on your system if you have permission to execute the standard Oracle PL/SQL package called *dbms_monitor*. This package gives you a lot of control over which sessions you trace. Here are some of its procedures:

session_trace_enable
  Enable tracing for either the database session from which the procedure is called, or a specific session identified by its session identifier and serial number.

database_trace_enable
  Enable tracing for a specific instance or a whole database.

Oracle provides a disable procedure to match each enable procedure.

When you use *dbms_monitor*, I recommend that you use the default value of `waits=>true`. If you use the value `waits=>false`, you'll be using SQL trace, but not extended SQL trace. You'll get a trace of the Oracle database calls your application makes, but not the OS calls that Oracle makes. Without a record of those OS calls in your trace file, you'll not be able to account for potentially significant amounts of response time.

I also recommend that you use the non-default value `binds=>true`. Setting `binds=>true` causes the Oracle Database to emit the values that the application bound to its placeholder variables into the trace data stream. For example, if someone has executed the following SQL statement:

```
1  update salary set amount = :v1 where id = :v2
```

...Then your trace data will show what values were assigned to v1 and v2. This is invaluable information for creating reproducible test cases for solving problems. However, be aware of the data security implication of emitting bind data into a trace file; when you do it, you are copying potentially sensitive data from your database to your file system.

SESSION TRACING

One of the nice things about Oracle tracing is that you're not required to change an application in order to use it. Even if the application you're using is completely un-modifiable

Chapter 3. Oracle Extended SQL Trace

and was in no way designed to cooperate with tracing, you still have the following very powerful tools at your disposal:

dbms_monitor.session_trace_enable

With *session_trace_enable*, you can trace any session on your system if you know its session id and serial number. You just have to be meticulous to enable the trace immediately before the user begins the task you want to diagnose, and then disable the trace immediately after the task completes.

Triggers

For fast-moving sessions that don't give you time to identify their session ids before they begin doing work (like that Pro*C program that runs for 20 seconds, but that should run in 2), triggers are a convenient tool for inserting code to enable tracing. You can, for example, create an *after logon* trigger whose body uses:

```
 2  session_trace_enable(
 3    session_id => null,
 4    serial_num => null,
 5    …
 6  )
```

This code will enable tracing for the session that's logging on. There's no need for a corresponding before logoff trace disablement, by the way, because logging off automatically disables the trace.

sys_context

The Oracle *sys_context* function gives you dozens of hooks you can use inside of a trigger body to identify the session that's logging in. For example,

```
 7  sys_context('USERENV','IP_ADDRESS')
```

…returns the IP address of the machine from which the client is connected. With *sys_context*, you can write PL/SQL code in your *after logon* trigger body that can decide to trace only logins originating from a specific IP address, only logins requested by certain client OS users, or logins matching any of the other criteria that *sys_context* makes available to you.

Running suspicious SQL in your own session

There are lots of ways you can identify suspicious SQL statements: you'll find them in OEM, in your AWR or ADDM reports, or by querying *v$sqlstat*. Copy them and run them in *sqlplus* or Oracle SQL Developer. You can plug in whatever bind variable values you need and trace to your heart's content.[4]

dbms_monitor.database_trace_enable

If all else fails, there's always the thermonuclear option of tracing everything that happens over some time interval you choose. Beware, however: enabling trace for a whole instance or database will only activate tracing for new sessions that log in after you enable the trace. It won't enable tracing for sessions that are already logged in. Of course, even with these omissions, the big problem with enabling database-wide tracing is that you'll get so many trace files (and some of those trace files will be so large) that you won't be able to make sense of them all.

---

[4] …Subject, naturally, to constraints on whether you are permitted access to the objects manipulated by the statement, and so on. Also, please make sure that, before you execute a SQL statement that might change rows in the database, you do not have an *auto-commit* feature enabled.

END-TO-END TRACING

There are three major milestones in the history of tracing in the Oracle Database:

- In 1988, Oracle version 6 introduced SQL trace, which let us discover the start and end time of every database call an application executed.
- In 1993, Oracle version 7 introduced extended SQL trace, which let us discover the duration of every system call the database executed.
- In 2003, Oracle version 10 introduced end-to-end extended SQL trace, which let us activate tracing, not just for sessions whose session ids we knew, but for sessions with specific attribute values.

The third milestone—end-to-end tracing—makes it possible for you to specify the intent to trace a business task in advance of that task ever running. Then, the Oracle Database will automatically enable tracing for any session that executes the task you have specified.

The way you specify the standing order to trace certain tasks is with the following *dbms_monitor* procedures:

client_id_trace_enable
: Enable tracing for any database session whose client identifier matches the one you specify.

serv_mod_act_trace_enable
: Enable tracing for any database session whose service, module, and action names match the ones you specify.

For example, if you wanted to trace any user whose application had set the Oracle *client_id* field to 192.168.1.104, you'd use:

```
 8  dbms_monitor.client_id_trace_enable(
 9      client_id  => '192.168.1.104',
10      waits      => true,
11      binds      => true,
12      plan_stat  => 'ALL_EXECUTIONS'
13  )
```

...And that's that. No matter when the next person whose *client_id* was set to 192.168.1.104 (presumably the user's actual IP address), his work would be traced. If you wanted to trace any business task whose service is called FINAPPS, whose module is called GLPPOS, and whose action is called Concurrent Request, you'd execute:

```
14  dbms_monitor.serv_mod_act_trace_enable(
15      service_name  => 'FINAPPS',
16      module_name   => 'GLPPOS',
17      action_name   => 'Concurrent Request'
18      waits         => true,
19      binds         => true,
20      plan_stat     => 'ALL_EXECUTIONS'
21  )
```

...Then you'd be set to trace your GL Posting runs until you disabled the trace with *dbms_monitor.serv_mod_act_trace_disable*.

Before end-to-end tracing, the hardest thing about tracing was getting a trace file that represents exactly the business task that the user is experiencing right there at her keyboard. When you trace a session based on its session id, you almost always capture either more trace data than you really want, or not enough. That's because it takes you a little time to identify the session's id before you can execute the *session_trace_enable* call.

However, when you activate tracing for a specific client id or service-module-action name combination, you create a standing order to Oracle, instructing the kernel to begin tracing any session that changes its client id to your specific value, or whenever it changes its server-module-action name combination to your specific values. And then Oracle will stop tracing immediately when that session changes its identifying information to something different. Pure magic.

Chapter 3. Oracle Extended SQL Trace

END-TO-END PREREQUISITES

But there's a catch with end-to-end tracing. How can *dbms_monitor* know a session's client id or service-module-action names? The answer: your application has to provide those attribute values. If your application doesn't name its tasks or set the client id attribute for its sessions in a useful way, then you can't use the *dbms_monitor* end-to-end tracing features.

If you're using an off-the-shelf application, your only recourse may be to live without the end-to-end tracing features (though you can still use the techniques described in "Session Tracing" on page 49) and lobby your vendor to instrument a future version of your application in the manner I'm about to describe. If you can change your application source code yourself, instrumenting for end-to-end tracing is not hard to do. The only thing you really have to do is have each session set what Oracle calls its user session handle attributes. There are several ways to do it.

One way you can set those session handle attributes for your code is to use these standard Oracle PL/SQL packages:

dbms_session
> The *set_identifier* procedure lets you set the calling session's client identifier.

dbms_application_info
> The *set_action* procedure lets you set the calling session's action name, and the *set_module* procedure lets you set the calling session's module and action names together.

If you prefer a simpler approach to setting your session handle attributes, you can use the Instrumentation Library for Oracle (ILO), a free open-source project that Method R Corporation maintains at SourceForge. ILO gives you PL/SQL packages that make it dead simple for an application developer to define where in an application's code path each business task begins and ends. It sets all the "hooks" that your systems DBAs will need later to trace specific business tasks by name. ILO gives you several extra features as well, which are detailed in the project's documentation.

If it bothers you to insert additional database calls into your application (and if you're building an application that will serve thousands of database requests per second, it should), then you should choose another option. Some Oracle APIs allow you to pass service-module-action names and a client-id from the application to the database as an attribute of each of the database calls that you were already determined to make.

The Oracle user session handle attributes you'll need to set are these:

```
OCI_ATTR_CLIENT_IDENTIFIER
OCI_ATTR_SERVICE
OCI_ATTR_MODULE
OCI_ATTR_ACTION
```

You can set them, for example, with the Oracle Call Interface (OCI) *OCIAttrSet* function, or with the JDBC *setEndToEndMetrics* method. These are client-side function calls that don't require a round-trip to the database. Once you have made a call to set your user session handle attributes, each database call that your application code makes after that is marked with the identifying information that *dbms_monitor* needs.

Setting your Oracle user session handle attributes yourself enables you to instrument your application with no extra database calls at all, which means no extra network round-trips between the application and the database. It's the most scalable way to instrument your code.

To summarize, you can instrument your application code for end-to-end tracing by calling standard Oracle PL/SQL procedures (or calling them through someone else's package, like ILO), or you can do it with no extra database calls by setting session handle attributes directly with an Oracle API like OCI or JDBC.

If your application is not designed to set these attributes for your sessions, then you won't be able to use the *client_id_trace_enable* or *serv_mod_act_trace_enable* procedures in *dbms_monitor*. You'll have to use only the *session_trace_enable* and *database_trace_enable* procedures instead, until you can convince the people who built your application to instrument the application so that you can measure and manage its performance while you operate it. Until then, not only will you not be able to trace as flexibly, you also won't be able to group application performance statistics using other applications like Oracle Enterprise Manager.

Finding Your Trace File

Once you've traced your code, you'll need to find your trace file. The process running your Oracle kernel code writes your trace file to the operating system directory named by an Oracle instance parameter. In Oracle version 11, the Oracle kernel will write your files into a directory that you can identify by using the following SQL statement:

```
22  select * from v$diag_info where name='Diag Trace'
```

In older versions of Oracle, you can identify your trace file directories by using this statement:

```
23  select * from v$parameter where name in ('user_dump_dest','background_dumnp_dest')
```

In Oracle version 10 and prior, the *user_dump_dest* directory is probably where most of your trace files will be. If you use Oracle parallel execution features, then you'll find some of your trace files in the *background_dump_dest* directory.

Different ports of Oracle use different naming conventions for trace files. Your trace file names will probably look something like one of the following:

```
xe_ora_10840.trc
prod7_23389_ora.trc
ora_1492_delta1.trc
ORA01215.trc
fin1_ora_11297_POSTING.trc
MERKUR_S7_FG_ORACLE_013.trc
```

Trace files may look different on different platforms and on different versions of Oracle, but you can count on your trace file names containing at least some of the following elements:

- The string *ora*.
- Your Oracle instance name.
- Your Oracle kernel process id (on Microsoft Windows, it will be your process's thread id).
- If you set a *tracefile_identifier* within your Oracle session (with an *alter session* command), then the string value of that parameter.
- The suffix *.trc*.

If you're writing code that will connect to an Oracle instance that someone else manages, you'll need to coordinate with that person to get permissions to read your trace files. Without access to your trace files, optimizing the code you write is going to be a lot more expensive for your company.

Performance Intrusion

One thing that people always want to know is, "What is the performance penalty of tracing?" People get a little nervous about all those extra timer calls that their Oracle kernel processes must execute when you turn trace on.

What they don't realize is that their Oracle kernel process is making many of those timer calls anyway, whether tracing is activated or not. How else could it publish the timing information you see in fixed views like *v$sesstat*, *v$session_event*, and *v$session_wait*? The actual performance intrusion of tracing is dominated by the cost of the additional I/O calls required to persist to your trace file the information Oracle is already collecting.

Most people should trace only a few sessions at a time. If you don't have specialized tools, you'll never in your life be able to sift through all the trace files that an Oracle Database system can generate in a good, busy hour of work. If you want to trace a lot of sessions at once (and there are legitimate reasons for wanting to), you can trace as many sessions as your hardware capacity will allow. If you trace infrequently, then you don't have to be too careful about your trace file destination. If you trace a lot of sessions simultaneously, then just make sure you write your trace files to a drive array that has all the storage capacity and throughput capacity you need, and then trace all you want.

Unless you're using a version of Oracle that has a trace-related performance bug (Oracle bug 3009359, introduced in version 9.2.0.2, was a famous one), your program will probably run with ±5% of the duration that it takes to run it without tracing.[5] If a program's response time gets more than 10% worse when you trace it, then you should check whether the I/O subsystem to which you're writing trace files is ok, check whether your session's setting of *statistics_level* is what you want it to be, and check the Oracle Support database for bugs.

People who ask about the performance intrusion of tracing generally ask because they're fearful that they'll get into trouble if they do anything that might make performance worse than it already is. However, your goal in tracing is to learn how much faster a program ought to be running. Isn't that information worth at least as much as a one-time response time penalty induced by a trace? I've seen people work on problems for months on end without trace data, when they could have cleared everything up with just a single one-time trace. Even if tracing imposed five times the performance penalty that it does, I wouldn't use it any less.

Tracing in Multiplexed Architectures

I mentioned in "What Happens When You Trace" on page 48 that tracing is an attribute of the Oracle session. However, many systems these days have many layers of software between the user and the Oracle session, and many of those layers employ pooling technologies that conceal the user's identity from her Oracle session.

The solution, in general, is this: where there's a will, there's a way. If you are committed to tracing a specific user's specific business task, it can be done. Here are some techniques you can use to do it:

User session handle attributes
> The service, module, action, and client id attributes are the right and proper cure for tracing in pooled architectures. When the application identifies its users to the Oracle database, the *dbms_monitor* package lets you enable tracing for exactly the tasks you want traced, and then tools like Oracle's *trcsess* help you do the work of concatenating the various fragments of trace data that will describe how your task spent its time.

Session isolation
> If your application doesn't set its session handle attributes that allow you to distinguish the business task you're interested in from the thousands of other business tasks running at the same time, then isolate your user into a configuration where you can make the distinction. For example, instead of your user connecting to her usual *www.app.com*

---

[5] That's right, plus *or minus*. Sometimes a program will run faster when you trace it. It sounds nice, but it's usually not what you want.

site, where her task gets stripped of her identity as it enters some session pool or connection pool with a thousand other tasks, have her connect to *www.app.com:88*, where her task is the only task in a session pool or connection pool with a pool size of exactly one. You can trace every session connecting to the database through port 88, which, at the time you're doing your analysis, you know will be nobody else but the one user you're analyzing.

TRACING WHILE YOU DEVELOP

The most important time for a developer to trace is early in the software development life cycle, where defects are cheaper and easier to fix than any other time in your project.[6] Fortunately, tracing is easiest in the development environment.

I can remember since my earliest days of working with Oracle having some kind of *sqlplus* script that will turn trace on or off when you call it. It could be as simple as two scripts *traceon.sql* and *traceoff.sql* that look like this:

```
24  $ cat traceon.sql
25  exec dbms_monitor.session_trace_enable(binds=>true);
26  $ cat traceoff.sql
27  exec dbms_monitor.session_trace_disable();
```

When you write your code, it works like this:

```
28  @traceon
29  -- Your code goes here
30  @traceoff
```

Nowadays, I use the Method R Trace extension for Oracle SQL Developer ("MR Trace").[7] When MR Trace is enabled, every Run Script button click creates a trace file, which MR Trace automatically fetches for you from your database server to your workstation. It also lets you tag your local trace files to make them easy to find later.

The best thing a developer can do to promote high performance over an application's long lifespan is to make it easy to trace the application throughout its production life cycle. Of course, you do this by coding the application to set its own user session handle attributes, as I've described in "End-to-End Prerequisites" on page 52.

Applications work better when the world works like this:

1. Developers trace their SQL and PL/SQL code as they write it. They study their trace files to ensure that the code they're writing is efficient.

2. Developers become fluent in understanding what the trace files mean, which results in more efficient application code.

3. Developers code applications to set their user session handle attributes.

4. Developers and database administrators participate together during integration testing to trace the application code (which is easy with the user session handle attributes all set) and study the trace files to ensure that the code is efficient under load and that there are no unwanted performance interdependencies among competing sessions.

5. Production system administrators (database administrators, for example) trace the application code periodically in production when the application is behaving well, to record a baseline of how each application task is supposed to perform (which is easy with the user session handle attributes all set).

6. During performance problem episodes, production operators trace problem business tasks (session handle attributes make this easy) and work together with application

---

[6] Barry Boehm, *Software Engineering Economics*, 40.

[7] Method R Trace, at *http://method-r.com/software/mrtrace*.

Chapter 3. Oracle Extended SQL Trace

developers—who are already familiar with what the trace file for the given task normally looks like—to solve problems quickly.

With habitual tracing throughout a software life cycle, applications tend to have fewer performance problems, and they tend to get fixed more quickly on the rare occasion when they do have a problem. They tend to evolve toward being fast, optimized systems that can last a long time. ...Much like the Oracle Database, which is itself heavily performance instrumented.

Trace File Guided Tour

Once you have your trace file in hand, the real fun begins. Now you have a call-by-call description of what the Oracle Database did throughout your entire response time.

If your only interface to the Oracle Database has been SQL or PL/SQL executed through client software like *sqlplus* or Oracle SQL Developer, you may not know about the distinct steps that Oracle uses to process a single statement. The following figure shows the steps from the perspective of the Oracle Call Interface:

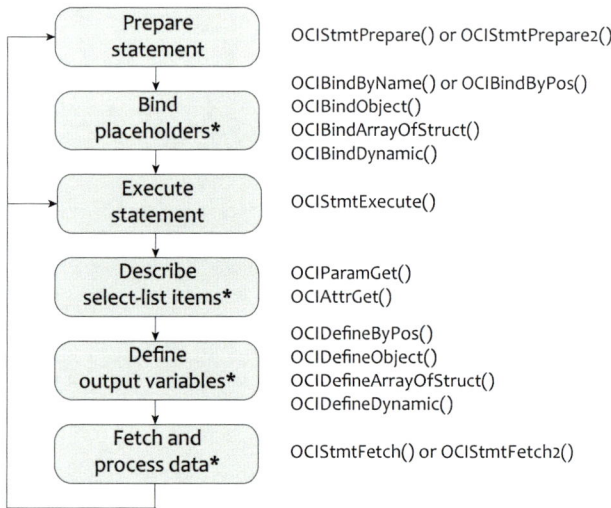

*These steps are performed only if necessary.

Steps in processing a SQL statement.[8]

You can see this sequence of activity whenever you trace even a simple SQL statement like "`select 'Hello world' from dual`". An Oracle 11.2.0.2.0 trace file for an execution of this SQL statement is shown in its entirety in "Trace File: Hello World" on page 63. Here are some highlights.

On line 34, you can see the "Hello world" query itself. Lines 36–45 show how Oracle processed the query:

```
32 =====================
33 PARSING IN CURSOR #7285244 len=30 dep=0 uid=5 oct=3 lid=5 tim=1294688002747560 hv=1604528588 ad='3d526cd8' sqlid='guthms1gu6afc'
34 select 'Hello world' from dual
35 END OF STMT
36 PARSE #7285244:c=0,e=70,p=0,cr=0,cu=0,mis=0,r=0,dep=0,og=1,plh=1388734953,tim=1294688002747559
37 EXEC #7285244:c=0,e=112,p=0,cr=0,cu=0,mis=0,r=0,dep=0,og=1,plh=1388734953,tim=1294688002747793
38 WAIT #7285244: nam='SQL*Net message to client' ela= 2 driver id=1650815232 #bytes=1 p3=0 obj#=-1 tim=1294688002747865
39 FETCH #7285244:c=0,e=8,p=0,cr=0,cu=0,mis=0,r=1,dep=0,og=1,plh=1388734953,tim=1294688002747910
40 STAT #7285244 id=1 cnt=1 pid=0 pos=1 obj=0 op='FAST DUAL  (cr=0 pr=0 pw=0 time=4 us cost=2 size=0 card=1)'
41 WAIT #7285244: nam='SQL*Net message from client' ela= 375 driver id=1650815232 #bytes=1 p3=0 obj#=-1 tim=1294688002748453
42 FETCH #7285244:c=0,e=1,p=0,cr=0,cu=0,mis=0,r=0,dep=0,og=0,plh=1388734953,tim=1294688002748493
43 WAIT #7285244: nam='SQL*Net message to client' ela= 1 driver id=1650815232 #bytes=1 p3=0 obj#=-1 tim=1294688002748520
```

---

[8] Oracle Corporation, "Oracle Call Interface Programmer's Guide 11*g* Release 2," at *http://docs. oracle.com/cd/E14072_01/appdev.112/e10646/title.htm*.

```
44 WAIT #7285244: nam='SQL*Net message from client' ela= 1627 driver id=1650815232 #bytes=1 p3=0 obj#=-1 tim=1294688002750168
45 XCTEND rlbk=0, rd_only=1, tim=1294688002750230
```

Here, you can see the query being prepared (the PARSE line), which consumed 70 μs.[9] Next, it was executed (regarding "Steps in processing a SQL statement." on page 56, there was no bind necessary, since my query didn't contain any placeholders), which consumed 112 μs. Then, on line 38, the Oracle kernel process issued an OS write call to send the result of the prepare-execute call pair back to the client (which Oracle calls *SQL*Net message to client*).

On line 39 is a *fetch* call, which consumed 8 μs and returned 1 row. Line 40 shows the execution plan that Oracle used to process my query. Line 41 shows the Oracle kernel blocked on an OS read call for 375 μs, awaiting another database call from the client (which Oracle calls *SQL*Net message from client*).

On line 42, the kernel has processed a second fetch call, consuming 1 μs and fetching no rows. Line 43 shows that the kernel issued another OS write call to send the zero-row result set back to the client (which of course informs the client that there are no more rows to be had from the query). Line 44 shows the kernel blocked for 1,627 μs on another OS read call, awaiting instructions for what to do next. Line 45 shows that the next action was a *commit*, which *sqlplus* issued automatically upon disconnecting from Oracle.

The remainder of the trace file is interesting, because it shows something you might not have expected: the session inserted a row into *sys.aud$*. From this, I can tell that my instance is set up for session-level auditing. I didn't have to work my way down a checklist to figure that out; plus, my trace data will show me exactly the cost of that overhead upon my response time.

```
46 =====================
47 PARSING IN CURSOR #7386176 len=447 dep=1 uid=0 oct=2 lid=0 tim=1294688002750383 hv=1097020010 ad='3d7e77d4' sqlid='f711myt0q6cma'
48 insert into sys.aud$( sessionid,entryid,statement,ntimestamp#, userid,userhost,terminal,action#,returnco
   de, logoff$lread,logoff$pread,logoff$lwrite,logoff$dead, logoff$time,comment$text,spare1,clientid,sessioncpu,proxy$
   sid,user$guid, instance#,process#,auditid,dbid) values(:1,:2,:3,SYS_EXTRACT_UTC(SYSTIMESTAMP),       :4,:5,:6,:7,:8,
   :9,:10,:11,:12,    cast(SYS_EXTRACT_UTC(systimestamp) as date),:13,:14,:15,:16,:17,:18,    :19,:20,:21,:22)
49 END OF STMT
50 PARSE #7386176:c=0,e=93,p=0,cr=0,cu=0,mis=0,r=0,dep=1,og=4,plh=0,tim=1294688002750382
```

On line 48, you can see the SQL statement. Line 50 shows that the prepare call for that statement consumed 93 μs. On lines 51–156 (see "Trace File: Hello World" on page 63), you can see the values that were bound into the statement's placeholder variables (:1, :2, ..., :22) within that statement.

```
157 EXEC #7386176:c=0,e=1733,p=0,cr=1,cu=2,mis=0,r=1,dep=1,og=4,plh=0,tim=1294688002752264
158 STAT #7386176 id=1 cnt=0 pid=0 pos=1 obj=0 op='LOAD TABLE CONVENTIONAL  (cr=1 pr=0 pw=0 time=155 us)'
159 CLOSE #7386176:c=0,e=5,dep=1,type=0,tim=1294688002752341
160 WAIT #0: nam='log file sync' ela= 153 buffer#=5673 sync scn=1046841 p3=0 obj#=-1 tim=1294688002752632
161 CLOSE #7285244:c=0,e=9,dep=0,type=0,tim=1294688002752690
162 CLOSE #7248564:c=0,e=30,dep=0,type=0,tim=1294688002752740
```

Line 157 shows that the execute call for the insert took 1,733 μs. Line 158 shows the execution plan for the insert, and line 159 shows that the close call for the insert took 5 μs. Line 160 shows that the OS call Oracle uses to implement its *log file sync* event consumed 153 μs, and the final two lines of the trace file show two more *close* calls, which consumed 9 μs and 30 μs.

I hope you can see from just this little tour how it is possible to use trace data to see exactly where your time has gone. You just need to know how to read them. Let's begin with the alphabet.

---

[9] Call durations in trace files are expressed in microseconds, abbreviated *μs*. 1 μs = .000001 seconds, or 1/1,000,000th of a second.

Trace File Alphabet

Trace files look plenty ugly when you first meet them, but it's not too difficult to figure out what they mean. There are really only two types of lines in the trace file that tell you where time has gone:

Database call lines

> Database call lines begin with the keyword PARSE, EXEC, FETCH, CLOSE, UNMAP, SORT UNMAP, LOBREAD, or LOBARRTMPFRE (Oracle Corporation adds new ones from time to time). Such a line indicates that an application client has made a database call, and that the Oracle Database has responded to it.

System call lines

> System call lines begin with the keyword WAIT. Such a line indicates that the Oracle kernel process has made an OS call, and that the OS has responded to it.

That's it; just two.

Trace File Alphabet: Database Calls

With exception of the *close* call, which doesn't contain all the fields that the other database calls do, all contain the same fields. They look like this:

```
FETCH #12390720:c=8000,e=1734,p=1,cr=7,cu=0,mis=0,r=1,dep=2,og=4,plh=3992920156,tim=1294438818783887
```

Here's what the fields mean:

FETCH

> This was a *fetch* call (not a *parse* or *exec* or some other kind).

#12390720

> The call's cursor handle id is 12390720. To find the definition of this cursor, you'd seek backward in the trace file to the first PARSING IN CURSOR #12390720 that you find.

c=8000

> This call consumed 8,000 ±10,000 μs of CPU time.[10]

e=1734

> This call consumed 1,734 ±1 μs of elapsed time. (Yes, Oracle actually measured the call as having consumed more CPU time than the call's actual elapsed duration.)

p=1

> This call obtained 1 Oracle block via OS read calls.

cr=7

> This call executed 7 "consistent mode" accesses upon the Oracle database buffer cache.

cu=0

> This call executed 0 "current mode" accesses upon the Oracle database buffer cache.

ms=0

> This call encountered 0 misses upon the Oracle library cache.

---

[10] For a detailed description of why the CPU consumption statistic is accurate to only ±10,000 μs, see Millsap and Holt *Optimizing Oracle Performance* (O'Reilly 2003), 161–165. There is a mistake in the book that I should clean up, however. Until recently, I believed that Oracle Database kernels running on Solaris with microstate accounting turned on would result in *c* statistic values accurate to ±1 μs. However, since Oracle on Solaris (at least through Oracle Database version 11.2) uses the *times* system call instead of *getrusage*, even with microstate accounting available from the OS, Oracle's *c* statistic is accurate to only ±10,000 μs.

`r=1`
: This call returned 1 row.

`dep=2`
: There were 2 levels of database calls below this call in the database call stack. That is, this call is a child of another db call, which in turn is a child of another db call.

`og=4`
: This call's Oracle optimizer goal is *choose*. The four choices are, in order: *all*, *first*, *rule*, and *choose*.

`plh=3992920156`
: This call's execution plan hash value is 3992920156.

`tim=1294438818783887`
: This call completed at time 1,294,438,818,783,887 ±1 µs. The *tim* value is given in microseconds, but the answer to "microseconds since what?" varies by platform. All that really matters is for the *tim* values to be consistent within a given trace file, which they usually are.[11]

TRACE FILE ALPHABET: SYSTEM CALLS

All syscall lines resemble this:

```
WAIT #12397272: nam='db file sequential read' ela= 221 file#=1 block#=2735 blocks=1 obj#=423 tim=1294438818791494
```

Here's what the fields mean:

`WAIT`
: This call is a syscall, not a database call.[12]

`#12397272`
: The call's cursor handle id is 12397272. To find the definition of this cursor, you'd seek backward in the trace file to the first `PARSING IN CURSOR #12397272` that you find.

`nam='db file sequential read'`
: This call was a read of a database file that retrieved one or more blocks and stored them contiguously somewhere in memory. Oracle Corporation gives each syscall its kernel makes a distinct name, and the company documents the meanings of those names so you can more easily understand what's going on.

`ela= 221`
: This call consumed 221 ±1 µs of elapsed time.

`file#=1 block#=2735 blocks=1`
: This read call (probably a *pread* call—you can tell by using *strace*) read 1 block from Oracle file id 1, beginning at block id 2735. Each call has three parameters like these, which are named differently depending on the call name. These three parameters give you contextual information about what the call was meant to accomplish.

---

[11] They're most likely not to be consistent within a given file on Microsoft Windows systems, where *tim* values wrap (that is, get as large as they can go and then start over at 0) more frequently than on other systems.

[12] I've had good fun explaining why the word *wait* is the wrong word to use in this context. See for example my essay, "Dang it people, they're syscalls, not 'waits'..." at *http://carymillsap.blogspot.com/2009/02/dang-it-people-theyre-syscalls-not.html*.

Chapter 3. Oracle Extended SQL Trace

`obj#=423`

This call operated upon the Oracle object with id 423. When a call operated upon no object in particular, the Oracle kernel will emit `obj#=-1`.

`tim=1294438818791494`

This call completed at time 1,294,438,818,791,494 ±1 μs.

TRACE FILE FLOW

The Oracle kernel emits trace lines as calls complete. You have to know this to determine the parent-child relationships among calls. For example, what can you know about the following trace data stream?

```
1  PARSE #2:…,e=1,…,tim=5
2  EXEC  #2:…,e=2,…,tim=8
3  FETCH #2:…,e=4,…,tim=15
4  PARSE #1:…,e=15,…,tim=17
```

From just the data shown here, you can determine the start and end time of each call. A call's end time is its *tim* value, and its begin time is *tim – e*. From that, you can work out the parent-child relationships among these calls:

Time	Call
2	parse #1 {
4	parse #2 {
5	}
6	exec #2 {
8	}
11	fetch #2 {
15	}
17	}

You can work out call parent-child relationships by computing call begin and end times.

Before Oracle version 10.2, when there were no *tim* values on the syscall lines, we inferred call parent-child hierarchy from the *dep* values on database call lines and from the lines' relative locations. We attributed each *dep* = 1 call as the child of the *dep* = 0 call that followed it in the trace data stream. With *tim* values on all our call lines, it is no longer necessary to do that. You can determine all the parent-child information you need now just by noticing at what time each call begins and ends.

TRACE FILE ARITHMETIC: PART 1

Now you know the trace file alphabet and how trace file lines flow forth at the completion of the database calls your client application makes and the OS calls your Oracle kernel makes. The next step is to understand a few details about how time works in Oracle trace files.

First, a database call's total duration (*e*) is approximately the sum of the time it spends using CPU (*c*) plus the sum of the durations of the OS calls made by the database call (ela_j for each *j* in the set of syscalls that are children of the database call). The equation is only approximate, primarily because of the ±10,000 μs on the CPU time measurement. Expressed as a precise equality, we have, for a given database call *i*:

$$e_i = c_i + \sum_{j \in \text{Children}(i)} ela_j + \Delta_i \qquad (1)$$

The term Δ_i there at the end is the time within the known duration of the call that is unaccounted for (unexplained, if you prefer) by Oracle. It can be positive or negative or zero. As much as you'd like for this unaccounted-for duration to be zero, it just won't be. However, in the aggregate, unaccounted-for time won't usually be a material contributor to total response time. When it is, it's an indication that:

- Either you have forgotten to trace the OS calls (as with `waits=>false` in your call to a *dbms_monitor* function);
- Or you have an un-patched Oracle bug;
- Or you have a process preemption problem (perhaps too much paging or swapping).

Here's how the arithmetic works out in a two-line trace file excerpt:

```
69 WAIT #124367516: nam='Disk file operations I/O' ela= 124 FileOperation=2 fileno=4 filetype=2 obj#=-1 tim=1294702369858445
70 FETCH #124367516:c=0,e=386,p=0,cr=6,cu=0,mis=0,r=14,dep=0,og=1,plh=3956160932,tim=1294702369858666
```

Here, you have an OS call on line 1 that is a child of the database call on line 2. You can prove that by comparing *tim* and duration values:

Time (microseconds)	Call
1294702369858280	fetch #124367516 {
1294702369858321	wait #124367516 {
1294702369858445	}
1294702369858666	}

Parent-child relationships among calls, using call begin and end time data.

For the database call (a fetch), we have $e = 386$, and $c = 0$. The sum of the OS call durations is simply 124. Using the equation above, this leaves an unaccounted-for duration of $\Delta = 262$. Here's what the call's response time looks like in the form of a profile table:

Call	Duration (microseconds)	
unaccounted-for within calls	262	67.9%
Disk file operations I/O	124	32.1%
fetch	0	0.0%
Response time	386	100.0%

Response time profile for the *fetch* database call, using Equation 1.

You can extend the same logic from this simple example to database calls that are parents of many more OS calls, or even calls that are parents of one or more levels of other database calls.

TRACE FILE ARITHMETIC: PART 2

The second relationship you need to understand is that the total response time described by a trace file is simply the time elapsed from the beginning of the first call to the end of the final call. Remember that the Oracle kernel doesn't emit call begin times—only call end times. But you can compute the begin time of a call by subtracting its duration from its end time:

$$R = tim_{final} - \left(tim_{first} - e_{first}\right) \qquad (2)$$

Chapter 3. Oracle Extended SQL Trace

Note that although Equation 2 refers to the duration of the first call as *e*, if the first call in the file is an OS call, you'll need to use its *ela* field.

The values tim_{first} and e_{first} refer to fields associated with the first call to begin in the process being traced. Because the Oracle kernel emits trace lines when calls end (not when they begin), the first call to begin is not necessarily the first call listed in the trace file. The two lines of trace data profiled in the prior section illustrate how that can happen.

TRACE FILE ARITHMETIC: PART 3

The final category of response time to describe is the time that is unaccounted-for between the top-level database and OS calls. This one is simple:

$$\Delta_{between} = R - \sum_{i \in TopLevelCalls} e_i \quad (3)$$

That is, the total between-call unaccounted-for duration is the total response time that we know has passed minus the time accounted for by top-level calls (both database and OS) in the trace file. So Equation 1 gives you most of the detail that you need to make up your profile. Equation 2 gives you the total response time that you need to account for. And Equation 3 gives you the label to which to assign the remainder of the unexplained duration. These are the three elements you need to create a complete response time profile.

TRACING TRAPS

When performance is the question, tracing is usually my answer. However, it's not always easy. Here are some of the pitfalls to avoid.

Data collection

> By far, the most common problem we encounter in the field is the trace file whose response time doesn't match the response time of the end user's experience that you're trying to diagnose. We get a lot of trace files whose overall response times are dominated by either a small number of long-duration *SQL*Net message from client* calls or a small number of unaccounted-for gaps in the action. The most important thing to remember about collecting trace data is you want the response time of your trace file to exactly match the response time of your end user's experience.

Oracle microseconds

> A microsecond is 1/1,000,000th of a second, or 1,000 ns (nanoseconds). On some platforms, an Oracle microsecond is 1/976,563th of a second, or 1,024 ns. Being off by 2.4% may not sound like too big of a problem, but if you want to regard an Oracle *tim* value as a number of microseconds that have elapsed since the Unix epoch (1970-01-01T00:00:00.000000Z in ISO 8601 form), you need to multiply your *tim* value by 1.024 before calculating the date and time it represents. Otherwise, for *tim* values generated in 2011, you will be off by almost a year:

```
31  $ mrtim 1290919161132812  -u1024ns
32  2011-11-21T12:47:00.999999-0600
33  $ mrtim 1290919161132812
34  2010-11-27T22:39:21.132812-0600
```

> The *tim* value 1290919161132812 represents the time at which I'm writing this paragraph, expressed in 1,024-ns units, the way versions of the Oracle Database prior to 11.2.0.2.0 would do it. The *mrtim* command from the Method R Tools software package makes it easy to see that this *tim* value, interpreted in the way Oracle constructed it (using -u1024ns as the unit of measure), represents 2011-11-21 (the right answer). However, interpreting the same *tim* value as a number of real microseconds yields the date 2010-11-27, which is incorrect by approximately one year.

Oracle bugs

> The Oracle 11.1 era was especially unkind to trace file users. Bug 7522002 causes OS call time values to come from a 1,000-ns-per-μs clock, while database call time values come from a 1,024-ns-per-μs clock. This causes the sequence of calls in a trace file to zigzag back and forth in time. This problem is correctable, because the numbers are merely rendered in different scales. The Method R Tools program *mrtimfix* can correct the problem for you.
>
> However, bug 8342329 is not correctable, because it conceals data.[13] It causes the Oracle kernel to emit the same *tim* value repeatedly for multiple distinct database calls, which is debilitating. Happily, these bugs in 11.1 have patches and are fixed in version 11.2.0.2.0.

COMMERCIAL TRACE FILE TOOLS

There's generally too much detail in a trace file for a human to process without software assistance. The most famous trace file software tool of all is Oracle Corporation's *tkprof* utility, which Oracle ships with the Oracle Database (all releases, all editions). The *tkprof* tool aggregates by SQL statement, and it allows you to sort those SQL statements in its output report by any of several criteria. This can work out okay, as long as:

- You care about inefficient SQL more than you care about response time (which is often a mistake).
- You sort by the right thing (`sort=prsela,exeela,fchela` is almost always the right thing).
- Your problem doesn't involve parent-child relationships among database calls (so-called recursive SQL).

I used *tkprof* extensively for the first ten years of my career. However, I spent a lot of time looking at raw trace data, too, because there's a lot of information inside a trace file that *tkprof* ignores (as well as the newer, much handsomer *trcanalzr*), and the format of the *tkprof* output is not particularly friendly to my response time focus. So, I've helped to design and write a few software tools in the past ten years, including:

Method R Profiler

> The Method R Profiler is software that Jeff Holt and I wrote about in our book *Optimizing Oracle Performance*. It produces an HTML report that unambiguously explains the response time accounted in a trace file, no matter what the cause (whether SQL or not), using color to direct your attention.

Method R Tools *mrskew*

> The Method R Skew Analyzer, called *mrskew*, is a data-mining tool for trace files. With *mrskew*, you can use group and filter functions to drill into trace files with practically any analysis perspective you want. For example, you can group a whole directory full of trace files by SQL statement hash values, or database file ids, or hash latch address values, or library cache miss counts, or block counts per read call, or service-module-action names, or prepare call durations, ...anything you like.

TRACE FILE: HELLO WORLD

Here is the complete listing of the trace file from the "hello world" query:

```
1  Trace file /opt/oracle/diag/rdbms/v11202/V11202/trace/V11202_ora_21089.trc
2  Oracle Database 11g Enterprise Edition Release 11.2.0.2.0 - Production
3  With the Partitioning, OLAP, Data Mining and Real Application Testing options
```

---

[13] See also patches 9415425 for Oracle 11.1.0.7.1 on Solaris and 9941786 for Oracle 11.1.0.7.4 on Solaris.

Chapter 3. Oracle Extended SQL Trace

```
  4  ORACLE_HOME = /opt/oracle/product/11.2.0.2
  5  System name:    Linux
  6  Node name:      rhel01.dev.method-r.com
  7  Release:        2.6.18-92.1.13.el5xen
  8  Version:        #1 SMP Thu Sep 4 04:20:55 EDT 2008
  9  Machine:        i686
 10  VM name:        Xen Version: 3.1 (PVM)
 11  Instance name: V11202
 12  Redo thread mounted by this instance: 1
 13  Oracle process number: 30
 14  Unix process pid: 21089, image: oracle@rhel01.dev.method-r.com (TNS V1-V3)
 15
 16
 17  *** 2011-01-10 13:33:22.746
 18  *** SESSION ID:(19.1247) 2011-01-10 13:33:22.746
 19  *** CLIENT ID:() 2011-01-10 13:33:22.746
 20  *** SERVICE NAME:(SYS$USERS) 2011-01-10 13:33:22.746
 21  *** MODULE NAME:(SQL*Plus) 2011-01-10 13:33:22.746
 22  *** ACTION NAME:() 2011-01-10 13:33:22.746
 23
 24  =====================
 25  PARSING IN CURSOR #7285244 len=60 dep=0 uid=5 oct=47 lid=5 tim=1294688002745892 hv=1548041990 ad='3d51df50' sqlid='31wf1v9f4ags6'
 26  BEGIN dbms_monitor.session_trace_enable(binds=>true); END;
 27  END OF STMT
 28  EXEC #7285244:c=0,e=845,p=0,cr=0,cu=0,mis=1,r=1,dep=0,og=1,plh=0,tim=1294688002745889
 29  WAIT #7285244: nam='SQL*Net message to client' ela= 2 driver id=1650815232 #bytes=1 p3=0 obj#=-1 tim=1294688002746391
 30  WAIT #7285244: nam='SQL*Net message from client' ela= 931 driver id=1650815232 #bytes=1 p3=0 obj#=-1 tim=1294688002747354
 31  CLOSE #7285244:c=0,e=55,dep=0,type=0,tim=1294688002747449
 32  =====================
 33  PARSING IN CURSOR #7285244 len=30 dep=0 uid=5 oct=3 lid=5 tim=1294688002747560 hv=1604528588 ad='3d526cd8' sqlid='guthms1gu6afc'
 34  select 'Hello world' from dual
 35  END OF STMT
 36  PARSE #7285244:c=0,e=70,p=0,cr=0,cu=0,mis=0,r=0,dep=0,og=1,plh=1388734953,tim=1294688002747559
 37  EXEC #7285244:c=0,e=112,p=0,cr=0,cu=0,mis=0,r=0,dep=0,og=1,plh=1388734953,tim=1294688002747793
 38  WAIT #7285244: nam='SQL*Net message to client' ela= 2 driver id=1650815232 #bytes=1 p3=0 obj#=-1 tim=1294688002747865
 39  FETCH #7285244:c=0,e=8,p=0,cr=0,cu=0,mis=0,r=1,dep=0,og=1,plh=1388734953,tim=1294688002747910
 40  STAT #7285244 id=1 cnt=1 pid=0 pos=1 obj=0 op='FAST DUAL  (cr=0 pr=0 pw=0 time=4 us cost=2 size=0 card=1)'
 41  WAIT #7285244: nam='SQL*Net message from client' ela= 375 driver id=1650815232 #bytes=1 p3=0 obj#=-1 tim=1294688002748453
 42  FETCH #7285244:c=0,e=1,p=0,cr=0,cu=0,mis=0,r=0,dep=0,og=0,plh=1388734953,tim=1294688002748493
 43  WAIT #7285244: nam='SQL*Net message to client' ela= 1 driver id=1650815232 #bytes=1 p3=0 obj#=-1 tim=1294688002748520
 44  WAIT #7285244: nam='SQL*Net message from client' ela= 1627 driver id=1650815232 #bytes=1 p3=0 obj#=-1 tim=1294688002750168
 45  XCTEND rlbk=0, rd_only=1, tim=1294688002750230
 46  =====================
 47  PARSING IN CURSOR #7386176 len=447 dep=1 uid=0 oct=2 lid=0 tim=1294688002750383 hv=1097020010 ad='3d7e77d4' sqlid='f711myt0q6cma'
 48  insert into sys.aud$( sessionid,entryid,statement,ntimestamp#, userid,userhost,terminal,action#,returnco
     de, logoff$lread,logoff$pread,logoff$lwrite,logoff$dead, logoff$time,comment$text,spare1,clientid,sessioncpu,proxy$
     sid,user$guid, instance#,process#,auditid,dbid) values(:1,:2,:3,SYS_EXTRACT_UTC(SYSTIMESTAMP),      :4,:5,:6,:7,:8,
     :9,:10,:11,:12,       cast(SYS_EXTRACT_UTC(systimestamp) as date),:13,:14,:15,:16,:17,:18,       :19,:20,:21,:22)
 49  END OF STMT
 50  PARSE #7386176:c=0,e=93,p=0,cr=0,cu=0,mis=0,r=0,dep=1,og=4,plh=0,tim=1294688002750382
 51  BINDS #7386176:
 52   Bind#0
 53    oacdty=02 mxl=22(22) mxlc=00 mal=00 scl=00 pre=00
 54    oacflg=08 fl2=0001 frm=00 csi=00 siz=24 off=0
 55    kxsbbbfp=0070ac04  bln=22  avl=04  flg=05
 56    value=63843
 57   Bind#1
 58    oacdty=02 mxl=22(22) mxlc=00 mal=00 scl=00 pre=00
 59    oacflg=08 fl2=0001 frm=00 csi=00 siz=24 off=0
 60    kxsbbbfp=0070abe0  bln=24  avl=02  flg=05
 61    value=2
 62   Bind#2
 63    oacdty=02 mxl=22(22) mxlc=00 mal=00 scl=00 pre=00
 64    oacflg=08 fl2=0001 frm=00 csi=00 siz=24 off=0
 65    kxsbbbfp=0070abbc  bln=24  avl=02  flg=05
 66    value=1
 67   Bind#3
 68    oacdty=01 mxl=32(06) mxlc=00 mal=00 scl=00 pre=00
 69    oacflg=18 fl2=0001 frm=01 csi=178 siz=32 off=0
 70    kxsbbbfp=006df248  bln=32  avl=06  flg=09
 71    value="SYSTEM"
 72   Bind#4
 73    oacdty=01 mxl=32(23) mxlc=00 mal=00 scl=00 pre=00
 74    oacflg=18 fl2=0001 frm=01 csi=178 siz=32 off=0
 75    kxsbbbfp=006df1c2  bln=32  avl=23  flg=09
 76    value="rhel01.dev.method-r.com"
 77   Bind#5
 78    oacdty=01 mxl=32(05) mxlc=00 mal=00 scl=00 pre=00
 79    oacflg=18 fl2=0001 frm=01 csi=178 siz=32 off=0
 80    kxsbbbfp=635ffd04  bln=32  avl=05  flg=09
 81    value="pts/0"
 82   Bind#6
 83    oacdty=02 mxl=22(22) mxlc=00 mal=00 scl=00 pre=00
 84    oacflg=08 fl2=0001 frm=00 csi=00 siz=24 off=0
 85    kxsbbbfp=0070ab98  bln=24  avl=03  flg=05
 86    value=101
 87   Bind#7
 88    oacdty=02 mxl=22(22) mxlc=00 mal=00 scl=00 pre=00
 89    oacflg=08 fl2=0001 frm=00 csi=00 siz=24 off=0
 90    kxsbbbfp=0070ab74  bln=24  avl=01  flg=05
 91    value=0
 92   Bind#8
 93    oacdty=02 mxl=22(22) mxlc=00 mal=00 scl=00 pre=00
 94    oacflg=08 fl2=0001 frm=00 csi=00 siz=24 off=0
 95    kxsbbbfp=0070ab40  bln=24  avl=02  flg=05
 96    value=44
 97   Bind#9
 98    oacdty=02 mxl=22(22) mxlc=00 mal=00 scl=00 pre=00
```

```
 99      oacflg=08 fl2=0001 frm=00 csi=00 siz=24 off=0
100      kxsbbbfp=0070ab1c  bln=24  avl=01  flg=05
101      value=0
102    Bind#10
103      oacdty=02 mxl=22(22) mxlc=00 mal=00 scl=00 pre=00
104      oacflg=08 fl2=0001 frm=00 csi=00 siz=24 off=0
105      kxsbbbfp=0070aaf8  bln=24  avl=02  flg=05
106      value=4
107    Bind#11
108      oacdty=02 mxl=22(22) mxlc=00 mal=00 scl=00 pre=00
109      oacflg=08 fl2=0001 frm=00 csi=00 siz=24 off=0
110      kxsbbbfp=0070aad4  bln=24  avl=01  flg=05
111      value=0
112    Bind#12
113      oacdty=01 mxl=32(00) mxlc=00 mal=00 scl=00 pre=00
114      oacflg=18 fl2=0001 frm=01 csi=178 siz=32 off=0
115      kxsbbbfp=00000000  bln=32  avl=00  flg=09
116    Bind#13
117      oacdty=01 mxl=32(06) mxlc=00 mal=00 scl=00 pre=00
118      oacflg=18 fl2=0001 frm=01 csi=178 siz=32 off=0
119      kxsbbbfp=635ffc98  bln=32  avl=06  flg=09
120      value="oracle"
121    Bind#14
122      oacdty=01 mxl=32(00) mxlc=00 mal=00 scl=00 pre=00
123      oacflg=18 fl2=0001 frm=01 csi=178 siz=32 off=0
124      kxsbbbfp=00000000  bln=32  avl=00  flg=09
125    Bind#15
126      oacdty=02 mxl=22(22) mxlc=00 mal=00 scl=00 pre=00
127      oacflg=08 fl2=0001 frm=00 csi=00 siz=24 off=0
128      kxsbbbfp=0070aab0  bln=24  avl=02  flg=05
129      value=1
130    Bind#16
131      oacdty=02 mxl=22(00) mxlc=00 mal=00 scl=00 pre=00
132      oacflg=08 fl2=0001 frm=00 csi=00 siz=24 off=0
133      kxsbbbfp=0070aa8c  bln=24  avl=00  flg=05
134    Bind#17
135      oacdty=01 mxl=32(00) mxlc=00 mal=00 scl=00 pre=00
136      oacflg=18 fl2=0001 frm=01 csi=178 siz=32 off=0
137      kxsbbbfp=00000000  bln=32  avl=00  flg=09
138    Bind#18
139      oacdty=02 mxl=22(22) mxlc=00 mal=00 scl=00 pre=00
140      oacflg=08 fl2=0001 frm=00 csi=00 siz=24 off=0
141      kxsbbbfp=0070aa58  bln=24  avl=01  flg=05
142      value=0
143    Bind#19
144      oacdty=01 mxl=32(05) mxlc=00 mal=00 scl=00 pre=00
145      oacflg=18 fl2=0001 frm=01 csi=178 siz=32 off=0
146      kxsbbbfp=bfc1b840  bln=32  avl=05  flg=09
147      value="21089"
148    Bind#20
149      oacdty=01 mxl=32(00) mxlc=00 mal=00 scl=00 pre=00
150      oacflg=18 fl2=0001 frm=01 csi=178 siz=32 off=0
151      kxsbbbfp=00000000  bln=32  avl=00  flg=09
152    Bind#21
153      oacdty=02 mxl=22(22) mxlc=00 mal=00 scl=00 pre=00
154      oacflg=08 fl2=0001 frm=00 csi=00 siz=24 off=0
155      kxsbbbfp=0070a7f8  bln=24  avl=06  flg=05
156      value=518865609
157  EXEC #7386176:c=0,e=1733,p=0,cr=1,cu=2,mis=0,r=1,dep=1,og=4,plh=0,tim=1294688002752264
158  STAT #7386176 id=1 cnt=0 pid=0 pos=1 obj=0 op='LOAD TABLE CONVENTIONAL  (cr=1 pr=0 pw=0 time=155 us)'
159  CLOSE #7386176:c=0,e=5,dep=1,type=0,tim=1294688002752341
160  WAIT #0: nam='log file sync' ela= 153 buffer#=5673 sync scn=1046841 p3=0 obj#=-1 tim=1294688002752632
161  CLOSE #7285244:c=0,e=9,dep=0,type=0,tim=1294688002752690
162  CLOSE #7248564:c=0,e=30,dep=0,type=0,tim=1294688002752740
```

4 Oracle Database Timed Event Reference

Through its extended SQL tracing mechanism, the Oracle Database allows you to view details about "timed events" that take place within the Oracle kernel. These timed events are internally instrumented database calls (dbcalls) and operating system calls (syscalls) executed by the Oracle kernel. You can learn about Oracle timed events in the standard Oracle Database documentation set, but you can learn more by using an operating system tracing tool like strace. This chapter shows how to use strace to explain the meaning of syscalls you will encounter in working with Oracle Database-based applications.

Where to Begin

You can learn a lot in a ten-minute session looking at Oracle trace data, but what happens when you see an Oracle timed event name that you don't understand? This chapter contains advice that will guide you through the most common code paths that you'll see described in your trace files. First, you'll find a list of timed events that you'll see commonly in your profiles, and you'll see a brief description of what to do when you encounter each one. Later, you'll see how you can use *strace* and your operating system's documentation to earn a deeper understanding of how the Oracle Database spends your time.

For calls not listed in this chapter, the best online sources are probably Google and Oracle.com (in that order). However, you'll learn more reliably by learning to use a tool like Dtrace or *strace* (or *truss*, *sctrace*, *tusc*, …whatever OS call tracing tool your platform gives you) to see what OS call each Oracle timed event name maps to. Once you're to that point, it's easy: there is lots of reliable documentation for OS calls available all over the place, all the way down to the source code level for many operating systems. Understanding your performance in terms of core OS function calls will give you more power to prevent and solve problems.

Responding to Commonly Occurring Timed Events

Here is an alphabetized list of some of the timed events (dbcalls and syscalls) that you'll see over and over again, with a brief bit of advice about what to do when that's the type of call that dominates your task's response time:

buffer busy waits syscall

> Your response time should never be dominated by *buffer busy wait* syscalls. They happen to a program when it tries to change an in-memory block in the database buffer cache, but some other process is in the midst of modifying that buffer. Fix the problem by working with your developers and data designer to make the most competed-for database blocks less interesting to so many concurrent Oracle sessions. A common cause of *buffer busy waits* is the application that uses tables with *select for update* statements to generate keys instead of using a sequence object.

db file scattered read syscall

> It is entirely appropriate to see *db file scattered read* calls occupy a prominent position in your response time profile, but you should generally not see them consume more

than about 20% of your response time. The call indicates a read of two or more Oracle blocks in a single OS call. Conventional advice instructs your database administrator to make the database buffer cache bigger when he sees lots of this kind of OS call. Better advice is to write more efficient queries that follow the rule-of-ten advice explained in the *fetch* section.

db file sequential read syscall

It is entirely appropriate to see *db file sequential read* calls occupy a prominent position in your response time profile, but you should generally not see them consume more than about 20% of your response time. The call normally indicates the read of a single Oracle block with a single OS call. If you can eliminate unnecessary buffer cache visits as directed in the *fetch* section, you'll naturally eliminate *db file sequential read* calls as well.

direct path read syscall

It is entirely appropriate to see *direct path read* calls occupy a prominent position in your response time profile, but you should generally not see them consume more than about 20% of your response time. The call normally indicates the read of two or more Oracle blocks with a single OS call. If you can eliminate unnecessary buffer cache visits as directed in the *fetch* section, you'll naturally eliminate *direct path read* calls as well.

enqueue syscall

Your response time should never be dominated by *enqueue* calls. Each call indicates that a timeout has occurred while your code is trying to change a row that another Oracle session has locked. If you wrote the program that's holding the lock, then rewrite it to hold the lock for a smaller total duration. For example, don't allow any end-user data entry opportunities to occur between an *insert*, *update*, *delete*, or *merge* SQL statement and its subsequent *commit*. If you didn't write the code that's holding the lock, then find out who did.

exec dbcall

It is perfectly reasonable for most of your task's response time to be consumed by *exec* calls. However, make sure that your *exec* call work is *efficient*. If your execution has a query component (like an *update* statement with a complex query built into it), see the advice in the *fetch* entry. If you are executing a PL/SQL package with no real time consuming SQL statements within it, then use the Oracle *dbms_profiler* package to identify which lines of PL/SQL are costing you the most time.

fetch dbcall

It is perfectly reasonable for most of your task's response time to be consumed by *fetch* calls. However, make sure that your *fetch* call work is *efficient*. Don't visit the buffer cache (the value $cr + cu$ from your Oracle extended SQL trace data) more than 10 times per row returned per data source. For example, a 4-table join that returns 3 rows should have $cr + cu \leq 120$.

latch.* syscall (call names with the word *latch* in them)

Your response time should never be dominated by *latch.** calls. You'll see *shared pool* or *library cache* latch waits (maybe both of them) when you run code that makes too many parse calls. You'll see *cache buffers chains* or *cache buffers lru chain* latch waits when you run inefficient SQL that visits the database buffer cache too many times. Don't do those things.

In Oracle version 10 and beyond, the names of many latch-related OS calls each contain the name of the latch, as in *latch: cache buffers chains*. Prior to version 10, all latch-related OS calls were recorded under the call name *latch free*, and the type of the latch was listed as the value of the p2 field in the WAIT line.

log file sync syscall
> Your response time should never be dominated by *log file sync* calls. The call indicates *commit* call processing, which you can easily abuse when, for example, you write applications that use *auto-commit* or that explicitly commit one row at a time (such as most service-bus architectures do).

parse dbcall
> Your response time should never be dominated by *parse* calls. Parsing too often prevents an application from scaling to large user counts, no matter how many CPUs your system might happen to have. It's because parsing is a software-serialized operation. A good application never parses (that is, prepares) a given SQL statement more than once per session. A great application never parses a given SQL statement more than once per Oracle instance startup.

SQL*Net message from client syscall
> Your response time should almost never be dominated by *SQL*Net message from client* calls. Each call indicates a network round-trip. Don't make unnecessary network round-trips. For example, it's almost never a good idea to write applications that process only one database row at a time. If you're sloppy in how you collect your trace data for interactive applications, then some of the time included in your *SQL*Net message from client* durations will be time that the end user spends regarding the data just presented to him. This is a false negative performance indicator that you should fix by being more careful about how you collect your trace data. Scope your trace data collecting to include only the time that your end user is waiting on the application to execute a task.

SQL*Net more data to client syscall
> Your response time should never be dominated by *SQL*Net more data to client* calls. This call is what you'll see when you crank up your array fetch size for programs that select a lot of rows. It's like a *SQL*Net message to client*, except it's in the context of a single data transfer that's already in progress.

unaccounted-for time
> Your response time should never be dominated by *unaccounted-for* time. If you use a commercial profiling tool like the Method R Profiler or the Method R Tools *mrskew* utility, the presence of *unaccounted-for* time almost always indicates time that your process has spent preempted by the operating system. Fix it by making your program (and the programs it competes against for CPU time) use as little CPU as possible. Eliminate unnecessary parse calls, process data in sets instead of row-by-row, and ensure that your SQL visits the database buffer cache as few times as possible.

ORACLE TIMED EVENT INSTRUMENTATION

Oracle Database timed event instrumentation is ingenious. For syscalls, it works like this:

```
 1  function syscall {
 2      ela0 = gettime();                                       # mark the time before the call
 3
 4      ...                                                     # execute the syscall here
 5
 6      ela1 = gettime();                                       # mark the time after the call
 7      nam = …;                                                # name assigned to the code path by some Oracle developer
 8      cid = …;                                                # cursor handle id
 9      ela = ela1 - ela0;                                      # elapsed duration between wall times
10      write(TRC, "WAIT #%d: nam='%s'…", cid, nam, ela, …);    # write the syscall record to the trace file
11  }
```

Chapter 4. Oracle Database Timed Event Reference

And for dbcalls, the instrumentation works like this:

```
12  function dbcall {
13      e0 = gettime();                                     # mark the time before the call
14      c0 = getrusage();                                   # mark the CPU time consumed before the call
15
16      ...                                                 # execute the dbcall here; maybe make calls to dbcall() or syscall()
17
18      e1 = gettime();                                     # mark the time after the call
19      c1 = getrusage();                                   # mark the CPU time consumed after the call
20      nam = …;                                            # name assigned to the call: PARSE, EXEC, FETCH, …
21      cid = …                                             # cursor handle id
22      e = e1 - e0;                                        # elapsed duration between wall times
23      c = (c1.utime + c1.stime) - (c0.utime + c0.stime)   # CPU time consumed by the call
24      write(TRC, "%s #%d:c=%d,e=%d…", nam, cid, c, e, …); # write the dbcall record to the trace file
25  }
```

Having both dbcalls and syscalls instrumented this way means that you can create a profile for the response time that the Oracle Database consumes on behalf of the application that uses it.

Understanding how the Oracle Database instruments itself is vital if you're going to compare database statistics with other statistics generated on your system. You can't have an informed conversation about performance with your OS or network or storage administrators if you don't know where your Oracle Database numbers are coming from.

TRACING ORACLE KERNEL SYSTEM CALLS

What can you do when you've reached a problem where you documentation doesn't help you? …When your Google search doesn't produce anything at all, or when it gives you information of suspicious quality? Or when your software might have changed more recently than anything you can find out about it online? That's when it's good to know how to view your Oracle kernel process through the lens of a system call tracing utility like *strace*. With *strace* and the online manual pages for your operating system's syscalls, you can learn details that you can't find anywhere else about how Oracle works. With *strace*, you can improve the conversations you'll have with your non-Oracle colleagues, like your system administrators, storage administrators, and network administrators.

Just about every system has system call tracing tool, but different tools on different systems have different names. Here is the tool you'll need to find on your system:

Operating system	System call tracing tool
Linux	*strace*
Solaris	*dtruss* or *truss*
HP-UX	*tusc*
IBM AIX	*sctrace*
Microsoft Windows	*Process Monitor*, *straceNT*, or *strace*
Mac OS X	*dtruss*

System call tracing tool by operating system.

I'll show how to trace Oracle kernel system calls on a Linux server running Oracle Database 12c. First, here's a *sqlplus* query that will show the operating system process id for its own *sqlplus* process and the dedicated Oracle kernel process to which it is attached:

```
26  SQL> r
27    1  select s.process "sqlplus pid", p.spid "kernel pid"
28    2  from v$session s, v$process p
29    3* where s.paddr = p.addr and s.audsid=sys_context('userenv','sessionid')
30
31  sqlplus pid            kernel pid
32  ---------------------- ----------------------
33  15195                  15197
```

Here is how you can attach *strace* to the Oracle kernel:

```
34  $ nohup strace -s132 -o strace.txt -p15197 &
35  [1] 15388
36  $ nohup: ignoring input and appending output to `nohup.out'
```

Now *strace* will generate output to *strace.txt* for every system call that the Oracle kernel makes in response to the *sqlplus* session. If you *tail* the *strace.txt* file, you'll see Oracle blocking on a *read* call, like this:

```
37  $ tail -f strace.txt
38  read(36,
```

If you look up the *read* syscall, you'll find this:

```
39  $ man 2 read
40  READ(2)                        Linux Programmer's Manual                        READ(2)
41
42  NAME
43         read - read from a file descriptor
44
45  SYNOPSIS
46         #include <unistd.h>
47
48         ssize_t read(int fd, void *buf, size_t count);
49
50  DESCRIPTION
51         read() attempts to read up to count bytes from file descriptor fd into the buffer starting at buf.
52
53         If count is zero, read() returns zero and has no other results.  If count is greater than SSIZE_MAX,
54         the result is unspecified.
55
56  RETURN VALUE
57         On  success,  the  number  of  bytes  read  is  returned (zero indicates end of file), and the file
58         position is advanced by this number.  It is not an error if this number is smaller than the number
59         of bytes requested; this may happen for example because fewer bytes are actually available right
60         now (maybe because we were close to end-of-file, or because we are reading from a pipe, or from a
61         terminal), or because read() was interrupted by a signal.  On error, -1 is returned, and errno is
62         set appropriately.  In this case it is left unspecified whether the file position (if any) changes.
```

So, the first argument to *read* is a file descriptor. With the *lsof* command, you can see which file it is that file descriptor 36 describes:

```
63  $ lsof -p15197 -ad36
64  COMMAND     PID   USER   FD   TYPE DEVICE SIZE/OFF NODE NAME
65  oracle_15 15197 oracle  36u  IPv6 402529      0t0  TCP oel02.dev.method-r.com:ncube-lm->oel02.dev.method-r.com:41083 (ESTABLISHED)
```

File descriptor 36 is a network connection. Here's how you can find out what's on the other end, if the other end is on the same machine, which in this case it will be (you can tell by the NAME value):

```
66  $ lsof | head -1; lsof | grep oel02.dev.method-r.com:41083
67  COMMAND     PID   USER   FD   TYPE  DEVICE SIZE/OFF NODE NAME
68  sqlplus   15195 oracle  10u   IPv4  402528      0t0  TCP oel02.dev.method-r.com:41083->oel02.dev.method-r.com:ncube-lm (ESTABLISHED)
69  oracle_15 15197 oracle  36u   IPv6  402529      0t0  TCP oel02.dev.method-r.com:ncube-lm->oel02.dev.method-r.com:41083 (ESTABLISHED)
```

File descriptor 36 on the Oracle kernel process is connected to the *sqlplus* process. The *strace* output is telling you that the Oracle kernel is simply waiting for the *sqlplus* session to tell it what to do next.

It is particularly interesting to use *strace* in conjunction with Oracle extended SQL tracing. So, I'll activate the trace from within *sqlplus*:

```
70  SQL> exec dbms_monitor.session_trace_enable(null, null, true, true)
71
72  PL/SQL procedure successfully completed.
```

This stimulates a flurry of activity in the *strace* output:

```
73  read(36, "\0\0\1x\6\0\0\0\0\21i5\376\377\377\377\377\377\377\377\1\0\0\0\0\0\0\10\0\0\0\3^6!\0\4\0\0\0\0\0\376\377\377\377\377\377\377
    G\0\0\0\0\0\0\376\377\377\377\377\377\377\r\0\0\0\0\0\0\376\377\377\377\377\377\377\0\376\377\377\377\377\377\377\0\0\0\0\1\0\0
    \0\0\0\0\0\0\0\0\0\0\0\0\0\0\0\0\0\0\0\0\0\0\0\0\0\0\0\0\0\0\0"..., 8208) = 376
74  clock_gettime(CLOCK_MONOTONIC, {280953, 700139065}) = 0
75  times(NULL)                             = 457492550
76  gettimeofday({1378232348, 693922}, NULL) = 0
77  lseek(10, 0, SEEK_CUR)                  = 275559
78  write(10, "\n*** 2013-09-03 13:19:08.693\n", 29) = 29
79  write(11, "7?As4f9~z1T\n", 12)          = 12
80  lseek(10, 0, SEEK_CUR)                  = 275588
81  write(10, "WAIT #139778455421104: nam='SQL*Net message from client' ela= 161761044 driver
    id=1413697536 #bytes=1 p3=0 obj#=440 tim=280953700139", 132) = 132
82  write(11, "I?U2+L-r7Y1~042\n", 16)      = 16
83  write(10, "\n", 1)                      = 1
84  getrusage(0x1 /* RUSAGE_??? */, {ru_utime={0, 586910}, ru_stime={0, 182972}, ...}) = 0
85  times(NULL)                             = 457492550
86  clock_gettime(CLOCK_MONOTONIC, {280953, 702381070}) = 0
```

Chapter 4. Oracle Database Timed Event Reference

```
 87  getrusage(0x1 /* RUSAGE_??? */, {ru_utime={0, 586910}, ru_stime={0, 182972}, ...}) = 0
 88  clock_gettime(CLOCK_MONOTONIC, {280953, 702806463}) = 0
 89  getrusage(0x1 /* RUSAGE_??? */, {ru_utime={0, 586910}, ru_stime={0, 182972}, ...}) = 0
 90  lseek(10, 0, SEEK_CUR)                  = 275721
 91  write(10, "CLOSE #139778455421104:c=0,e=425,dep=0,type=0,tim=280953702806", 62) = 62
 92  write(11, "3?Db~1-\n", 8)               = 8
 93  lseek(10, 0, SEEK_CUR)                  = 275783
 94  write(10, "\n", 1)                      = 1
 95  write(11, "3?x0~01\n", 8)               = 8
 96  clock_gettime(CLOCK_MONOTONIC, {280953, 703950300}) = 0
 97  getrusage(0x1 /* RUSAGE_??? */, {ru_utime={0, 587910}, ru_stime={0, 182972}, ...}) = 0
 98  getrusage(0x1 /* RUSAGE_??? */, {ru_utime={0, 587910}, ru_stime={0, 182972}, ...}) = 0
 99  times(NULL)                             = 457492550
100  getrusage(0x1 /* RUSAGE_??? */, {ru_utime={0, 587910}, ru_stime={0, 182972}, ...}) = 0
101  times(NULL)                             = 457492550
102  clock_gettime(CLOCK_MONOTONIC, {280953, 706693775}) = 0
103  clock_gettime(CLOCK_MONOTONIC, {280953, 706779699}) = 0
104  getrusage(0x1 /* RUSAGE_??? */, {ru_utime={0, 587910}, ru_stime={0, 182972}, ...}) = 0
105  times(NULL)                             = 457492550
106  getrusage(0x1 /* RUSAGE_??? */, {ru_utime={0, 587910}, ru_stime={0, 182972}, ...}) = 0
107  getrusage(0x1 /* RUSAGE_??? */, {ru_utime={0, 588910}, ru_stime={0, 182972}, ...}) = 0
108  times(NULL)                             = 457492550
109  clock_gettime(CLOCK_MONOTONIC, {280953, 708000579}) = 0
110  clock_gettime(CLOCK_MONOTONIC, {280953, 708083037}) = 0
111  getrusage(0x1 /* RUSAGE_??? */, {ru_utime={0, 588910}, ru_stime={0, 182972}, ...}) = 0
112  clock_gettime(CLOCK_MONOTONIC, {280953, 708605024}) = 0
113  lseek(10, 0, SEEK_CUR)                  = 275784
114  write(10, "=====================", 21)  = 21
115  write(11, "3??E1~0L\n", 9)              = 9
116  write(10, "\n", 1)                      = 1
117  write(10, "PARSING IN CURSOR #139778455421104 len=71 dep=0 uid=105 oct=47 lid=105 tim=280953708605 hv=2873426773 ad='7a545768' sqlid='0kmzfbu
     pn"..., 137) = 137
118  write(10, "\n", 1)                      = 1
119  lseek(10, 0, SEEK_CUR)                  = 275944
120  write(10, "BEGIN dbms_monitor.session_trace_enable(null, null, true, true); END;", 69) = 69
121  write(11, "N?MH~B251\n", 10)            = 10
122  write(10, "\n", 1)                      = 1
123  write(10, "END OF STMT", 11)            = 11
124  write(10, "\n", 1)                      = 1
125  write(10, "PARSE #139778455421104:c=1000,e=1304,p=0,cr=0,cu=0,mis=0,r=0,dep=0,og=1,plh=0,tim=280953708083", 94) = 94
126  write(10, "\n", 1)                      = 1
127  getrusage(0x1 /* RUSAGE_??? */, {ru_utime={0, 588910}, ru_stime={0, 182972}, ...}) = 0
128  clock_gettime(CLOCK_MONOTONIC, {280953, 710823208}) = 0
129  clock_gettime(CLOCK_MONOTONIC, {280953, 710907906}) = 0
130  getrusage(0x1 /* RUSAGE_??? */, {ru_utime={0, 588910}, ru_stime={0, 182972}, ...}) = 0
131  clock_gettime(CLOCK_MONOTONIC, {280953, 711582680}) = 0
132  times(NULL)                             = 457492551
133  times(NULL)                             = 457492551
134  times(NULL)                             = 457492551
135  times(NULL)                             = 457492551
136  times(NULL)                             = 457492551
137  times(NULL)                             = 457492551
138  times(NULL)                             = 457492551
139  times(NULL)                             = 457492551
140  gettimeofday({1378232348, 706105}, NULL) = 0
141  gettimeofday({1378232348, 707183}, NULL) = 0
142  gettimeofday({1378232348, 707363}, NULL) = 0
143  gettimeofday({1378232348, 707786}, NULL) = 0
144  gettimeofday({1378232348, 707947}, NULL) = 0
145  clock_gettime(CLOCK_MONOTONIC, {280953, 715175458}) = 0
146  clock_gettime(CLOCK_MONOTONIC, {280953, 715543904}) = 0
147  getrusage(0x1 /* RUSAGE_??? */, {ru_utime={0, 590910}, ru_stime={0, 182972}, ...}) = 0
148  lseek(10, 0, SEEK_CUR)                  = 276121
149  write(10, "EXEC #139778455421104:c=2000,e=4636,p=0,cr=0,cu=0,mis=0,r=1,dep=0,og=1,plh=0,tim=280953715543", 93) = 93
150  write(11, "N?SM1~i1T1\n", 11)           = 11
151  write(10, "\n", 1)                      = 1
152  times(NULL)                             = 457492551
153  times(NULL)                             = 457492551
154  times(NULL)                             = 457492551
155  times(NULL)                             = 457492551
156  clock_gettime(CLOCK_MONOTONIC, {280953, 716860977}) = 0
157  clock_gettime(CLOCK_MONOTONIC, {280953, 717077935}) = 0
158  getrusage(0x1 /* RUSAGE_??? */, {ru_utime={0, 590910}, ru_stime={0, 182972}, ...}) = 0
159  getrusage(0x1 /* RUSAGE_??? */, {ru_utime={0, 590910}, ru_stime={0, 182972}, ...}) = 0
160  times(NULL)                             = 457492551
161  clock_gettime(CLOCK_MONOTONIC, {280953, 717491241}) = 0
162  clock_gettime(CLOCK_MONOTONIC, {280953, 717542098}) = 0
163  lseek(10, 0, SEEK_CUR)                  = 276215
164  write(10, "WAIT #139778455421104: nam='SQL*Net message to client' ela= 51 driver id=1413697536 #bytes=1 p3=0 obj#=440 tim=280953717542", 123)
     = 123
165  write(11, "J?wK~1x1\n", 9)              = 9
166  write(10, "\n", 1)                      = 1
167  clock_gettime(CLOCK_MONOTONIC, {280953, 717921697}) = 0
168  write(36, "\0\0\0\275\6\0\0\0\0\0\10\6\0\322\204N\0\0\0\0\0\7\0\0\0\0\0\0\0\0\0\0\0\0\0\0\0\0\4\1\0\0004\0\1\1\0\0\0\0\0\0\
     0\0\7\0\0/\0\0\0\0\0\0\0\0\0\0\0\0\0\0\0\0\0\0\0\0\0006\0\0\1\0\0\0006\1\0\0\0\0\0\0\0\0\0\0\0\0\340\320\237\265 \177\0\0\0\0\
     \0\0\0\0\0\0"..., 189) = 189
169  read(36,
```

We can see lots of activity, *lseek* calls and *write* calls, for example, upon file descriptor 10:

```
170  $ lsof -p15197 -ad10
171  COMMAND     PID   USER   FD   TYPE DEVICE SIZE/OFF    NODE NAME
172  oracle_15 15197 oracle  10w   REG  253,0   276339 1186168 /opt/oracle/diag/rdbms/v120100/v120100/trace/v120100_ora_15197.trc
```

...Which is the Oracle trace file. Thus, you can see the information that the Oracle kernel process writes to its trace file, as that information is written.

SOME TRICKS

Getting *strace* to show you what you want to see isn't always easy:

- Tools like *strace* show only system calls. Sometimes, the Oracle kernel code path that will dominate your response time has nothing to do with system calls. In this case, you might find the *ltrace* utility helpful.

    Example: If your program is spending the bulk of its time processing a database *fetch* call that needs to visit your database buffer cache billions of times (which don't require system calls), then *strace* is going to show you very little output.

- Tools like *strace* don't always show you *all* your system calls.

    Example: In newer versions of Red Hat Enterprise Linux, *strace* conceals the abundance of timer calls to which we'd all grown accustomed when tracing Oracle. They just don't show up! ...That is, unless you adjust a Linux kernel parameter.[1]

    Example: In Oracle 11g, Oracle uses some asynchronous read calls that are not completely instrumented either by Oracle extended SQL trace data or *strace*.[2]

ORACLE TIMED EVENT EXAMPLE

Here is a segment of strace output that shows the execution of a *db file scattered read* event.

```
173 write(19, "\n", 1)                              = 1
174 clock_gettime(CLOCK_MONOTONIC, {202800, 340027170}) = 0
175 clock_gettime(CLOCK_MONOTONIC, {202800, 340112075}) = 0
176 clock_gettime(CLOCK_MONOTONIC, {202800, 340140657}) = 0
177 pread(258, "\6\242\0\0\0\t@\0\16\204\23\0\0\0\2\4\300\233\0\0\2\0\0\0001\1\0\0\16\204\23\0\0\0\1\0\2\0\0\0\0\1\0\0\0\354\3\0\0\33\6@\1\2
    02\0\2\0\0\200\0\0\16\204\23\0\2\0\200\2\2\0\0\0\2\0 \0a\37A\37\263(A\0\0\0\0\0x\37\0\0a\37k\37T\37H\37<\0370\37$\37\30\37\r\37\3\37\370\36\3
    54\36\340\36\324\36\311\36\275\36\261\36\245\36\231\36\216\36\202\36w\36k\36_\36S\36G\36;\36/\36#\36\27\36v\36\377\35\363\35\347\35\333\35\3
    17\35\303\35\270\35\254\35\240\35\225\35\211\35~\35s\35h\35]\35R\35G\35<\0350\35$\35\31\35\r\35\1\35\366\34\353\34\340\34\324\34\310\34\274\3
    4\261\34\245\34\232\34\217\34\204\34y\34m\34b\34V\34J\34?\0343\34'\34\33\34\17\34\3\34\367\33\353\33\337\33\323\33\307\33\274\33\263\33\247\33
    \233\33\220\33\205\33z\33n\33b\33W\33K\33?\0334\33(\33\34\34\20\33\5\33\371\32\355\32\341\32\326\32\312\32\276\32\262\32\247\32\233\32\217\32\
    203\32x\32l\32a\32V\32J\32?\0324\32(\32\35\32\21\32\6\32\372\31\356\31\342\31\326\31\312\31\277\31\263\31\250\31\235\31\221\31\205\31z\31n\31
    c\31X\31M\31B\0316\31*\31\36\31\23\31\10\31\373\30\356\30\341\30\324\30\310\30\274\30\257\30\242\30\230\30\213\30~\30q\30e\30Y\30L\30?\0303\3
    08\30\31\30\f\30\0\30\364\27\350\27\333\27\316\27\301\27\264\27\247\27\232\27\216\27\201\27t\27g\27Z\27M\27@\0273\27&\27\31\27\f\27\377\26\36
    2\26\345\26\330\26\313\26\277\26\263\26\246\26\231\26\215\26\200\26s\26g\26Z\26M\26@\0263\26'\26\32\26\r\26\0\26\363\25\351\25\334\25\317\25\
    302\25\265\25\250\25\233\25\216\25\201\25t\25g\25Z[\25N\25A\0254\25'\25\32\25\r\25\1\25\366\24\352\24\335\24\320\24\304\24\267\24\252\24\235\2
    4\220\24\203\24v\24i\24]\24P\24C\0246\24)\24\34\24\17\24\2\24\365\23\350\23\333\23\316\23\301\23\264\23\247\23\232\23\215\23\201\23t\23h\23\
    \23P\23C\0236\23)\23\35\23\20\23\4\23\367\22\352\22\335\22\320\22\303\22\266\22\252\22\235\22\221\22\205\22z\22k\22^\22R\22F\22:\0220\22$\22\
    30\22\f\22\0\22\364\21\350\21\334\21\320\21\303\21\266\21\251\21\234\21\217\21\202\21u\21h\21[\21N\21D\0217\21*\21\35\21\20\21\3\21\366\20\35
    1\20\334\20\317\20\302\20\265\20\250\20\233\20\216\20\201\20t\20g\20Z\20M\20@\0203\20&\20\31\20\f\20\367\17\353\17\341\17\324\17\310\17\
    273\17\256\17\241\17\224\17\207\17z\17m\17 \17S\17F\0179\17,\17\37\17\22\17\5\17\370\16\353\16\336\16\321\16\304\16\270\16\256\16\241\16\224\
    16\212\16~\16t\16h\16\\\16P\16C\0167\16*\16\36\16\21\16\5\16\371\r\354\r\340\r\324\r\310\r\274\r\257\r\243\r\226\r\211\r\|\ro\rb\rU\rH\r>\r1\r
    $\r\27\r\n\r\375\f\360\f\343\f\326\f\311\f\274\f\257\f\242\f\225\f\210\f{\fn\fa\fT\fG\f:\f-\f \f\23\f\6\f\371\v\355\v\340\v\324\v\307\v\273\v
    \257\v\242\v\225\v\210\v|\vp\vc\vV\vJ\v=\v0\v#\v\26\v\t\v\374\n\357\n\342\n\325\n\310\n\273\n\256\n\241\n\224\n\210\n{\no\nc\nW\nJ\n=\n0\n#\n
    \31\n\f\n\377\t\362\t\345\t\330\t\313\t\276\t\261\t\244\t\227\t\213\t\177\ts\tf\tZ\tM\tA\t4\t(\t\33\t"..., 57344, 19537920) = 57344
178 clock_gettime(CLOCK_MONOTONIC, {202800, 340430846}) = 0
179 write(19, "WAIT #140590364442984: nam='db file scattered read' ela= 290 file#=1 block#=2385 blocks=7 obj#=305 tim=202800340430", 115) = 115
180 write(19, "\n", 1)                              = 1
```

In Oracle Database release 11 and prior, we saw the Oracle kernel on Linux collect its time information by using pairs of *gettimeofday* system calls. In release 12, we see times collected with pairs of *clock_gettime* calls. In this example, the Oracle kernel has executed the *db file scattered read* event with an operating system *pread* call that consumed 290 μs. The

---

[1] Morle, James, "Who stole gettimeofday() system calls from Oracle strace() sessions?" at *http://www.scaleabilities.co.uk/2012/12/18/who-stole-gettimeofday-from-oracle-straces/*.

[2] Hoogland, Frits, "Getting to know Oracle wait events in Linux" at *http://fritshoogland.wordpress.com/2012/04/26/getting-to-know-oracle-wait-events-in-linux/*.

Chapter 4. Oracle Database Timed Event Reference

clock_gettime calls that immediately precede and follow the *pread* call provide the values used to compute the duration of the call:

$$\begin{array}{r}202{,}800.340\ 430\ 846\\ -\ 202{,}800.340\ 140\ 657\\ \hline 0.000\ 290\ 189\end{array}$$

The *pread* call is an operating system call that works as follows:

```
181  $ man 2 pread
182  PREAD(2)                    Linux Programmer's Manual                    PREAD(2)
183
184  NAME
185         pread, pwrite - read from or write to a file descriptor at a given offset
186
187  SYNOPSIS
188         #define _XOPEN_SOURCE 500
189
190         #include <unistd.h>
191
192         ssize_t pread(int fd, void *buf, size_t count, off_t offset);
193
194         ssize_t pwrite(int fd, const void *buf, size_t count, off_t offset);
195
196  DESCRIPTION
197         pread() reads up to count bytes from file descriptor fd at offset offset (from the start of the
198         file) into the buffer starting at buf.  The file offset is not changed.
199
200         pwrite() writes up to count bytes from the buffer starting at buf to the file descriptor fd at
201         offset offset.  The file offset is not changed.
202
203         The file referenced by fd must be capable of seeking.
204
205  RETURN VALUE
206         On  success,  the number of bytes read or written is returned (zero indicates that nothing was
207         written, in the case of pwrite(), or end of file, in the case of pread(), or -1 on error, in
208         which case errno is set to indicate the error.
```

In our case, the Oracle kernel has read 7 Oracle blocks (count = 7 × 8,192 = 57,344 bytes) from file descriptor 258. You can find the name of the file associated with this file descriptor by using the *lsof* command; for me, it was */opt/oracle/oradata/v120100/system01.dbf*. The read began at Oracle internal file id 1 (no surprise, given the file name), block number 2385.

SQL*Net message from client

When an Oracle kernel process awaits a client application's instruction, it is spending time that will be logged (upon completion of the wait) to the event called *SQL*Net message from client*. In "Tracing Oracle Kernel System Calls" on page 70, when the Oracle kernel blocked on a *read* call awaiting its next instruction from *sqlplus*, Oracle logged that read to its trace data as a *SQL*Net message from client* call.

Traditional Oracle authors and teachers tell us that the *SQL*Net message from client* event conveys no meaningful information to the performance diagnostician. To the contrary, this timed event is very valuable in quantifying the performance penalties incurred by applications that execute too many database calls. For example, applications that execute Oracle parse calls inside of loops consume significant extra end-user response time just transmitting the calls from the application client process to the Oracle server process. The *SQL*Net message from client* timed event shows you how much time you spend doing that.

Here is *strace* output showing a *SQL*Net message from client* call:

```
209  write(5, "\n", 1)                       = 1
210  times(NULL)                             = 53663644
211  gettimeofday({1105481879, 577241}, NULL) = 0
212  gettimeofday({1105481879, 577302}, NULL) = 0
213  getrusage(RUSAGE_SELF, {ru_utime={1, 410000}, ru_stime={5, 30000}, ...}) = 0
214  getrusage(RUSAGE_SELF, {ru_utime={1, 410000}, ru_stime={5, 30000}, ...}) = 0
215  times(NULL)                             = 53663644
216  gettimeofday({1105481879, 577549}, NULL) = 0
217  gettimeofday({1105481879, 577598}, NULL) = 0
218  times(NULL)                             = 53663644
219  write(5, "WAIT #9: nam=\'SQL*Net message to client\' ela= 48 p1=1650815232 p2=1 p3=0", 72) = 72
220  write(5, "\n", 1)                       = 1
221  times(NULL)                             = 53663644
222  gettimeofday({1105481879, 577887}, NULL) = 0
223  write(10, "\0\204\0\0\6\0\0\0\0\4\1\0\0\0\34\0\1\1\0\0\0{\5\0\0\0\t\0\0\0\3\0\0\0\0\0\0\0\0\0\0\0\0\0\0\0\0\0\0\0\36\0\0\1\
```

```
    0\0\0006\1\0\0\0\0\0\300\257\375\v\0\0\0\0\0\0\0\0\0\0"..., 132) = 132
224 read(7, "\0\300\0\0\6\0\0\0\0\0\21i\37@3\364\10\1\0\0\0\t\0\0\0\3^ !\200\0\0\0\0\0\214W\364\10\37\0\0\0\354t\362\10\r\0\0\0\0\0\0 u\362\1
    0\0\0\0\0\1\0\0\0\0\0\0\0\0\0\0\0\0\0\0\0\0\0\0\0\0\0\0\0"..., 2064) = 192
225 gettimeofday({1105483109, 742217}, NULL) = 0
226 times(NULL)                              = 53786660
227 times(NULL)                              = 53786660
228 gettimeofday({1105483109, 742370}, NULL) = 0
229 times(NULL)                              = 53786660
230 write(5, "*** 2005-01-11 16:38:29.742", 27) = 27
231 write(5, "\n", 1)                        = 1
232 times(NULL)                              = 53786660
233 write(5, "WAIT #9: nam=\'SQL*Net message from client\' ela= 1201332353 p1=1650815232 p2=1 p3=0", 82) = 82
234 write(5, "\n", 1)                        = 1
```

In this example, the read call consumed a tremendous amount of time (1,201.332353 seconds). In this case, though, this is not an indication of an application performance problem; it's an indication of an inattentive user (me) who remained connected to Oracle but inactive (from the Oracle kernel process's perspective) for about 20 minutes. This kind of trace file time scoping mistake is what causes people to believe that they should ignore all *SQL*Net message from client* events. However, if your trace file is properly time scoped, the event becomes an important and meaningful measurement in your overall response time profile.

In all versions of Oracle through 12, there is a bug in how *SQL*Net message from client* and *SQL*Net message to client* calls are reported. Unfortunately, the Oracle kernel reports a duration in excess of the actual duration of the read call that the *SQL*Net message from client* event is meant to cover. You can see on that the p2=1 value for the *SQL*Net message from client* event is also incorrect; the value should be 192 (the number of bytes read by—and the return value of—the *read* call on line 16). See the next section for details.

THE BUG WITH SQL*NET MESSAGE TO CLIENT

The Oracle *SQL*Net message to client* event is supposed to cover the duration required to transmit data from the Oracle kernel process to the application client process. Unfortunately, Oracle doesn't work this way. Here is *strace* output showing a *SQL*Net message to client* call:

```
235 write(10, "\n", 1)                       = 1
236 times(NULL)                              = 457476376
237 times(NULL)                              = 457476376
238 times(NULL)                              = 457476376
239 times(NULL)                              = 457476376
240 clock_gettime(CLOCK_MONOTONIC, {280791, 938477175}) = 0
241 mmap(0x7f20b50ff000, 262144, PROT_NONE, MAP_PRIVATE|MAP_FIXED|MAP_NORESERVE, 6, 0x270000) = 0x7f20b50ff000
242 clock_gettime(CLOCK_MONOTONIC, {280791, 938830480}) = 0
243 getrusage(0x1 /* RUSAGE_??? */, {ru_utime={0, 585910}, ru_stime={0, 182972}, ...}) = 0
244 getrusage(0x1 /* RUSAGE_??? */, {ru_utime={0, 585910}, ru_stime={0, 182972}, ...}) = 0
245 times(NULL)                              = 457476376
246 clock_gettime(CLOCK_MONOTONIC, {280791, 938948713}) = 0
247 clock_gettime(CLOCK_MONOTONIC, {280791, 938982608}) = 0
248 write(10, "WAIT #139778455421104: nam='SQL*Net message to client' ela= 34 driver
    id=1413697536 #bytes=1 p3=0 obj#=440 tim=280791938982", 123) = 123
249 write(10, "\n", 1)                       = 1
250 clock_gettime(CLOCK_MONOTONIC, {280791, 939095347}) = 0
251 write(36, "\0\0\0\275\6\0\0\0\0\0\10\6\0\211\204N\0\0\0\0\10\0\0\0\0\0\0\0\0\0\0\0\0\0\0\0\0\0\0\0\0\0\4\1\0\0\0002\0\1\1\0\0\0\0\0\0
    \0\0\10\0\0\0\0\0\0\0\0\0\0\0\0\0\0\0\0\0\4\0\0\1\0\0\0006\1\0\0\0\0\0\0\0\0\0\0\0\340\320\237\265 \177\0\0
    \0\0\0\0\0\0"..., 189) = 189
252 read(36, "\0\0\1x\6\0\0\0\0\0\0\0\21i5\376\377\377\377\377\377\377\377\1\0\0\0\0\0\10\0\0\0\3^6!\0\4\0\0\0\0\376\377\377\377\377\377\377
    G\0\0\0\0\0\0\376\377\377\377\377\377\377\r\0\0\0\0\0\376\377\377\377\377\377\377\376\377\377\377\377\377\0\0\0\0\1\0\0\1
    0\0\0\0\0\0\0\0\0\0\0\0\0\0\0\0\0\0\0\0\0\0\0\0\0\0\0"..., 8208) = 376
253 clock_gettime(CLOCK_MONOTONIC, {280953, 700139065}) = 0
254 times(NULL)                              = 457492550
255 gettimeofday({1378232348, 693922}, NULL) = 0
256 lseek(10, 0, SEEK_CUR)                   = 275559
257 write(10, "\n*** 2013-09-03 13:19:08.693\n", 29) = 29
258 write(11, "7?As4f9~z1T\n", 12)            = 12
259 lseek(10, 0, SEEK_CUR)                   = 275588
260 write(10, "WAIT #139778455421104: nam='SQL*Net message from client' ela= 161761044 driver
    id=1413697536 #bytes=1 p3=0 obj#=440 tim=280953700139", 132) = 132
261 write(11, "I?U2+L-r7Y1~042\n", 16)        = 16
262 write(10, "\n", 1)                       = 1
```

We'll need this, too:

```
263 $ lsof -p15197 -ad36
264 COMMAND      PID    USER    FD   TYPE DEVICE SIZE/OFF NODE NAME
265 oracle_15  15197  oracle   36u   IPv6 402529      0t0  TCP oel02.dev.method-r.com:ncube-lm->oel02.dev.method-r.com:41083 (ESTABLISHED)
```

Chapter 4. Oracle Database Timed Event Reference

The call trace proves concisely that there's a bug in how the Oracle kernel reports both *SQL*Net message to client* and *SQL*Net message from client* durations. Notice the call trace shows the following sequence of Oracle kernel actions:

1. Write to the trace file a *SQL*Net message to client* event with duration 34 μs.

2. Execute a *write* call upon file descriptor 36 (the connection to the client) of 189 bytes.

3. Execute the *read* call, also upon file descriptor 36 (the connection to the client) of 376 bytes.

4. Write to the trace file a *SQL*Net message from client* event with duration 161,761,044 μs.

Do you see the problem? The *SQL*Net message to client* was supposed to have reported on the performance of the *write* call, but the *write* had not yet occurred when Oracle wrote the *SQL*Net message to client* event to the trace file. How can a kernel process report on how long a *write* call took at a time when the *write* hasn't yet occurred? This explains two persistent problems with *SQL*Net message to client* data that you may have experienced:

- *SQL*Net message to client* durations are always very small, even when the server process has to communicate massive amounts of data back to the client. Oracle reports only a few microseconds for this event—in this case, 34 μs.

- *SQL*Net message to client* byte counts parameter are almost always wrong. Oracle's documentation states that the *#bytes* value is supposed to be the number of bytes communicated back to the client. In my experience, the Oracle *#bytes* value for this event is invariably 1. In the case shown here, the actual byte count is 189 (the return value of the *write* call).

The *write* call duration is tallied into the *SQL*Net message from client* event duration, which already contains more types of time consumption than we'd like, even if everything worked perfectly: network latency, application code path execution time, and end-user think time. However, it's only a minor inconvenience to the performance analyst.

When you repair an application that makes too many database calls, you'll typically eliminate *...from client* and *...to client* events in pairs. In cases like this, the pair can be considered as an atomic unit, so the fact that the time accounting between the two events is messed up doesn't matter too much.

5 Cases in Oracle Trace Data Analysis

This chapter presents a sequence of case studies representing interesting performance problems from across a wide range of applications and Oracle Database versions. The goal of this chapter is to stimulate your interest and imagination by showing innovative performance improvements available to users of the Method R Tools software package with Oracle extended SQL trace data.

The commands described in this chapter are illustrated using the Bash Unix shell. If you use a different shell, you may need to use different quotation marks than the ones shown here. See the "OS Dependencies" section of the *mrskew* manual page for details.[1]

IMPORTANCE OF CAREFUL TIME SCOPING

The first goal of the person who collects the Oracle trace file for a given problem is to collect lines of trace data that explain exactly where the *time that the end-user cares about* has gone: no more, and no less. It's not always easy to do that. Consider the typical example of a query that you want to run in *sqlplus*. This case takes you through what happens when you don't time-scope your trace data collection carefully enough.

> Task name: *sqlplus @myscript*
> Response time: ~2.5 seconds
> Trace file size: 3.7 MB
> Trace file line count: 35,085
> Typical *mrskew* execution duration: 2 seconds

When people trace a SQL or PL/SQL block in *sqlplus*, they commonly do it this way:

```
1  SQL> ...execute a command to activate SQL tracing
2  SQL> @myscript
3  ...output from myscript goes here
4  SQL> ...execute a command to deactivate SQL tracing
```

The result is a trace file, but the begin time and end time of the trace do not coincide with the begin time and end time of the script. The trace file will contain duration occurring before the beginning of the script, and additional duration occurring after the end of the script. How *much* duration will depend on a number of factors including—bizarrely—how quickly the person typed the "disable" command, and whether he went for a coffee break between activating and deactivating the trace.

The trace file for a ~2.5-second experience (the duration that *myscript* consumed) thus looks like this:

```
5  $ mrls ora_10358_SNMFC.trc
6      R   ORA                    START                          END FILE
7  31.931  11.2  2011-08-18T14:36:21.577-0500  2011-08-18T14:36:53.507-0500  ora_10358_SNMFC.trc
```

The trace file accounts for 31.931 s.

---

[1] Method R Corporation, "*mrskew* Documentation" at *http://method-r.com/component/content/article/126*.

Chapter 5. Cases in Oracle Trace Data Analysis

The Method R Profiler output for the file looks like this:

	Subroutine	Duration seconds	% R	Cumulative duration seconds	% R	Call count	Duration per call (seconds) mean	min	skew	max	Drill-down
1	SQL*Net message from client [think time]	28.946	90.7%	28.946	90.7%	2	14.472881	8.824256		20.121507	SQL
2	SQL*Net message from client	2.073	6.5%	31.019	97.1%	10,001	0.000207	0.000023		0.016861	SQL
3	unaccounted-for between dbcalls	0.404	1.3%	31.422	98.4%	10,013	0.000040	-0.000045		0.200446	
4	CPU service, unreported call(s)	0.285	0.9%	31.707	99.3%	1	0.284542	0.284542		0.284542	
5	direct path read	0.111	0.3%	31.817	99.6%	10,000	0.000011	0.000004		0.020533	
6	CPU service, FETCH calls	0.083	0.3%	31.900	99.9%	5,002	0.000017	0.000000		0.001000	
7	unaccounted-for within dbcalls	0.017	0.1%	31.918	100.0%	5,011	0.000003	-0.000983		0.000402	
8	SQL*Net message to client	0.009	0.0%	31.927	100.0%	10,003	0.000001	0.000000		0.000061	
9	CPU service, PARSE calls	0.002	0.0%	31.929	100.0%	3	0.000667	0.000000		0.002000	
10	CPU service, EXEC calls	0.002	0.0%	31.931	100.0%	3	0.000667	0.000000		0.001000	
11	CPU service, CLOSE calls	0.000	0.0%	31.931	100.0%	3	0.000000	0.000000		0.000000	
12	Total (11)	31.931	100.0%								

Note that the Profiler reports exactly the same 31.931-second response time as *mrls* reported. The *mrskew* output for the file looks like this:

```
 8  $ mrskew ora_10358_SNMFC.trc
 9  CALL-NAME                   DURATION       %   CALLS        MEAN       MIN        MAX
10  -------------------------  ---------  ------  ------  ----------  --------  ---------
11  SQL*Net message from client 31.018640  99.3%  10,003    0.003101  0.000023  20.121507
12  direct path read             0.110575   0.4%  10,000    0.000011  0.000004   0.020533
13  FETCH                        0.081993   0.3%   5,001    0.000016  0.000000   0.001000
14  SQL*Net message to client    0.008804   0.0%  10,003    0.000001  0.000000   0.000061
15  PARSE                        0.003999   0.0%       2    0.001999  0.000000   0.003999
16  EXEC                         0.001000   0.0%       2    0.000500  0.000000   0.001000
17  CLOSE                        0.000000   0.0%       2    0.000000  0.000000   0.000000
18  -------------------------  ---------  ------  ------  ----------  --------  ---------
19  TOTAL (7)                   31.225011 100.0%  35,013    0.000892  0.000000  20.121507
```

Note that *mrskew* reports a duration total that's slightly different from the response time reported by mrls or the Profiler. That's because both *mrls* and the Profiler report the file's response time, but *mrskew* reports the sum of the file's call durations (see R and $\sum$ terms, respectively, in equation 3 on page 62). The difference, $\Delta_{between}$, is the sum of three durations in the Profile report:

> *unaccounted-for between dbcalls*
> *CPU service, unreported call(s)*
> *unaccounted-for within dbcalls*

The *mrskew* tool does not report these quantities. To notice them without the Profiler requires you to notice the difference between the response time reported by *mrls* and the call duration total reported by *mrskew*.

In both reports, the reported response time is dominated by *SQL*Net message from client* calls. The problem, though, is that the reported duration isn't the duration we're interested in. We're interested in a ~2.5-second experience. This trace file reports a 31.931-second-experience. The surplus of time in the trace file is caused by sloppy collection of the trace data. The trace file includes all the following durations:

A. The duration a person waited after entering a *session_trace_enable* command and before pressing Enter for the *@myscript* command;

B. The duration that the *myscript* execution consumed;

C. The duration that the person waited to begin typing the *session_trace_disable* command;

D. The duration that the person spent typing the *session_trace_disable* command, pressing Enter, and waiting for the Oracle kernel to execute the command.

The following picture illustrates the problem.

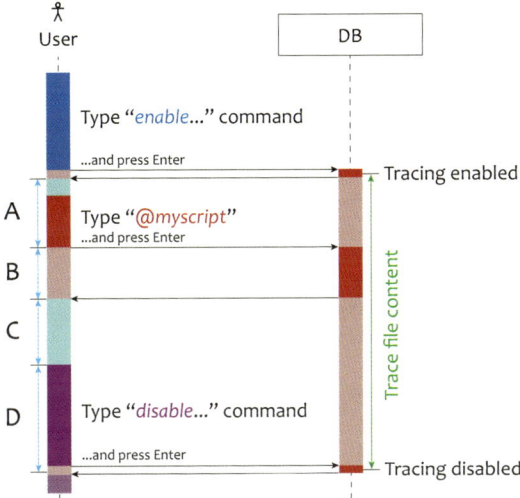

We want for the trace file content (green) to account for only step B, but it covers steps A through D, from when tracing is enabled to when tracing is disabled, including all the time in between waiting for the user to type.

All these steps combined consumed 31.225 s. If you take the profile literally (which you should always be able to), it screams out that the best way to reduce the response time of this process is to stop wasting so much time in steps A, C, and D. However, the process A–D is not what you need to optimize. You want to reduce the response time of step B. So therefore, you need to isolate the trace data that accounts for the time consumed executing step B.

If you're a classically trained Oracle DBA, you know the answer: "You're supposed to ignore all the *SQL*Net message from client* duration." Let's try that:

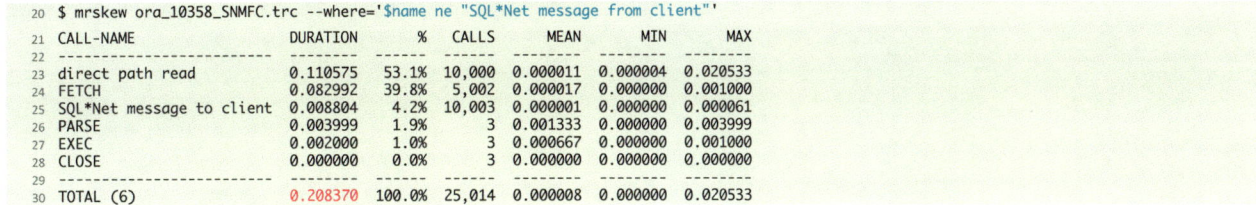

But that won't work, because the response time of the *myscript* execution wasn't 0.208 s, either.

The *First Rule of Using Trace Data*: The duration your trace file explains must match the duration of the end-user experience you want to diagnose.

Of course, fixing the time scoping problem for a trace file executed from within *sqlplus* is simple: just move the commands to enable and disable the trace into *myscript.sql* itself. That way, the trace file will contain exactly the experience you're trying to analyze; no more, no less. It's a trickier situation when the poorly scoped trace files are the result of a user using application menu items to enable and disable traces (for example, in the form of **Help → Debug → Trace Enable** and **Help → Debug → Trace Disable**). Then, unless you

Chapter 5. Cases in Oracle Trace Data Analysis

can change how the application works, your only option will be to manipulate the poorly scoped trace file after it has been created.

The first thing you need to know when you meet a new trace file is how the trace file was created, but sometimes there's nobody around who can tell you that. In those cases, when someone just hands you a trace file and asks you to diagnose it, you have to figure out how the file was created by looking at the file itself.

The Profiler output gave you a big clue, with its two big *SQL*Net message from client [think time]* calls. By default, the Profiler adds this "[think time]" suffix to any *SQL*Net message from client* call whose duration is greater than or equal to 1.0 seconds. The two such calls with durations 8.824256 and 20.121507 (see the min and max columns) account for where the durations in the picture labeled A and C–D went. The trick now is to find where those calls are in the trace file. Here is the *mrskew* query that lets us find out:

```
31  $ mrskew ora_10358_SNMFC.trc --name='SQL\*Net message from client' --group='$line' --gl=LINE#
32         LINE#    DURATION       %   CALLS      MEAN       MIN       MAX
33  ------------  ----------  ------  ------  --------  --------  --------
34            26   20.121507   64.9%       1  20.121507 20.121507 20.121507
35         35078    8.824256   28.4%       1   8.824256  8.824256  8.824256
36         26560    0.016861    0.1%       1   0.016861  0.016861  0.016861
37         29276    0.016698    0.1%       1   0.016698  0.016698  0.016698
38          7544    0.016511    0.1%       1   0.016511  0.016511  0.016511
39         34029    0.016343    0.1%       1   0.016343  0.016343  0.016343
40         32671    0.016149    0.1%       1   0.016149  0.016149  0.016149
41         13657    0.016055    0.1%       1   0.016055  0.016055  0.016055
42         12978    0.015923    0.1%       1   0.015923  0.015923  0.015923
43         10260    0.015778    0.1%       1   0.015778  0.015778  0.015778
44   9,993 others    1.942559    6.3%   9,993   0.000194  0.000023  0.015340
45  ------------  ----------  ------  ------  --------  --------  --------
46  TOTAL (10,003)  31.018640  100.0%  10,003   0.003101  0.000023 20.121507
```

Note that in the *mrskew --where* option earlier, I referred to the string `"SQL*Net message from client"`, whereas here in the *--name* option, I used a backslash character in the string `'SQL\*Net message from client'`. The difference is that the *--name* option expects a regular expression as its argument. The '*' character is a regular expression operator, so we have to escape it (remove its magic) by preceding it with '\'. Without the '\', the pattern `'SQL*Net message from client'` would match the string "SQ", followed by zero or more occurrences of the letter 'L', followed by the string "Net message from client", which would in fact *not* match the call name that we want.

Two comparatively gigantic *SQL*Net message from client* calls are responsible for 93.3% (64.9% + 28.4%) of the total time spent executing *SQL*Net message from client* calls. One call was near the beginning of the file, on line 26, and the other was much deeper into the file, on line 35,078. Let's see how deep that is:

```
47  $ wc -l ora_10358_SNMFC.trc
48     35085 ora_10358_SNMFC.trc
```

The whole file has only 35,085 lines in it, so line 35,078 is very near the end. Let's look at the first 26 lines of the file, and then lines 35,078 through the end. Here are the first 26:

```
49  $ head -26 ora_10358_SNMFC.trc
50  # version=mrtrace2.0.0.16|cpu_count=1|project=|author=carymillsap|platform_name=Linux IA (32-bit)|date_added
    =1313696690154|description=|instance_name=sumneva|node_name=local-orcl|oracle_release=11.2.0.1.0
51  Oracle Database 11g Enterprise Edition Release 11.2.0.1.0 - Production
52  With the Partitioning, OLAP, Data Mining and Real Application Testing options
53  ORACLE_HOME = /app/oracle/product/11.2.0/db_1
54  System name:    Linux
55  Node name:      local-orcl
56  Release:        2.6.18-194.el5
57  Version:        #1 SMP Mon Mar 29 20:06:41 EDT 2010
58  Machine:        i686
59  Instance name: sumneva
60  Redo thread mounted by this instance: 1
61  Oracle process number: 25
62  Unix process pid: 10358, image: oracle@local-orcl (TNS V1-V3)
63
64
65  *** 2011-08-18 14:36:21.576
66  *** SESSION ID:(23.42) 2011-08-18 14:36:21.576
67  *** CLIENT ID:() 2011-08-18 14:36:21.576
68  *** SERVICE NAME:(SYS$USERS) 2011-08-18 14:36:21.576
69  *** MODULE NAME:(SQL*Plus) 2011-08-18 14:36:21.576
70  *** ACTION NAME:() 2011-08-18 14:36:21.576
71
72  WAIT #8: nam='SQL*Net message to client' ela= 1 driver id=1650815232 #bytes=1 p3=0 obj#=-1 tim=1313696181576631
```

Importance of Careful Time Scoping

```
73
74 *** 2011-08-18 14:36:41.698
75 WAIT #8: nam='SQL*Net message from client' ela= 20121507 driver id=1650815232 #bytes=1 p3=0 obj#=-1 tim=1313696201698518
```

...And here are the lines 35,078 through the end of the file:

```
76 $ tail +35078 ora_10358_SNMFC.trc
77 WAIT #5: nam='SQL*Net message from client' ela= 8824256 driver id=1650815232 #bytes=1 p3=0 obj#=86815 tim=1313696213506522
78 CLOSE #5:c=0,e=22,dep=0,type=0,tim=1313696213506643
79 =====================
80 PARSING IN CURSOR #2 len=55 dep=0 uid=84 oct=42 lid=84 tim=1313696213506753 hv=2217940283 ad='0' sqlid='06nvwn223659v'
81 alter session set events '10046 trace name context off'
82 END OF STMT
83 PARSE #2:c=0,e=70,p=0,cr=0,cu=0,mis=0,r=0,dep=0,og=0,plh=0,tim=1313696213506752
84 EXEC #2:c=1000,e=354,p=0,cr=0,cu=0,mis=0,r=0,dep=0,og=0,plh=0,tim=1313696213507146
```

From these two segments of trace data, you can fill in the story of how this trace file was created. First, the user activated tracing. It was 20.121507 seconds before he actually ran the query he was trying to measure. When the query finished, another 8.824256 s elapsed before he deactivated the trace with an *alter session* command. These two *SQL*Net message from client* calls were not part of the end-user's response time at all.

There are two ways to leave them out. With *mrskew*, we could *where*-clause our way around them, using *$line* as a key:

```
85 $ mrskew ora_10358_SNMFC.trc --where='$line != 26 and $line != 35078'
86 CALL-NAME                DURATION       %    CALLS      MEAN       MIN       MAX
87 ----------------------   --------   -----   ------   -------   -------   -------
88 SQL*Net message from client  2.072877  90.9%  10,001  0.000207  0.000023  0.016861
89 direct path read         0.110575    4.9%  10,000  0.000011  0.000004  0.020533
90 FETCH                    0.081993    3.6%   5,001  0.000016  0.000000  0.001000
91 SQL*Net message to client  0.008804   0.4%  10,003  0.000001  0.000000  0.000061
92 PARSE                    0.003999    0.2%       2  0.001999  0.000000  0.003999
93 EXEC                     0.001000    0.0%       2  0.000500  0.000000  0.001000
94 CLOSE                    0.000000    0.0%       2  0.000000  0.000000  0.000000
95 ----------------------   --------   -----   ------   -------   -------   -------
96 TOTAL (7)                2.279248  100.0%  35,011  0.000065  0.000000  0.020533
```

Ah, that's much better. The 2.279-second response time reported here matches the ~2.5-second user experience. That method will work, but it's going to get tedious having to type in that huge *where* expression every time we pass *mrskew* through this file. You could put the *where* expression in a .rc file in the directory where this trace file is, but that's dangerous, because *mrskew* processes .rc file contents silently, and we don't want to silently ignore lines 26 and 35,078 in other trace files.

A better way to solve the problem is with *mrcallrm*:

```
97 $ mrcallrm ora_10358_SNMFC.trc --lines=26,35078 >ora_10358_SNMFC-repaired.trc
```

Now let's look at the repaired file. Here's the top:

```
 98 $ head -26 ora_10358_SNMFC-repaired.trc
 99 # version=mrtrace2.0.0.16|cpu_count=1|project=|author=carymillsap|platform_name=Linux IA (32-bit)|date_added
    =1313696690154|description=|instance_name=sumneva|node_name=local-orcl|oracle_release=11.2.0.1.0
100 Oracle Database 11g Enterprise Edition Release 11.2.0.1.0 - Production
101 With the Partitioning, OLAP, Data Mining and Real Application Testing options
102 ORACLE_HOME = /app/oracle/product/11.2.0/db_1
103 System name:    Linux
104 Node name:      local-orcl
105 Release:        2.6.18-194.el5
106 Version:        #1 SMP Mon Mar 29 20:06:41 EDT 2010
107 Machine:        i686
108 Instance name: sumneva
109 Redo thread mounted by this instance: 1
110 Oracle process number: 25
111 Unix process pid: 10358, image: oracle@local-orcl (TNS V1-V3)
112
113
114 *** 2011-08-18T14:36:21.576000-0500
115 *** SESSION ID:(23.42) 2011-08-18T14:36:21.576000-0500
116 *** CLIENT ID:() 2011-08-18T14:36:21.576000-0500
117 *** SERVICE NAME:(SYS$USERS) 2011-08-18T14:36:21.576000-0500
118 *** MODULE NAME:(SQL*Plus) 2011-08-18T14:36:21.576000-0500
119 *** ACTION NAME:() 2011-08-18T14:36:21.576000-0500
120
121 WAIT #8: nam='SQL*Net message to client' ela= 1 driver id=1650815232 #bytes=1 p3=0 obj#=-1 tim=1313696181576631
122
123 *** 2011-08-18T14:36:41.698000-0500
124 WAIT #8: nam='SQL*Net message from client' ela= 0 driver id=1650815232 #bytes=1 p3=0 obj#=-1 tim=1313696181577011
```

Notice that the *SQL*Net message from client* call is still there, but instead of the 20,121,507-ms duration it had before, now it has a 0 ms duration. The call has been wiped out. If you look closely, you might also notice that the *tim* value is now

Chapter 5. Cases in Oracle Trace Data Analysis

1313696181577011, where before it was 1313696201698518. This change is vital to any tool that pays attention to the clock values within a trace file, like *mrls* or the Method R Profiler.

Here is the bottom of the repaired file:

```
125  $ tail +35078 ora_10358_SNMFC-repaired.trc
126  WAIT #5: nam='SQL*Net message from client' ela= 0 driver id=1650815232 #bytes=1 p3=0 obj#=86815 tim=1313696184560759
127  CLOSE #5:c=0,e=22,dep=0,type=0,tim=1313696184560880
128  =====================
129  PARSING IN CURSOR #2 len=55 dep=0 uid=84 oct=42 lid=84 tim=1313696184560990 hv=2217940283 ad='0' sqlid='06nvwn223659v'
130  alter session set events '10046 trace name context off'
131  END OF STMT
132  PARSE #2:c=0,e=70,p=0,cr=0,cu=0,mis=0,r=0,dep=0,og=0,plh=0,tim=1313696184560989
133  EXEC #2:c=1000,e=354,p=0,cr=0,cu=0,mis=0,r=0,dep=0,og=0,plh=0,tim=1313696184561383
```

Again, the *SQL*Net message from client* call duration has been replaced with 0, and the duration changes have propagated throughout all of the *tim* values in the file.

Now, we can use *mrskew* on the repaired file and continue our analysis:

```
134  $ mrskew ora_10358_SNMFC-repaired.trc
135  CALL-NAME                 DURATION       %   CALLS      MEAN       MIN       MAX
136  ------------------------  --------  ------  ------  --------  --------  --------
137  SQL*Net message from client  2.072877  90.9%  10,003  0.000207  0.000000  0.016861
138  direct path read          0.110575    4.9%  10,000  0.000011  0.000004  0.020533
139  FETCH                     0.081993    3.6%   5,001  0.000016  0.000000  0.001000
140  SQL*Net message to client 0.008804    0.4%  10,003  0.000001  0.000000  0.000061
141  PARSE                     0.003999    0.2%       2  0.001999  0.000000  0.003999
142  EXEC                      0.001000    0.0%       2  0.000500  0.000000  0.001000
143  CLOSE                     0.000000    0.0%       2  0.000000  0.000000  0.000000
144  ------------------------  --------  ------  ------  --------  --------  --------
145  TOTAL (7)                 2.279248  100.0%  35,013  0.000065  0.000000  0.020533
```

This profile is the same as the one with the complicated *where* expression, except that the *SQL*Net message from client* call count includes the calls whose durations were zeroed out by *mrcallrm*. Much easier. Furthermore, with the trace file fixed, we can run the Method R Profiler on the file and see total response time, including the various unaccounted-for durations:

Subroutine	Duration seconds	Duration % R	Cumulative duration seconds	Cumulative duration % R	Call count	Duration per call (seconds) mean	Duration per call (seconds) min	Duration per call (seconds) skew	Duration per call (seconds) max	Drill-down
1. SQL*Net message from client	2.073	69.4%	2.073	69.4%	10,003	0.000207	0.000000		0.016861	SQL
2. unaccounted-for between dbcalls	0.404	13.5%	2.477	83.0%	10,013	0.000040	-0.000045		0.200446	SQL
3. CPU service, unreported call(s)	0.285	9.5%	2.761	92.5%	1	0.284542	0.284542		0.284542	SQL
4. direct path read	0.111	3.7%	2.872	96.2%	10,000	0.000011	0.000004		0.020533	
5. CPU service, FETCH calls	0.083	2.8%	2.955	99.0%	5,002	0.000017	0.000000		0.001000	
6. unaccounted-for within dbcalls	0.017	0.6%	2.972	99.6%	5,011	0.000003	-0.000983		0.000402	
7. SQL*Net message to client	0.009	0.3%	2.981	99.9%	10,003	0.000001	0.000000		0.000061	
8. CPU service, PARSE calls	0.002	0.1%	2.983	99.9%	3	0.000667	0.000000		0.002000	
9. CPU service, EXEC calls	0.002	0.1%	2.985	100.0%	3	0.000667	0.000000		0.001000	
10. CPU service, CLOSE calls	0.000	0.0%	2.985	100.0%	3	0.000000	0.000000		0.000000	
11. Total (10)	2.985	100.0%								

So, what's consuming the 2.985 seconds? It's still dominantly *SQL*Net message from client* duration. Had we discarded all the *SQL*Net message from client* duration from our original trace file (like most performance tools for Oracle do), we would have discarded data we'd need to diagnose our problem, too.

> You can't ignore *SQL*Net message from client* calls—or any calls, for that matter—if they contribute to your response time.

How efficient is this program at the work that it does? Let's find out first by determining how many rows this program manipulated:

```
146  $ mrskew ora_10358_SNMFC-repaired.trc --select='$row' --sl=ROWS --pre=0 --name=dbcall
147  CALL-NAME     ROWS       %  CALLS  MEAN  MIN  MAX
148  ---------    -----  ------  -----  ----  ---  ---
149  FETCH        5,000  100.0%  5,001     1    0    1
150  PARSE            0    0.0%      2     0    0    0
151  CLOSE            0    0.0%      2     0    0    0
152  EXEC             0    0.0%      2     0    0    0
153  ---------    -----  ------  -----  ----  ---  ---
154  TOTAL (4)    5,000  100.0%  5,007     1    0    1
```

The program returns 5,000 rows in 5,001 fetch calls. Already, I can see a problem here: the program should be returning more than one row per network round-trip. This is why the *SQL*Net message from client* calls are dominating the program's response time. For more analysis on how to fix such a problem, see "Java-Based Report" on page 84.

Conclusion

The most common problem that our customers have with analyzing Oracle trace files is dealing with improperly time scoped trace data. The first question you must ask before you analyze any trace file is, "Does this file account for the response time of the business task I'm trying to diagnose?" If the answer is no, as it was in this case, then it adds to the analysis work you have to do.

The case in this section illustrated a common problem: the person who traced the task activated the trace too early and then deactivated it too late. Trace activation and deactivation should tightly bracket the business task so that the duration explained by the trace data is exactly the duration that the user has experienced.

Many people have learned in official Oracle training that to fix time-scoping problems, they should simply ignore the durations of "idle events" like *SQL*Net message from client* calls. However, in many cases, like the one here, such calls are important contributors to response time, and ignoring them prevents you from detecting performance improvement opportunities in your programs.

Tools like *mrskew* and *mrcallrm* help you find and fix trace file time-scope problems. However, time-scope problems go away entirely if you instrument carefully as you develop an application. Instrumentation should fit snugly around the code path that implements a business task. The Instrumentation Library for Oracle (ILO) project maintained by Method R Corporation at SourceForge is a PL/SQL package that makes good Oracle instrumentation easy.[2] For scripts that you run in Oracle *sqlplus*, activate your trace in your script immediately before the block of code you mean to analyze, and deactivate your trace immediately afterward. For scripts that you run in Oracle SQL Developer, use Method R Trace, which time-scopes and retrieves your trace files automatically for you.

Exercises

1. Describe some reasons that would cause trace files at your business to have time-scope errors.

2. Why does *mrcallrm* need to manipulate *tim* values when it zeroes out a call's elapsed duration?

---

[2] Method R Corporation, "ILO: Instrumentation Library for Oracle," at *http://method-r.com/software/ilo*.

Chapter 5. Cases in Oracle Trace Data Analysis

JAVA-BASED REPORT

This business task is one that my team at Method R Corporation wrote to simulate a problem that we commonly see in our field experience. It is a report, written in Java, that returns several thousand rows to its user. It is the first case that I described in chapter 2.

Task name: Java-based report
Response time: 24 seconds
Trace file size: 4.3 MB
Trace file line count: 42,799
Typical *mrskew* execution duration: 2 seconds

Let's begin with a *mrls* command to see some general information about the trace file:

```
1  $ mrls xe_ora_9024_METHODR_TESTING_.trc
2      R  ORA                    START                          END  FILE
3  23.966 10.2 2008-11-25T11:12:29.682-0600 2008-11-25T11:12:53.649-0600 xe_ora_9024_METHODR_TESTING_.trc
```

The 23.966-second duration explained by the trace file closely matches the end-user experience, so this is good trace data with which to proceed. Next, let's see where the time was spent. Here is the Profiler's rendition:

	Subroutine	Duration seconds	% R	Cumulative duration seconds	% R	Call count	Duration per call (seconds) mean	min	skew	max	Drill-down
1.	**SQL*Net message from client**	**20.070**	**85.8%**	20.070	85.8%	**14,254**	0.001408	0.000862		0.243156	SQL
2.	unaccounted-for between dbcalls	1.789	7.6%	21.859	93.4%	28,507	0.000063	-0.000239		0.002762	SQL
3.	CPU service, FETCH calls	1.652	7.1%	23.511	100.5%	14,252	0.000116	0.000000		0.001000	SQL
4.	SQL*Net message to client	0.033	0.1%	23.543	100.6%	14,254	0.000002	0.000000		0.000322	
5.	CPU service, EXEC calls	0.001	0.0%	23.544	100.6%	3	0.000333	0.000000		0.001000	
6.	CPU service, PARSE calls	0.001	0.0%	23.545	100.6%	2	0.000500	0.000000		0.000999	
7.	unaccounted-for within dbcalls	-0.141	-0.6%	23.405	100.0%	14,254	-0.000010	-0.000923		0.018841	
8.	Total (7)	23.405	100.0%								

This time, notice that the Profiler's total duration (23.405 seconds) doesn't exactly match the duration reported by *mrls* (23.966 seconds). The culprit here is a measurement error caused by Oracle Database 10.2.0.1.0 on our Linux machine, which causes Oracle timings to be off by a factor of 1.024 ("Tracing Traps" on page 62). The Method R Tools utilities automatically correct for the problem, but the Profiler doesn't. You can see evidence of the self-correction using the *mrls --units* option:

```
4  $ mrls xe_ora_9024_METHODR_TESTING_.trc --units
5      R    SIZE   SEC/TIM    OFFSET ZONE ZONE-NAME  M  ORA START                          FILE
6  23.966 4343855 0.000001024 -21600.000 -0600     MDT cB 10.2 2008-11-25T11:12:29.682-0600 xe_ora_9024_METHODR_TESTING_.trc
```

The "SEC/TIM" value of 0.000001024 indicates that *mrls* has detected that in this trace file, each *tim* unit accounts for 1.024 microseconds. You could fix the trace file with the following *mrtimfix* command:

```
7  $ mrtimfix --all xe_ora_9024_METHODR_TESTING_.trc >xe_ora_9024_METHODR_TESTING_-fixed.trc
```

The resulting profile matches the *mrls* output:

	Subroutine	Duration seconds	% R	Cumulative duration seconds	% R	Call count	Duration per call (seconds) mean	min	skew	max	Drill-down
1.	**SQL*Net message from client**	**20.552**	**85.8%**	20.552	85.8%	**14,254**	0.001442	0.000883		0.248992	SQL
2.	unaccounted-for between dbcalls	1.832	7.6%	22.384	93.4%	28,506	0.000064	-0.000246		0.002828	SQL
3.	CPU service, FETCH calls	1.652	6.9%	24.036	100.3%	14,252	0.000116	0.000000		0.001000	SQL
4.	SQL*Net message to client	0.033	0.1%	24.068	100.4%	14,254	0.000002	0.000000		0.000330	
5.	CPU service, EXEC calls	0.001	0.0%	24.069	100.4%	3	0.000333	0.000000		0.001000	
6.	CPU service, PARSE calls	0.001	0.0%	24.070	100.4%	2	0.000500	0.000000		0.000999	
7.	unaccounted-for within dbcalls	-0.104	-0.4%	23.966	100.0%	14,254	-0.000007	-0.000921		0.019317	
8.	Total (7)	23.966	100.0%								

Here is the *mrskew* report:

```
 8 $ mrskew xe_ora_9024_METHODR_TESTING_.trc
 9 CALL-NAME                    DURATION      %   CALLS       MEAN       MIN       MAX
10 -------------------------    --------  -----  ------  ---------  --------  --------
11 SQL*Net message from client  20.551541  92.4%  14,254   0.001442  0.000883  0.248992
12 FETCH                         1.651750   7.4%  14,252   0.000116  0.000000  0.001000
13 SQL*Net message to client     0.032850   0.1%  14,254   0.000002  0.000000  0.000330
14 EXEC                          0.001000   0.0%       2   0.000500  0.000000  0.001000
15 PARSE                         0.000999   0.0%       2   0.000500  0.000000  0.000999
16 -------------------------    --------  -----  ------  ---------  --------  --------
17 TOTAL (5)                    22.238140 100.0%  42,764   0.000520  0.000000  0.248992
```

So *mrskew* leaves 1.727860 s (23.966 − 22.238140) of the task's response time unexplained. You can quickly see where the difference comes from by comparing the *mrskew* report with the Profiler report. There are two types of measurement errors in trace files that produce this unaccounted-for time phenomenon: there are (1) durations *within* database calls that are unaccounted for, and (2) durations *between* database calls that are unaccounted for. You can learn about the within-call unaccounted-for durations with this *mrskew* command:

```
18 $ mrskew xe_ora_9024_METHODR_TESTING_.trc --name=dbcall --select='$uafwc' --sl=UAFWC
19 CALL-NAME     UAFWC      %   CALLS       MEAN       MIN       MAX
20 ---------  ---------  -----  ------  ---------  --------  --------
21 PARSE      -0.000296   0.3%       2  -0.000148  -0.000553  0.000257
22 EXEC       -0.000821   0.8%       2  -0.000411  -0.000907  0.000086
23 FETCH      -0.102787  98.9%  14,252  -0.000007  -0.000921  0.019317
24 ---------  ---------  -----  ------  ---------  --------  --------
25 TOTAL (3)  -0.103904 100.0%  14,256  -0.000007  -0.000921  0.019317
```

The presence of only negative unaccounted-for durations in this report, totaling −.103904 s, means that the net error in measurements of dbcall durations is an overcounting of duration. That is, there's no missing duration in the dbcall reporting; on the contrary, there's double-counted duration in the dbcall reporting, which happens because of small, routine measurement inaccuracies in the Oracle trace data.[3]

You can learn about the between-call unaccounted-for durations with this *mrskew* command:

```
26 $ mrskew xe_ora_9024_METHODR_TESTING_.trc --group='$line' --gl='LINE' --select='$uafbc' --sl=UAFBC
27        LINE      UAFBC      %   CALLS       MEAN       MIN       MAX
28 -----------  ---------  -----  ------  ---------  --------  --------
29        6198   0.002870   0.2%       1   0.002870   0.002870  0.002870
30       33778   0.001853   0.1%       1   0.001853   0.001853  0.001853
31       19638   0.001583   0.1%       1   0.001583   0.001583  0.001583
32       13094   0.001559   0.1%       1   0.001559   0.001559  0.001559
33       15135   0.001021   0.1%       1   0.001021   0.001021  0.001021
34       36190   0.000928   0.1%       1   0.000928   0.000928  0.000928
35        5006   0.000877   0.0%       1   0.000877   0.000877  0.000877
36        5439   0.000802   0.0%       1   0.000802   0.000802  0.000802
37       21343   0.000792   0.0%       1   0.000792   0.000792  0.000792
38         984   0.000776   0.0%       1   0.000776   0.000776  0.000776
39 42,754 others 1.819250  99.3%  42,754   0.000043  -0.000919  0.000752
40 -----------  ---------  -----  ------  ---------  --------  --------
41 TOTAL (42,764) 1.832311 100.0% 42,764   0.000043  -0.000919  0.002870
```

The total unaccounted-for duration between database calls is 1.832311 s. The world makes sense, then:

Description	Duration (seconds)	%
Accounted-for duration	22.238140	92.8%
Unaccounted-for within calls	−0.103904	−0.4%
Unaccounted-for between calls	1.832311	7.6%
Total duration	23.966547	100.0%

Accounted-for time and unaccounted-for time (both types) sum to the total duration of the task.

---

[3] Cary Millsap and Jeff Holt, *Optimizing Oracle Performance*, chapter 7.

Chapter 5. Cases in Oracle Trace Data Analysis

About 7.6% of duration consumed by this task is occurring *between* dbcalls. Let's keep this in mind as a motive to see if we can eliminate any unnecessary dbcalls. With that in mind, let's look again at the 92.8% that *mrskew* explains in its default profile output:

```
42  $ mrskew xe_ora_9024_METHODR_TESTING_.trc
43  CALL-NAME                DURATION       %   CALLS      MEAN       MIN       MAX
44  ---------------------    --------    -----  ------  --------  --------  --------
45  SQL*Net message from client  20.551541  92.4%  14,254  0.001442  0.000883  0.248992
46  FETCH                     1.651750   7.4%  14,252  0.000116  0.000000  0.001000
47  SQL*Net message to client   0.032850   0.1%  14,254  0.000002  0.000000  0.000330
48  EXEC                      0.001000   0.0%       2  0.000500  0.000000  0.001000
49  PARSE                     0.000999   0.0%       2  0.000500  0.000000  0.000999
50  ---------------------    --------    -----  ------  --------  --------  --------
51  TOTAL (5)                22.238140  100.0%  42,764  0.000520  0.000000  0.248992
```

Here, the loudest line in the report shows that 14,254 executions of *SQL*Net message from client* calls have consumed 92.4% of the accounted-for time, consuming a grand total of 20.551541 seconds.

Let's see how many rows the program is returning to the user:

```
52  $ mrskew xe_ora_9024_METHODR_TESTING_.trc --select='$row' --sl=ROWS --name=dbcall --pre=0
53  CALL-NAME     ROWS      %    CALLS  MEAN  MIN  MAX
54  ---------  -------  ------  ------  ----  ---  ---
55  FETCH      142,517  100.0%  14,252    10    7   10
56  PARSE            0    0.0%       2     0    0    0
57  EXEC             0    0.0%       2     0    0    0
58  ---------  -------  ------  ------  ----  ---  ---
59  TOTAL (3)  142,517  100.0%  14,256    10    0   10
```

The program has fetched 142,517 rows across 14,252 *fetch* calls. Each fetch has returned between 7 and 10 rows. That's interesting, because the Java code appears to be doing row-by-row processing:

```
60  resultSet = statement.executeQuery(query);
61  while (resultSet.next()) {
62      // do your business upon resultSet
63  }
```

...But clearly, the trace file shows that the application is fetching an average of 10 rows at a time. This is a good thing. It's actually the JDBC driver doing its default buffering of rows, fetching them from the database 10 rows at a time, and then passing them to the Java code 1 row at a time in response to each *resultSet.next()* method call.

You can see how good this is by looking at the original 22.238-second profile again:

```
64  $ mrskew xe_ora_9024_METHODR_TESTING_.trc
65  CALL-NAME                DURATION       %   CALLS      MEAN       MIN       MAX
66  ---------------------    --------    -----  ------  --------  --------  --------
67  SQL*Net message from client  20.551541  92.4%  14,254  0.001442  0.000883  0.248992
68  FETCH                     1.651750   7.4%  14,252  0.000116  0.000000  0.001000
69  SQL*Net message to client   0.032850   0.1%  14,254  0.000002  0.000000  0.000330
70  EXEC                      0.001000   0.0%       2  0.000500  0.000000  0.001000
71  PARSE                     0.000999   0.0%       2  0.000500  0.000000  0.000999
72  ---------------------    --------    -----  ------  --------  --------  --------
73  TOTAL (5)                22.238140  100.0%  42,764  0.000520  0.000000  0.248992
```

If the program had done one *fetch* call and one *SQL*Net message from client* call for each row that the program processed—that is, 142,000+ calls each instead of just 14,200+ calls each—then the program would have spent 206 s in *SQL*Net message from client* calls instead of the 20.6 s that it did, and it would have spent 16.5 s in *fetch* calls instead of 1.65 s. Response time would have been ~200 s instead of ~20 s if the JDBC driver hadn't done its automatic optimization of fetching ten rows at a time instead of one. (We tested our program with 1-row *fetch* calls, and that's exactly what happened.)

This line of reasoning should lead you to wonder what would happen if we could make the Java code fetch, say, 100 rows at a time instead of just 10. Your expectation should be that the *SQL*Net message from client* and *fetch* call counts would fall from ~14,250 to ~1,426. We could hope, then, that the call duration would improve by a factor of ten, too. But, not so fast: skew in the call durations could invalidate that guess. Here's a query that answers the question, if we were to discard only the shortest-duration 1,426 *SQL*Net message from client* calls, then how much time would we save?

```
74 $ mrskew xe_ora_9024_METHODR_TESTING_.trc --name='SQL\*Net message from client' --group='$line' --gl=LINE# --top=1426 >t.txt
75 $ head -2 t.txt; tail -3 t.txt
76       LINE#    DURATION       %    CALLS      MEAN       MIN       MAX
77  --------------  ---------  ------  ------  --------  --------  --------
78  12,828 others  15.903364   77.4%  12,828  0.001240  0.000883  0.001750
79  --------------  ---------  ------  ------  --------  --------  --------
80  TOTAL (14,254) 20.551541  100.0%  14,254  0.001442  0.000883  0.248992
```

The answer is that, if by some kind of bad luck, the calls we eliminated were only the least expensive ones (that is, keeping the 1,426 most expensive ones), then we'd still save 15.903 s of execution time. The `head -2` and `tail -3` commands give me the first two lines from the *mrskew* output (the header lines) and the last three lines (containing the "12,828 others" information and the total line). Since the default sort order for *mrskew* is descending by duration, the 12,828 others that we see here are the fastest *SQL*Net message from client* calls in the file. It's our worst case that if we eliminate 12,828 calls at random, we'll eliminate only the fastest ones.

Likewise, we can find out the best-case estimate using a similar sequence of commands, this time sorting the output so that the *longest*-duration calls are grouped together in the "others" bucket:

```
81 $ mrskew xe_ora_9024_METHODR_TESTING_.trc --name='SQL\*Net message from client' --group='$line' --gl=LINE# --top=1426 --sort=2na >t.txt
82 $ head -2 t.txt; tail -3 t.txt
83       LINE#    DURATION       %    CALLS      MEAN       MIN       MAX
84  --------------  ---------  ------  ------  --------  --------  --------
85   12828 others  19.157293   93.2%   12828  0.001493  0.001031  0.248992
86  --------------  ---------  ------  ------  --------  --------  --------
87  TOTAL (14254)  20.551541  100.0%   14254  0.001442  0.000883  0.248992
```

Here, sorting in ascending order by the 2nd column (the duration) puts the longest-duration calls at the bottom of the report, which I've reported on again with `tail -3`. If we're lucky, then, we'll eliminate 19.157 s of execution time by eliminating all but 1,426 calls. So, now we know that eliminating all but 1,426 *SQL*Net message to client* calls will reduce response time by between 16 and 19 seconds, not counting any secondary effects.

Here's the same analysis for the *fetch* calls. First, sorted to show all but the 1,426 slowest calls:

```
88 $ mrskew xe_ora_9024_METHODR_TESTING_.trc --name=FETCH --group='$line' --gl=LINE# --top=1426 >t.txt
89 $ head -2 t.txt; tail -3 t.txt
90       LINE#    DURATION       %    CALLS      MEAN       MIN       MAX
91  --------------  ---------  ------  ------  --------  --------  --------
92  12,826 others   0.225774   13.7%  12,826  0.000018  0.000000  0.000999
93  --------------  ---------  ------  ------  --------  --------  --------
94  TOTAL (14,252)  1.651750  100.0%  14,252  0.000116  0.000000  0.001000
```

..And then sorted to show all but the 1,426 fastest calls.

```
95 $ mrskew xe_ora_9024_METHODR_TESTING_.trc --name=FETCH --group='$line' --gl=LINE# --top=1426 --sort=2na >t.txt
96 $ head -2 t.txt; tail -3 t.txt
97       LINE#    DURATION       %    CALLS      MEAN       MIN       MAX
98  --------------  ---------  ------  ------  --------  --------  --------
99  12,826 others   1.651750  100.0%  12,826  0.000129  0.000000  0.001000
100 --------------  ---------  ------  ------  --------  --------  --------
101 TOTAL (14,252)  1.651750  100.0%  14,252  0.000116  0.000000  0.001000
```

So then, eliminating all but 1,426 *fetch* calls will reduce response time by between 0.225 and 1.652 seconds.

Chapter 5. Cases in Oracle Trace Data Analysis

Our projected new response time after making this change, then, is:

Description	Worst-case (seconds)	Best-case (seconds)
SQL*Net message from client savings	15.903	19.157
fetch savings	0.225	1.652
Total savings	16.128	20.809
Original response time	23.966	23.966
Projected new response time	7.838	3.157

The expected worst-case and best-case response time savings from eliminating all but 1,426 *fetch* calls.

Response time should fall, then, to between 3.157 s and 7.838 s if we just use an array fetch size of 100 instead of the default value 10. It's worth a shot.

Here's how to specify, using the Oracle JDBC in Java, the array fetch size you want:

```
102  statement.setFetchSize(size);
103  resultSet = statement.executeQuery(query);
104  while (resultSet.next()) {
105      // do your business upon resultSet
106  }
```

The *setFetchSize* call sets the array fetch size for the statement (the query). Setting *size* = 100 produced the following result:

```
107  $ mrskew xe_ora_16470_QUERY_100.trc
108  CALL-NAME                   DURATION        %  CALLS     MEAN       MIN       MAX
109  -------------------------   --------   ------  -----  --------  --------  --------
110  SQL*Net message from client 3.598655    67.8%  1,428  0.002520  0.001499  0.020144
111  FETCH                       1.547763    29.2%  1,426  0.001085  0.000000  0.002000
112  SQL*Net more data to client 0.156718     3.0%  2,840  0.000055  0.000007  0.000227
113  SQL*Net message to client   0.005184     0.1%  1,428  0.000004  0.000001  0.000036
114  PARSE                       0.000000     0.0%      2  0.000000  0.000000  0.000000
115  EXEC                        0.000000     0.0%      2  0.000000  0.000000  0.000000
116  -------------------------   --------   ------  -----  --------  --------  --------
117  TOTAL (6)                   5.308320   100.0%  7,126  0.000745  0.000000  0.020144
```

The reported response time of 5.308 s is, as expected, exactly in the predicted range between 3.157 s and 7.838 s.

We further experimented with array fetch size values in the set {1, 2, 4, 8, 16, 32, ..., 16384} and found that the program's response time improved as we increased the *size* value up beyond *size* = 100 through *size* = 2048. Beyond 2,048, we saw no incremental improvement, so 2,048 is the array fetch size we chose. (The program crashed for *size* = 16384.) Here is the result of running the same program using a 2,048-row fetch size:

```
118  $ mrls xe_ora_28638_QUERY_2048.trc
119      R  ORA                  START                         END  FILE
120  2.458 10.2  2008-12-10T09:51:02.062-0600  2008-12-10T09:51:04.520-0600  xe_ora_28638_QUERY_2048.trc
```

The result is a 2.458 s response time, which is even better than our best-case prediction. Here's the detail of where the time went:

```
121  $ mrskew xe_ora_28638_QUERY_2048.trc
122  CALL-NAME                   DURATION        %  CALLS     MEAN       MIN       MAX
123  -------------------------   --------   ------  -----  --------  --------  --------
124  SQL*Net message from client 0.911041    36.5%     72  0.012653  0.000890  0.026857
125  SQL*Net more data to client 0.841897    33.7%  2,688  0.000313  0.000004  0.013287
126  FETCH                       0.744885    29.8%     70  0.010641  0.006999  0.012998
127  PARSE                       0.001000     0.0%      2  0.000500  0.000000  0.001000
128  SQL*Net message to client   0.000147     0.0%     72  0.000002  0.000001  0.000006
129  EXEC                        0.000000     0.0%      2  0.000000  0.000000  0.000000
130  -------------------------   --------   ------  -----  --------  --------  --------
131  TOTAL (6)                   2.498970   100.0%  2,906  0.000860  0.000000  0.026857
```

In this case, the *mrskew* accounted-for time (2.499 s) closely matches the *mrls*-reported response time (2.458 s). The *mrskew* accounted-for duration exceeds the *mrls*-reported duration by a little bit because of small, routine measurement inaccuracies in the Oracle trace data.

The ~7% of between-call unaccounted-for time that we had to cope with before is also gone. Eliminating thousands of calls also eliminated thousands of opportunities for unaccounted-for durations to exist between them.

So, is this the profile of an optimal task? It still spends only 29.8% of its time fetching, and the remainder of its time doing network I/O. The dominant response time consumer is still *SQL*Net message from client*, but now there's a new call in the profile, this *SQL*Net more data to client*. This call is in the profile because with an array fetch size of 2,048, there's too much data to fit into a single SQL*Net packet, so the data returned from the Oracle Database to the client returns via one *SQL*Net message from client* call for the first rows of the data, and then a sequence of *SQL*Net more data to client* calls to transport the remainder of the rows.

The fact is, there's just a lot of data to transport from the server to the client, and our database is faster than our network. The next phase of optimization for this business task, then, would be to answer the question, "Does this Java program really need to retrieve 142,517 rows from our database?" The answer to questions like this is often no.

CONCLUSION

This program is supposed to fetch 142,517 rows from a database. So why did it spend only less than 10% of that time doing that, and over 90% transporting those fetched rows? Drilling into the details of how this program was transporting rows from the server to the client revealed that it should be beneficial to fetch more rows per round trip. This is a common problem, because many application programmers never measure their code's response time. When database developers measure response times, their tools routinely discard the very information that you need to look at to notice that you have a problem like this.

EXERCISES

3. Is there a universal optimal array fetch size? What is it?
4. Should you always check your array fetch size to see if there's room for performance improvement? If not, then what should you do instead?

ORDER ENTRY BATCH JOB

This business task is a long-running batch job that deletes order entry application historical data that no longer needs to be stored in the database. It is a custom job based upon an Oracle E-Business Suite task.

Task name:	OE History Delete (customized)
Response time:	~20+ hours
Trace file size:	1.17 GB
Trace file line count:	11,147,993
Typical *mrskew* execution duration:	6 minutes

The first thing I like to do is run a quick *mrls* command to get my bearings about the trace file:

```
1  $ mrls prod_ora_14920.trc
2  mrls: estimating task start time in file 'prod_ora_14920.trc' using --scanmax=250
3         R   ORA                     START                       END  FILE
4  76939.572  11.1  2011-02-09T19:08:10.693+0000  2011-02-10T16:30:30.265+0000  prod_ora_14920.trc
```

The "estimating task start time…" message means that *mrls* has estimated the task start time instead of calculating it precisely. Precision is good, but it comes at the cost of speed,

Chapter 5. Cases in Oracle Trace Data Analysis

and *mrls* is a tool that we want to be able to use quickly and often, even for gargantuan trace files.[4] The response time of 76,939.572 s is roughly 21.4 h, which matches closely with the actual response time of the job, as recorded by the Oracle E-Business concurrent manager.

The next step is to find out where the time has gone. A simple *mrskew* call without any command line options tells us:

```
$ mrskew prod_ora_14920.trc
CALL-NAME                                              DURATION       %        CALLS       MEAN       MIN        MAX
------------------------------------------------  -------------   ------   ----------   --------   --------   --------
db file sequential read                           59,081.406102    76.6%   10,013,394   0.005900   0.000010  15.853019
log buffer space                                   6,308.758563     8.2%        9,476   0.665762   0.000004   1.010092
free buffer waits                                  4,688.730190     6.1%      200,198   0.023420   0.000004   1.021281
EXEC                                               4,214.190000     5.5%       36,987   0.113937   0.000000   5.400000
log file switch completion                         1,552.471890     2.0%        1,853   0.837815   0.000006   1.013093
db file parallel read                                464.976815     0.6%        7,641   0.060853   0.000030   8.964706
log file switch (checkpoint incomplete)              316.968886     0.4%          351   0.903045   0.000003   1.014777
rdbms ipc reply                                      244.937910     0.3%        2,737   0.089491   0.000001   2.010042
undo segment extension                               140.267429     0.2%        1,411   0.099410   0.000001   0.108950
log file switch (private strand flush incomplete)    112.680587     0.1%          134   0.840900   0.002781   1.000239
17 others                                             23.367228     0.0%       58,126   0.000402   0.000000   5.045291
------------------------------------------------  -------------   ------   ----------   --------   --------   --------
TOTAL (27)                                        77,148.755600   100.0%   10,332,308   0.007467   0.000000  15.853019
```

The calls in the trace file account for 77,148.755600 s. The difference in time reported and actual response time is 0.27%. Notice that the *mrskew* error, while minuscule, is greater than the *mrls* error. This is because *mrls* checks only the beginning and ending times in the file, which is both accurate and very fast. However, *mrskew* computes total response time by aggregating individual call durations throughout the file. The errors in double-counting and unaccounted-for durations in the individual call latencies accumulate to produce more error than *mrls*.[5] However, this duration closely matches the duration of the real-life experience, so the report has the proper time scope for our analysis.

The dominant response time consumer for the task was *db file sequential read* calls, consuming 76.6% of the execution time. The mean latency for these 10,013,394 calls is 0.0059 seconds per call, or 5.9 ms. Most SAN administrators would probably claim that less than 6 ms per I/O call is pretty good. But before we agree or disagree, let's check the skew in those read call latencies:

```
$ mrskew prod_ora_14920.trc --name=read --rc=p10
      RANGE {min ≤ e < max}      DURATION       %        CALLS       MEAN       MIN        MAX
   ------------------------   -------------   ------   ----------   --------   --------   --------
1.     0.000000     0.000001        0.000000    0.0%            0
2.     0.000001     0.000010        0.000000    0.0%            0
3.     0.000010     0.000100      199.789835    0.3%    9,351,360   0.000021   0.000010   0.000099
4.     0.000100     0.001000       21.638881    0.0%      109,453   0.000198   0.000100   0.000999
5.     0.001000     0.010000      612.690226    1.0%      106,356   0.005761   0.001000   0.009999
6.     0.010000     0.100000   11,216.210793   18.8%      315,370   0.035565   0.010000   0.099999
7.     0.100000     1.000000   26,267.753168   44.1%      131,181   0.200241   0.100002   0.999717
8.     1.000000    10.000000   21,050.466284   35.3%        7,401   2.844273   1.000184   9.900656
9.    10.000000   100.000000      192.219083    0.3%           17  11.307005  10.242772  15.853019
10.  100.000000 1,000.000000        0.000000    0.0%            0
11. 1,000.000000          +∞        0.000000    0.0%            0
   ------------------------   -------------   ------   ----------   --------   --------   --------
                 TOTAL (11)   59,560.768268  100.0%   10,021,138   0.005944   0.000010  15.853019
```

So 9,351,360 of the total 10,021,138 calls with the string `read` in their names have an average latency of 0.021 ms, which is spectacular. These are reads for which, clearly, one or more of the cache layers between the Oracle Database and the actual disks are paying off. However, this histogram also highlights some problems:

- 18.8% of time spent reading was consumed by 315,370 calls consuming between 10 ms and 100 ms apiece, with average latency of over 35 ms.
- 44.1% of time spent reading was consumed by 131,181 calls consuming between 100 ms and 1.000 s apiece, with average latency of 200 ms.

---

[4] You can use the *mrskew --scanmax* option to experiment with the time-precision tradeoff. A *--scanmax* value of 0 turns causes *mrls* to read the entire file for the most precise possible answer.

[5] See chapter 7 of Millsap and Holt, *Optimizing Oracle Performance* for details about errors in durations that the Oracle Database reports for various calls.

- 35.3% of time spent reading was consumed by 7,401 calls consuming between 1 s and 10 s apiece, with average latency of 2.844 seconds.
- Finally, 17 read calls consumed between 10.242 and 15.853 seconds apiece. They didn't consume a large percentage of the total response time, but over three minutes (192 s) were consumed by executing just seventeen *read* calls.

Let's see how much time was spent executing just *read* calls that each lasted longer than 100 ms:

```
37  $ mrskew prod_ora_14920.trc --name=read --where='$ela > .100'
38  CALL-NAME                 DURATION       %     CALLS      MEAN       MIN       MAX
39  -----------------------   -----------   ----- --------   --------  --------  --------
40  db file sequential read   47,054.520839  99.0% 137,796   0.341480  0.100002  15.853019
41  db file parallel read        443.056897   0.9%     775   0.571686  0.100538   8.964706
42  db file scattered read        12.860799   0.0%      28   0.459314  0.114605   5.045291
43  -----------------------   -----------   ----- --------   --------  --------  --------
44  TOTAL (3)                 47,510.438535 100.0% 138,599   0.342791  0.100002  15.853019
```

That's 13.19 hours (47,510 s) spent on calls lasting longer than 100 ms apiece.

Still, though, the SAN administrator might argue that the *read* calls lasting longer than 100 ms were probably large, multi-block database *read* calls, and therefore it's probably not really a problem. You don't have to settle for "probably"; you can *know*. How much time did the task spend on *read* calls of different sizes? You can find out by grouping by the *$p3* variable, which, for Oracle *read* calls, reports the number of Oracle blocks obtained with the call:[6]

```
45  $ mrskew prod_ora_14920.trc --name=read --where='$ela > .100' --group='$p3' --gl=BLKS/CALL
46  BLKS/CALL      DURATION        %     CALLS      MEAN       MIN       MAX
47  ----------   -------------   ----- --------   --------  --------  --------
48          1   47,054.520839   99.0% 137,796    0.341480  0.100002  15.853019
49          2        71.221733   0.1%     186    0.382913  0.101225   6.549107
50         16        33.640917   0.1%      47    0.715764  0.101777   5.222509
51         17        31.576042   0.1%      29    1.088829  0.103392   6.798100
52         21        25.475776   0.1%      30    0.849193  0.111009   7.776442
53          6        24.320426   0.1%      21    1.158116  0.104758   8.964706
54          9        24.163314   0.1%      35    0.690380  0.109095   7.816674
55         22        22.592579   0.0%      36    0.627572  0.109590   3.946032
56         10        18.398100   0.0%      17    1.082241  0.114605   6.597871
57         18        15.518177   0.0%      23    0.674703  0.102651   3.097042
58  16 others       189.010632   0.4%     379    0.498709  0.100538   4.634953
59  ----------   -------------   ----- --------   --------  --------  --------
60  TOTAL (26)   47,510.438535  100.0% 138,599    0.342791  0.100002  15.853019
```

Thus, 1-block *read* calls accounted for fully 99% of the time spent doing *read* calls with 0.100+ s latencies. This is definitely a SAN performance problem.

From the information we have now, we can compute how long those 1-block *read* calls would take if the read latencies were, say, 50 ms instead of 100+ ms apiece. From the report above, we know that there were 137,796 1-block *read* calls lasting 100+ ms apiece. If those calls consumed 50 ms each, then they would have consumed 6,889.8 s (137,796 × .050 s), which is only 1.91 h.

Only by directly measuring the response times of individual calls can you be this bold and specific about predicting response time savings. *You cannot do it* with just mean latencies and call counts.

Thus, if all this task's 1-block reads that did consume 100+ ms per call instead consumed 50 ms apiece (still ten times worse than we ought to expect), then the duration consumed

---

[6] You can learn what each *$p1*, *$p2*, and *$p3* variable means for each Oracle Database system call name by viewing the *parameter1*, *parameter2*, and *parameter3* columns of *v$event_name*. In Oracle Database versions 11.2 onward, the connotative names for these parameters are rendered right in the trace file.

Chapter 5. Cases in Oracle Trace Data Analysis

doing 1-block read calls would drop from 13.19 hours to just 1.19 hours, a savings of 12 hours.

So, what kinds of skew can we find within these 1-block *read* durations? Let's find out. This query shows us the top ten response time contributors by file id:

```
$ mrskew prod_ora_14920.trc --name=read --where='$p3 == 1' --group='$p1' --gl=FILE-ID
   FILE-ID       DURATION       %       CALLS       MEAN        MIN        MAX
---------- -------------- ------- ----------- ---------- ---------- ----------
       128    4,451.015619    7.5%     700,100   0.006358   0.000011  12.382647
       376    2,599.047622    4.4%     578,001   0.004497   0.000010   9.748775
       373    2,168.688252    3.7%     573,470   0.003782   0.000010   8.541436
       378    2,105.972762    3.6%     452,128   0.004658   0.000010  11.439730
       381    2,091.643974    3.5%     449,178   0.004657   0.000010   8.556457
       164    1,821.251729    3.1%     158,517   0.011489   0.000011   8.840377
       347    1,814.647914    3.1%     490,371   0.003701   0.000010   7.912530
       348    1,656.326662    2.8%     491,827   0.003368   0.000010   8.877727
        89    1,380.846165    2.3%      95,671   0.014433   0.000011  10.905847
       371    1,379.391200    2.3%     347,232   0.003973   0.000011  11.701320
147 others   37,612.574205   63.7%   5,676,899   0.006626   0.000010  15.853019
---------- -------------- ------- ----------- ---------- ---------- ----------
TOTAL (157) 59,081.406102  100.0%  10,013,394   0.005900   0.000010  15.853019
```

About twice as much time was spent reading from file 128 as from any other file, but that's not particularly noteworthy, because the mean, min, and max call durations look like those of most of the other files shown. Files 89 and 164 have particularly bad mean latencies, which might be worth a deeper look with the SAN administrator to see if these files might benefit from some specific attention. However, the max latency on each file shown here is quite atrocious, most being 10+ s for 1-block reads. It looks like this phenomenon is not discriminating among files; rather, it appears to be uniformly bad across files.

The next *mrskew* query shows whether there was a particular object that accounted for most of the bad *read* calls:

```
$ mrskew prod_ora_14920.trc --name=read --where='$p3 == 1' --group='$obj' --gl=OBJ
       OBJ       DURATION       %       CALLS       MEAN        MIN        MAX
---------- -------------- ------- ----------- ---------- ---------- ----------
     43376   17,588.084232   29.8%   2,015,422   0.008727   0.000010  10.905847
     85889    9,085.340377   15.4%   1,777,240   0.005112   0.000010   9.748775
    133503    8,013.926408   13.6%     782,486   0.010242   0.000011  15.853019
    561197    5,504.529047    9.3%   2,660,425   0.002069   0.000010  10.875894
    561206    5,122.174173    8.7%   2,170,061   0.002360   0.000011  12.382647
   1827327    3,578.365415    6.1%      98,305   0.036401   0.000011   9.641552
    133491    3,455.198273    5.8%     157,083   0.021996   0.000011  10.328413
    561718    2,805.824826    4.7%      76,254   0.036796   0.000013  11.923302
    133506    2,171.151145    3.7%     137,061   0.015841   0.000010  11.072676
    561201    1,588.085653    2.7%     129,460   0.012267   0.000011  11.701320
 12 others      168.726555    0.3%       9,597   0.017581   0.000012   6.658386
---------- -------------- ------- ----------- ---------- ---------- ----------
TOTAL (22)  59,081.406102  100.0%  10,013,394   0.005900   0.000010  15.853019
```

Three objects each accounted for double-digit percentage contributions, but the mean, min, and max durations are uniformly distributed across objects.

The next *mrskew* query tells us whether there was a particular *sqlid* value that accounted for more than its share of the bad read durations:

```
$ mrskew prod_ora_14920.trc --name=read --where='$p3 == 1' --group='$sqlid' --gl=SQLID
SQLID                  DURATION       %       CALLS       MEAN        MIN        MAX
-------------------- ------------ ------- ----------- ---------- ---------- ----------
8fst2g04wuaxy         36,486.916281   61.8%   4,122,730   0.008850   0.000010  11.923302
ckba0vzb9mvtd         22,398.275472   37.9%   5,879,398   0.003810   0.000010  15.853019
304j4y72hddq2             88.284323    0.1%       4,941   0.017868   0.000012   2.740762
1gp7sxw0a7k24             37.265947    0.1%       2,538   0.014683   0.000015   2.736111
4yhq514a4pavr             32.708237    0.1%       1,639   0.019956   0.000016   6.658386
9tgj4g8y4rwy8             29.095710    0.0%         419   0.069441   0.000020   8.298437
6aq34nj2zb2n7              2.867922    0.0%          15   0.191195   0.000023   2.571521
#5 prod_ora_14920.trc      1.716978    0.0%       1,399   0.001227   0.000013   0.042402
1gu8t96d0bdmu              0.839728    0.0%          23   0.036510   0.000022   0.289970
2q93zsrvbdw48              0.563430    0.0%          44   0.012805   0.000017   0.208028
16 others                  2.872076    0.0%         248   0.011581   0.000015   0.269592
-------------------- ------------ ------- ----------- ---------- ---------- ----------
TOTAL (26)            59,081.406102  100.0%  10,013,394   0.005900   0.000010  15.853019
```

Two SQL statements accounted for 99.7% of the total read time, which was no surprise to the users running the task. They already knew that the task was dominated by two SQL statements. It's easy to find those statements with a simple Unix command:

```
$ grep -A1 8fst2g04wuaxy prod_ora_14920.trc | grep -v PARSING | grep -v "^--" | head -1
DELETE FROM OE_ORDER_LINES_HISTORY WHERE HEADER_ID=:B2 AND VERSION_NUMBER=:B1
```

```
111 $ grep -A1 ckba0vzb9mvtd prod_ora_14920.trc | grep -v PARSING | grep -v "^--" | head -1
112 DELETE FROM OE_PRICE_ADJS_HISTORY WHERE HEADER_ID=:B2 AND VERSION_NUMBER=:B1
```

Here, the `grep -A1` command fetches the trace file line containing the given *sqlid* and the one line after it. The two `grep -v` commands eliminate visual clutter from the output, and the `head -1` command gives us only the first definition in the file for the given *sqlid*. This command is fast and efficient; even on this huge file, it runs very quickly.

The next query tells us whether there was a particular 1,000-second time interval during which the read durations were especially bad. The query uses the Perl *substr* function to group by the string containing all but the final nine digits of the *tim* value:

```
113 $ mrskew prod_ora_14920.trc --name=read --where='$p3 == 1' --group='substr($tim,0,-(9+1))' --gl=1000-S-RANGE
114 1000-S-RANGE       DURATION       %      CALLS      MEAN       MIN        MAX
115 ------------   -------------   ------   ---------   --------   --------   ---------
116         5644     937.793929     1.6%     130,429   0.007190   0.000010    7.488264
117         5691     937.403763     1.6%     185,502   0.005053   0.000011   12.382647
118         5646     931.074661     1.6%     125,979   0.007391   0.000011   11.264117
119         5674     914.356376     1.5%     188,986   0.004838   0.000011    8.685342
120         5671     911.101551     1.5%     156,185   0.005833   0.000011    9.092496
121         5624     902.501723     1.5%     153,665   0.005873   0.000011   11.171112
122         5628     897.357891     1.5%     165,021   0.005438   0.000010    7.131034
123         5690     891.321714     1.5%     106,367   0.008380   0.000011   11.164841
124         5675     890.971207     1.5%     325,054   0.002741   0.000011   10.875894
125         5638     882.191281     1.5%      79,304   0.011124   0.000013   11.072676
126   68 others  49,985.332008    84.6%   8,396,902   0.005953   0.000010   15.853019
127 ------------   -------------   ------   ---------   --------   --------   ---------
128    TOTAL (78) 59,081.406102   100.0%  10,013,394   0.005900   0.000010   15.853019
```

The *tim* value in a trace file is expressed in microseconds.[7] However, the *$tim* variable in *mrskew* is expressed in seconds, with a decimal point. Thus, to strip off the final nine digits of a *tim* value, we need to strip off 9+1 characters of the *tim*. This is what the "−(9+1)" argument to the Perl *substr* function does. The "+1" is to account for the decimal point that we also need to remove:

tim value in trace file	5618769717353
`$tim`	5618769.717353
`substr($tim,0,-6)`	5618769.
`substr($tim,0,-(6+1))`	5618769
`substr($tim,0,−(9+1))`	5618

You can use the Perl *substr* function upon *$tim* values to create ranges of duration. In this example, all *tim* values between 5,618,000.000000 and 5,618,999.999999 will be grouped into a single histogram bucket.

Notice that there is no appreciable skew in the durations across these 1,000-second time buckets. The next query groups the same way, except with wider 10,000-second intervals (using *substr* to omit (10+1) characters at the end of the *$tim* string), and this time, sorted not by duration but in the order the buckets occurred:

```
129 mrskew prod_ora_14920.trc --name=read --where='$p3 == 1' --group='substr($tim,0,-(10+1))' --gl=10000-S-RANGE --sort=1na
130 10000-S-RANGE      DURATION       %      CALLS      MEAN       MIN        MAX
131 ------------   -------------   ------   ---------   --------   --------   ---------
132          561     820.219019     1.4%     145,403   0.005641   0.000011    6.599569
133          562   8,005.823224    13.6%   1,095,352   0.007309   0.000010   11.171112
134          563   4,964.048981     8.4%   1,218,236   0.004075   0.000012   11.439730
135          564   8,366.752719    14.2%   1,004,028   0.008333   0.000010   11.264117
136          565   7,230.484805    12.2%   1,129,279   0.006403   0.000011    9.561822
137          566   8,100.820764    13.7%   1,384,063   0.005853   0.000011    9.641552
138          567   8,413.455543    14.2%   1,455,219   0.005782   0.000010   15.853019
139          568   8,205.348608    13.9%   1,509,057   0.005437   0.000010   11.923302
140          569   4,974.452441     8.4%   1,072,757   0.004637   0.000010   12.382647
141 ------------   -------------   ------   ---------   --------   --------   ---------
142    TOTAL (9) 59,081.406102   100.0%  10,013,394   0.005900   0.000010   15.853019
```

…Again, still no appreciable skew either in the durations or the average latencies across most of the 10,000-second buckets of time, except to say that there were significantly fewer read calls (145,403) and less time spent reading in the earliest 10,000 seconds of

---

[7] All *tim* values are expressed in microseconds in Oracle Database versions 9 and onward. In prior versions, *tim* values were specified in 0.01-second units.

Chapter 5. Cases in Oracle Trace Data Analysis

the task's execution (which would be calls with *$tim* values 5,610,000.000000 through 5,619,999.999999).

Had we seen skew here, it might have been evidence of competing workload whose effect is worse during a particular time interval, but here we see nothing but uniformity of durations across time intervals.

Conclusion

Finding uniform latencies for 1-block reads among all the dimensions we analyzed indicates that the SAN has a systemic performance problem that's affecting all files, all objects, all SQL statements, and even all time intervals uniformly. If the SAN can just deliver its 100+ ms 1-block read calls in 50 ms, then this task will run in 8 hours instead of 20.

Exercises

5. What are some possible culprits for the SAN's misbehavior?
6. Is it possible that inefficient SQL is causing the performance problems for this task? How would you find out?

Payroll Batch Job

The next business task to analyze is a long-running Oracle Payroll job called PYUGEN. The process was causing agony to the business because it was consuming roughly twice as much response time (or half as much throughput) as the business could afford.

> Task name: PYUGEN (Oracle Payroll)
> Response time: ~30 minutes
> Trace file size: 73 MB
> Trace file line count: 1,760,351
> Typical *mrskew* execution duration: 25 seconds

Let's begin with a *mrls* command to see some general information about the trace file:

```
1  $ mrls ora_922341.trc
2      R  ORA                    START                        END  FILE
3  1985.200  8.1  2001-09-12T14:10:27.530+0000  2001-09-12T14:43:32.730+0000  ora_922341.trc
```

The task within the file consumes roughly 1,985 seconds of response time, or roughly half an hour. This duration matches the end-user experience, so we will continue investigating this trace file.

This trace file was generated on an Oracle version 8.1 database. The tools in the Method R Tools suite automatically adjust to the appropriate trace file timing units, even for versions as old as Oracle version 7.

The first step is to find out where the time has gone:

```
4  $ mrskew ora_922341.trc
5  CALL-NAME                    DURATION         %     CALLS       MEAN       MIN       MAX
6  -------------------------  ------------   ------  --------  --------  --------  --------
7  SQL*Net message from client   984.010000   50.3%    95,161  0.010340  0.000000  0.310000
8  SQL*Net more data from client 418.820000   21.4%     3,345  0.125208  0.000000  0.270000
9  db file sequential read       279.340000   14.3%    45,084  0.006196  0.000000  0.050000
10 EXEC                          136.880000    7.0%    67,888  0.002016  0.000000  1.320000
11 PARSE                          74.490000    3.8%    10,098  0.007377  0.000000  0.090000
12 FETCH                          37.320000    1.9%    57,217  0.000652  0.000000  0.130000
13 latch free                     23.690000    1.2%    34,695  0.000683  0.000000  0.080000
14 log file sync                   1.090000    0.1%       506  0.002154  0.000000  0.050000
15 SQL*Net more data to client     0.830000    0.0%    15,982  0.000052  0.000000  0.020000
16 log file switch completion      0.280000    0.0%         3  0.093333  0.080000  0.110000
17 5 others                        0.720000    0.0%    95,338  0.000008  0.000000  0.020000
18 -------------------------  ------------   ------  --------  --------  --------  --------
19 TOTAL (15)                  1,957.470000  100.0%   425,317  0.004602  0.000000  1.320000
```

The *mrskew* output accounts for 1,957.47 s of response time, which is not exactly 1,985 s of response time, for reasons that I mentioned before, but the reported response time is within −1.4% of the *mrls* actual reported response time, which is plenty good enough to continue our analysis without bothering to dig into the detail about why it's off.

This profile came as quite a shock to the system management team in charge of trying to optimize this task. The database monitoring tool they used had clearly reported that the most popularly waited-for syscall on their system was the *latch free* call, so the team had spent several weeks trying to eliminate the *latch free* waiting time from their system. However, it is easy to see here that *latch free* calls consumed only 1.2% of the total response time for PYUGEN. If our priority is to fix the performance of PYUGEN, then *latch free* calls are definitely not where we should point our attention.

The dominant response time consumer is calls to *SQL*Net message from client*, which account for 50.3% of the task's total response time. Seeing a profile that is dominated by what so many Oracle practitioners have learned to call "idle events" can make new users of response time profiling tools a bit anxious. However, the rule to remember is much simpler than remembering about idle events: if it's part of the response time that the business cares about, then it's important; otherwise, it's not. In this case, 50.3% of the half hour that a user spent waiting on Payroll to run was consumed by *SQL*Net message from client* processing. "Idle" or not, this fact means that the calls are important.

Let's examine the skew of the call durations:

```
20  mrskew ora_922341.trc --name='SQL\*Net message from client' --rc=p10
21       RANGE {min ≤ e < max}      DURATION      %    CALLS      MEAN       MIN       MAX
22     ------------------------- ------------ ------ -------  --------  --------  --------
23   1.    0.000000     0.000001     0.000000   0.0%  75,988  0.000000  0.000000  0.000000
24   2.    0.000001     0.000010
25   3.    0.000010     0.000100
26   4.    0.000100     0.001000
27   5.    0.001000     0.010000
28   6.    0.010000     0.100000   232.180000  23.6%  15,058  0.015419  0.010000  0.090000
29   7.    0.100000     1.000000   751.830000  76.4%   4,115  0.182705  0.100000  0.310000
30   8.    1.000000    10.000000
31   9.   10.000000   100.000000
32  10.  100.000000  1,000.000000
33  11. 1,000.000000          +∞
34     ------------------------- ------------ ------ -------  --------  --------  --------
35                   TOTAL (11)    984.010000 100.0%  95,161  0.010340  0.000000  0.310000
```

Because this is an Oracle version 8 database, the resolution of the timing data in the trace file is 0.01 s instead of the 0.000 001-second resolution that we've grown accustomed to since version 9. Thus, calls consuming less than 0.01 s will be listed in the trace data as having consumed 0 s. In this case, 75,988 calls consumed less than 0.01 s. All the time consumed by *SQL*Net message from client* calls came from individual calls lasting between 0.01 s and 1 s.

The average latency of those calls is 0.010 s (10 ms), which is interesting because in our interview with the client's DBA, we learned that the PYUGEN process ran on the same Sun where the Oracle Database runs. We were not aware of much client-side processing taking place within PYUGEN, so we suspected that most of the 10 ms of *SQL*Net message from client* per call was network I/O time. But, since PYUGEN was running on the database server itself, we expected the average latency to be much less even than 1 ms. Thus, we suspected we might be looking at a network performance problem.

We looked at the *tnsnames.ora* configuration file and found that PYUGEN was connecting to its Oracle instance via a (PROTOCOL=TCP) adapter. We wanted to know how much time was being consumed by the multi-layer TCP/IP processing code path, so we devised a test for the DBA. We had him write a small *sqlplus* script that executed a few thousand small *select* statements. He ran it first from an Oracle session that used the (PROTOCOL=TCP) adapter. It required roughly 10 ms per *select*. He then ran it again from an Oracle session that connected through a (PROTOCOL=BEQ) adapter (nowadays we'd use IPC). This time, it required less than 1 ms per *select*. We found that using the BEQ adapter was roughly 55 times faster than using TCP for this test.

Chapter 5. Cases in Oracle Trace Data Analysis

Here is the original profile again:

```
36  mrskew ora_922341.trc
37  CALL-NAME                       DURATION       %    CALLS      MEAN       MIN       MAX
38  -------------------------  -------------  ------  -------  --------  --------  --------
39  SQL*Net message from client     984.010000  50.3%   95,161  0.010340  0.000000  0.310000
40  SQL*Net more data from client   418.820000  21.4%    3,345  0.125208  0.000000  0.270000
41  db file sequential read         279.340000  14.3%   45,084  0.006196  0.000000  0.050000
42  EXEC                            136.880000   7.0%   67,888  0.002016  0.000000  1.320000
43  PARSE                            74.490000   3.8%   10,098  0.007377  0.000000  0.090000
44  FETCH                            37.320000   1.9%   57,217  0.000652  0.000000  0.130000
45  latch free                       23.690000   1.2%   34,695  0.000683  0.000000  0.080000
46  log file sync                     1.090000   0.1%      506  0.002154  0.000000  0.050000
47  SQL*Net more data to client       0.830000   0.0%   15,982  0.000052  0.000000  0.020000
48  log file switch completion        0.280000   0.0%        3  0.093333  0.080000  0.110000
49  5 others                          0.720000   0.0%   95,338  0.000008  0.000000  0.020000
50  -------------------------  -------------  ------  -------  --------  --------  --------
51  TOTAL (15)                    1,957.470000 100.0%  425,317  0.004602  0.000000  1.320000
```

We expected that if changing the protocol adapter could make *SQL*Net message from client* average latency 55 times smaller, then we should see a response time reduction from 984 s to just 984 ÷ 55 ≈ 20 s, which should result in an overall time savings of about 984 s – 20 s ≈ 960 s, which would bring the total response time of this task down to 1,957 s – 960 s ≈ 1,000 s, which would be roughly half its original response time.

Conclusion

The configuration change we suggested made it through the client's change control process within about a week, and response time for the first payroll run improved by roughly 50%. One configuration change had doubled the throughput of PYUGEN. Looking at other data sources had cost the team several weeks, but the team made this perfectly targeted configuration change within 15 minutes of seeing our first PYUGEN profile.

Exercises

7. Should you always check your protocol adapter for possible configuration mistakes that might be causing a performance problem?

8. How could a commercial monitoring tool have so badly missed the target by implicating *latch free* as the cause of the PYUGEN performance problem, when it contributed such a minuscule duration to the total response time of PYUGEN?

Purchasing Batch Job

This business task is a batch job run within the Oracle Purchasing application package. The person who traced it had often wondered why this particular batch job had taken so long, so one day he had some free time, and he found out.

> Task name: Oracle Purchasing batch job
> Response time: 42 minutes
> Trace file size: 18 MB
> Trace file line count: 269,419
> Typical *mrskew* execution duration: 10 seconds

Let's begin with a *mrls* command to see some general information about the trace file:

```
1  $ mrls proa021_ora_3639.trc
2        R    ORA                       START                             END  FILE
3  2510.220  8.0  2001-06-06T17:02:09.600+0000  2001-06-06T17:43:59.820+0000  proa021_ora_3639.trc
```

The response time of 2,510 s matches the end-user experience of the 42-minute batch job. Where did the time go?

```
 4  $ mrskew proa021_ora_3639.trc
 5  CALL-NAME                        DURATION       %    CALLS      MEAN       MIN       MAX
 6  ------------------------------  -----------  -----  -------  --------  --------  --------
 7  EXEC                             1,084.960000 48.6%   3,935  0.275720  0.000000  6.900000
 8  db file sequential read            432.030000 19.3%  62,495  0.006913  0.000000  1.730000
 9  FETCH                              373.930000 16.7%   3,912  0.095585  0.000000  4.190000
10  global cache lock s to x            99.870000  4.5%   3,434  0.029083  0.000000  0.790000
11  global cache lock open s            85.930000  3.8%   3,507  0.024502  0.000000  0.820000
12  global cache lock open x            57.880000  2.6%   1,930  0.029990  0.000000  0.960000
13  latch free                          26.770000  1.2%   1,010  0.026505  0.000000  0.800000
14  SQL*Net message from client         19.110000  0.9%   6,714  0.002846  0.000000  0.450000
15  write complete waits                11.130000  0.5%     155  0.071806  0.000000  0.720000
16  row cache lock                      11.100000  0.5%     485  0.022887  0.000000  0.670000
17  14 others                           30.740000  1.4%   7,321  0.004199  0.000000  1.010000
18  ------------------------------  -----------  -----  -------  --------  --------  --------
19  TOTAL (24)                       2,233.450000 100.0% 94,898  0.023535  0.000000  6.900000
```

The response time of 2,233 s leaves about 11% of the 2,510-second duration unaccounted for, but we'll press on anyway. Even if we can't account for 11% of the duration, we have three lines of profile data that we care about more. From the profile here, we can begin to piece together a story that there's some hardworking SQL in this task.[8] Let's find out:

```
20  $ mrskew proa021_ora_3639.trc --group='substr($sql,0,60)'
21  'substr($sql,0,60)'                                              DURATION      %    CALLS      MEAN       MIN       MAX
22  ---------------------------------------------------------------  ----------- -----  -------  --------  --------  --------
23  update po_requisitions_interface set requisition_header_id=:     1,351.620000 60.5%  14,620  0.092450  0.000000  1.430000
24  select req_number_segment1 from po_requisitions_interface wh       770.730000 34.5%  60,772  0.012682  0.000000  4.190000
25  insert into po_requisition_lines(requisition_line_id,requisi        40.130000  1.8%   2,796  0.014353  0.000000  6.900000
26  insert into mtl_supply(supply_type_code,supply_source_id,las        13.900000  0.6%     518  0.026834  0.000000  5.690000
27  INSERT INTO PO_WF_DEBUG_VALUES ( PO_WF_DEBUG_S.NEXTVAL,SYSDA        10.740000  0.5%     388  0.027680  0.000000  0.670000
28  INSERT INTO WF_ITEM_ATTRIBUTE_VALUES ( ITEM_TYPE,ITEM_KEY,NA         6.390000  0.3%     307  0.020814  0.000000  0.410000
29  select po_requisition_headers_s.nextval into :b0 from dual          5.640000  0.3%   4,725  0.001194  0.000000  0.400000
30  update seq$ set increment$=:2,minvalue=:3,maxvalue=:4,cycle#         3.220000  0.1%      88  0.036591  0.000000  0.450000
31  update po_requisition_lines set line_num=:b0 where :b1=requi        2.480000  0.1%   4,723  0.000525  0.000000  0.060000
32  INSERT INTO WF_ITEM_ACTIVITY_STATUSES ( ITEM_TYPE,ITEM_KEY,P        2.340000  0.1%     112  0.020893  0.000000  0.330000
33  87 others                                                          26.260000  1.2%   5,849  0.004490  0.000000  1.540000
34  ---------------------------------------------------------------  ----------- -----  -------  --------  --------  --------
35  TOTAL (97)                                                       2,233.450000 100.0% 94,898  0.023535  0.000000  6.900000
```

One *update* statement consumes 60.5% of the total response time, and another *select* consumes 34.5%, which is nearly all the remainder. Let's get the *sqlid* values:

```
36  $ mrskew proa021_ora_3639.trc --group='$sqlid'
37  '$sqlid'         DURATION       %    CALLS      MEAN       MIN       MAX
38  --------------  -----------  -----  -------  --------  --------  --------
39  hv=704365403    1,351.330000  60.5%  14,616  0.092456  0.000000  1.430000
40  hv=3277176312     770.730000  34.5%  60,772  0.012682  0.000000  4.190000
41  hv=3705838826      40.130000   1.8%   2,796  0.014353  0.000000  6.900000
42  hv=1232791132      13.900000   0.6%     518  0.026834  0.000000  5.690000
43  hv=2434620459      10.740000   0.5%     388  0.027680  0.000000  0.670000
44  hv=229242746        5.920000   0.3%     295  0.020068  0.000000  0.410000
45  hv=4159616793       5.640000   0.3%   4,725  0.001194  0.000000  0.400000
46  hv=1425443843       3.220000   0.1%      88  0.036591  0.000000  0.450000
47  hv=4294347205       2.480000   0.1%   4,723  0.000525  0.000000  0.060000
48  hv=3685168867       2.340000   0.1%     112  0.020893  0.000000  0.330000
49  101 others         27.020000   1.2%   5,865  0.004607  0.000000  1.540000
50  --------------  -----------  -----  -------  --------  --------  --------
51  TOTAL (111)     2,233.450000 100.0%  94,898  0.023535  0.000000  6.900000
```

Whoops—I forgot—Oracle didn't have *sqlid* values in the trace data until recently, but *mrskew* has me covered. The SQL hash values are shown instead. We can use those in *where* clauses to drill down into a profile for each statement individually. Here is the first one (the *update*):

```
52  $ mrskew proa021_ora_3639.trc --where='$hv eq "704365403"'
53  CALL-NAME                        DURATION       %    CALLS      MEAN       MIN       MAX
54  ------------------------------  -----------  -----  -------  --------  --------  --------
55  EXEC                             1,066.430000 78.9%   1,166  0.914605  0.000000  1.430000
56  global cache lock s to x            86.540000  6.4%   2,787  0.031051  0.000000  0.790000
57  global cache lock open s            72.330000  5.4%   2,778  0.026037  0.000000  0.820000
58  global cache lock open x            33.510000  2.5%     741  0.045223  0.000000  0.960000
59  db file sequential read             32.570000  2.4%   3,530  0.009227  0.000000  0.440000
60  latch free                          23.630000  1.7%     826  0.028608  0.010000  0.800000
61  write complete waits                10.920000  0.8%     148  0.073784  0.000000  0.720000
62  SQL*Net message from client          7.000000  0.5%   1,166  0.006003  0.000000  0.400000
63  log file switch completion           6.980000  0.5%      14  0.498571  0.090000  1.010000
64  row cache lock                       3.520000  0.3%     160  0.022000  0.000000  0.400000
65  5 others                             7.900000  0.6%   1,300  0.006077  0.000000  0.510000
66  ------------------------------  -----------  -----  -------  --------  --------  --------
67  TOTAL (15)                       1,351.330000 100.0% 14,616  0.092456  0.000000  1.430000
```

---

[8] By the way, this profile is a fantastic example of why you should sort a profile in descending order of duration, not in descending order of the call count.

Let's see how much work that statement accomplished in the 1,351 seconds it consumed:

```
68 $ mrskew proa021_ora_3639.trc --where='$hv eq "704365403"' --select='$row' --sl=ROWS --name=dbcall --pre=0
69 CALL-NAME  ROWS      %     CALLS  MEAN  MIN  MAX
70 ---------  ----  ------    -----  ----  ---  ---
71 EXEC          0   0.0%     1,166     0    0    0
72 ---------  ----  ------    -----  ----  ---  ---
73 TOTAL (1)     0 100.0%     1,166     0    0    0
```

This statement processed 0 rows. None. The job executed some update statement 1,166 times, but not a single one ever processed a row. But look at how much work it did within the database buffer cache:

```
74 $ mrskew proa021_ora_3639.trc --where='$hv eq "704365403"' --name=dbcall --select='$lio' --sl=LIO --pre=0
75 CALL-NAME       LIO      %    CALLS  MEAN   MIN   MAX
76 ---------  ---------  ------  -----  -----  -----  -----
77 EXEC       8,216,887  100.0%  1,166  7,047  6,529  8,308
78 ---------  ---------  ------  -----  -----  -----  -----
79 TOTAL (1)  8,216,887  100.0%  1,166  7,047  6,529  8,308
```

The LIO count is 8,216,887 across 1,166 executions, which is an average of ~7,047 LIOs per execution. Let's look at the skew:

```
80 $ mrskew proa021_ora_3639.trc --where='$hv eq "704365403"' --name=dbcall --select='$lio' --sl=LIO --group='$line' --gl=LINE --pre=0
81        LINE        LIO     %  CALLS   MEAN    MIN    MAX
82 -----------  ---------  ----  -----  -----  -----  -----
83        3275      8,308  0.1%      1  8,308  8,308  8,308
84       12133      8,261  0.1%      1  8,261  8,261  8,261
85       25858      8,259  0.1%      1  8,259  8,259  8,259
86       25221      8,258  0.1%      1  8,258  8,258  8,258
87       48669      8,252  0.1%      1  8,252  8,252  8,252
88        4588      8,113  0.1%      1  8,113  8,113  8,113
89       49288      8,105  0.1%      1  8,105  8,105  8,105
90       28763      8,073  0.1%      1  8,073  8,073  8,073
91       39788      8,060  0.1%      1  8,060  8,060  8,060
92       12772      7,916  0.1%      1  7,916  7,916  7,916
93 1,156 others 8,135,282 99.0%  1,156  7,037  6,529  7,909
94 -----------  ---------  ----  -----  -----  -----  -----
95 TOTAL (1,166) 8,216,887 100.0% 1,166  7,047  6,529  8,308
```

That's a uniform distribution of LIO calls per *exec* call (one per line in the trace file, whose line numbers you can see here). Even the call that did the most (8,308) LIOs didn't do considerably more of them than the average number of LIOs per call (7,047, computed earlier). So all the calls are struggling from pretty much the same problem of doing lots of work for no productive results. Now, let's look at the SQL:

```
96 $ grep -A1 704365403 proa021_ora_3639.trc | grep -v PARSING | grep -v "^--" | head -1
97 update po_requisitions_interface  set requisition_header_id=:b0 where (req_number_segment1=:b1 and request_id=:b2)
```

We're lucky; that's some easy SQL to look at. It's of course the query part of the update that's inefficient. Before the update statement can actually update rows, the statement has to execute the query part of the statement to determine which rows need updating.

There is no execution plan in the trace file, but you can tell from the 3,530 *db file sequential read* calls in the prior profile that the statement is probably doing single-block reads.[9] Let's verify:

```
98  $ mrskew proa021_ora_3639.trc --where='$hv eq "704365403"' --name=read --group='$p3' --gl=BLKS/CALL
99  BLKS/CALL   DURATION     %    CALLS    MEAN       MIN       MAX
100 ---------  ---------  ------  -----  --------  --------  --------
101         1  32.570000  100.0%  3,530  0.009227  0.000000  0.440000
102 ---------  ---------  ------  -----  --------  --------  --------
103 TOTAL (1)  32.570000  100.0%  3,530  0.009227  0.000000  0.440000
```

That's right, all 3,530 calls were 1-block reads, so we can infer even before seeing an execution plan that the query was using an index. Investigation of an *explain plan* for the statement revealed that there was an index on the *request_id* column, but not the *req_number_segment1* column. The index on the *request_id* column was highly un-selective and therefore not helpful. The statement was reading virtually every block of the table being updated, looking for rows to update, but never finding any. Creation of a composite index on both columns ((request_id, req_number_segment1), in that order) will reduce the LIO count from an average of over 7,000 LIOs per *exec* call, to roughly 7 LIOs per *exec* call.

---

[9] *db file sequential read* calls are not *always* single-block read calls. So we verify.

Recall the statement's profile from before:

```
104  $ mrskew proa021_ora_3639.trc --where='$hv eq "704365403"'
105  CALL-NAME                        DURATION       %    CALLS      MEAN       MIN       MAX
106  -------------------------    ------------   -----   ------   --------  --------  --------
107  EXEC                         1,066.430000   78.9%    1,166   0.914605  0.000000  1.430000
108  global cache lock s to x        86.540000    6.4%    2,787   0.031051  0.000000  0.790000
109  global cache lock open s        72.330000    5.4%    2,778   0.026037  0.000000  0.820000
110  global cache lock open x        33.510000    2.5%      741   0.045223  0.000000  0.960000
111  db file sequential read         32.570000    2.4%    3,530   0.009227  0.000000  0.440000
112  latch free                      23.630000    1.7%      826   0.028608  0.010000  0.800000
113  write complete waits            10.920000    0.8%      148   0.073784  0.000000  0.720000
114  SQL*Net message from client      7.000000    0.5%    1,166   0.006003  0.000000  0.400000
115  log file switch completion       6.980000    0.5%       14   0.498571  0.090000  1.010000
116  row cache lock                   3.520000    0.3%      160   0.022000  0.000000  0.400000
117  5 others                         7.900000    0.6%    1,300   0.006077  0.000000  0.510000
118  -------------------------    ------------   -----   ------   --------  --------  --------
119  TOTAL (15)                   1,351.330000  100.0%   14,616   0.092456  0.000000  1.430000
```

Reducing the LIO count by a factor of ~1,000 should reduce the duration of our *exec* calls by a factor of ~1,000, too. So we should expect that the new *exec* call total duration will improve from 1,066 s to roughly 1 s. That's a ~1,065-second reduction in the task's total response time of ~2,500 seconds.

Another great thing about eliminating LIOs is the peripheral benefits this task will receive by eliminating the LIO-related processing time, too. For example, what are the *global cache lock…* events there for? To synchronize two or more database buffer caches in a multi-instance system. With fewer LIO calls to manage, the Oracle Database kernel will have fewer lock open and lock conversion calls to make, which should save most of the 86 + 72 + 33 seconds those calls are now consuming. Why are the *db file sequential read* events in the profile? Because there are so many LIO calls to the database buffer cache for database blocks that the cache doesn't contain, so the Oracle kernel has to read them from disk. With 99.9% of the LIO calls eliminated, it's reasonable to expect that 99.9% of the time spent reading will be eliminated, too, for a total savings of ~1,290 s.

Now, how about that second SQL statement?

```
120  $ mrskew proa021_ora_3639.trc --group='$sqlid'
121  '$sqlid'             DURATION       %    CALLS      MEAN       MIN       MAX
122  --------------   ------------   -----   ------   --------  --------  --------
123  hv=704365403     1,351.330000   60.5%   14,616   0.092456  0.000000  1.430000
124  hv=3277176312      770.730000   34.5%   60,772   0.012682  0.000000  4.190000
125  hv=3705838826       40.130000    1.8%    2,796   0.014353  0.000000  6.900000
126  hv=1232791132       13.900000    0.6%      518   0.026834  0.000000  5.690000
127  hv=2434620459       10.740000    0.5%      388   0.027680  0.000000  0.670000
128  hv=229242746         5.920000    0.3%      295   0.020068  0.000000  0.410000
129  hv=4159616793        5.640000    0.3%    4,725   0.001194  0.000000  0.400000
130  hv=1425443843        3.220000    0.1%       88   0.036591  0.000000  0.450000
131  hv=4294347205        2.480000    0.1%    4,723   0.000525  0.000000  0.060000
132  hv=3685168867        2.340000    0.1%      112   0.020893  0.000000  0.330000
133  101 others          27.020000    1.2%    5,865   0.004607  0.000000  1.540000
134  --------------   ------------   -----   ------   --------  --------  --------
135  TOTAL (111)      2,233.450000  100.0%   94,898   0.023535  0.000000  6.900000
```

Here is its text:

```
136  $ grep -A1 3277176312 proa021_ora_3639.trc | grep -v PARSING | grep -v "^--" | head -1
137  select req_number_segment1  from po_requisitions_interface where ((req_number_segment1
     is  not null  and requisition_header_id is null ) and  request_id=:b0)
```

Funny thing: it would benefit from the same (`request_id`, `req_number_segment1`) composite index as the update. Let's see how much time that should save for the second statement. First, let's see how much useful work the statement accomplishes:

```
138  $ mrskew proa021_ora_3639.trc --where='$hv eq "3277176312"' --select='$row' --sl=ROWS --name=dbcall --pre=0
139  CALL-NAME    ROWS       %    CALLS  MEAN  MIN  MAX
140  ---------   -----   ------   -----  ----  ---  ---
141  FETCH       1,165   100.0%   1,166     1    0    1
142  ---------   -----   ------   -----  ----  ---  ---
143  TOTAL (1)   1,165   100.0%   1,166     1    0    1
```

Chapter 5. Cases in Oracle Trace Data Analysis

It fetches 1,165 rows in 1,166 *fetch* calls. Want to see how many rows each *fetch* call returned? Seems like probably one row per *fetch* call except for the final *fetch*, which you might guess returns no rows. No need to guess; it's fast and easy to find out:

```
144 $ mrskew proa021_ora_3639.trc --where='$hv eq "3277176312"' --name=dbcall --select='$row' --sl=ROWS --group='$line' --gl=LINE --pre=0
145          LINE   ROWS     %   CALLS  MEAN  MIN  MAX
146 -------------  -----  ------  -----  ----  ---  ---
147         67521      1    0.1%      1     1    1    1
148         17188      1    0.1%      1     1    1    1
149          4379      1    0.1%      1     1    1    1
150         55430      1    0.1%      1     1    1    1
151         55226      1    0.1%      1     1    1    1
152         13975      1    0.1%      1     1    1    1
153         28530      1    0.1%      1     1    1    1
154         35476      1    0.1%      1     1    1    1
155         47033      1    0.1%      1     1    1    1
156         78218      1    0.1%      1     1    1    1
157   1,156 others  1,155   99.1%  1,156     1    0    1
158 -------------  -----  ------  -----  ----  ---  ---
159 TOTAL (1,166)  1,165  100.0%  1,166     1    0    1
```

There you go: never more than one row per *fetch* call. Now, how much effort in the buffer cache is required to fetch all these rows?

```
160 $ mrskew proa021_ora_3639.trc --where='$hv eq "3277176312"' --name=dbcall --select='$lio' --sl=LIO --pre=0
161 CALL-NAME        LIO       %    CALLS   MEAN  MIN    MAX
162 ---------  ---------  ------    -----  -----  ---  ------
163 FETCH      5,772,519  100.0%    1,166  4,951    0  35,627
164 ---------  ---------  ------    -----  -----  ---  ------
165 TOTAL (1)  5,772,519  100.0%    1,166  4,951    0  35,627
```

It took 5,772,519 database buffer cache touches to produce 1,166 rows, for an average LIO count of ~4,000 LIOs per row fetched. The index should reduce that number to about 7 LIOs per row, which is a time reduction for *fetch* calls (and the syscalls made by *fetch* calls) by a factor of ~600. Now, let's see the profile for the statement, so we can predict the savings:

```
166 $ mrskew proa021_ora_3639.trc --where='$hv eq "3277176312"'
167 CALL-NAME                   DURATION       %   CALLS      MEAN       MIN       MAX
168 -----------------------   ----------  ------  ------  --------  --------  --------
169 db file sequential read   389.980000   50.6%  57,213  0.006816  0.000000  1.730000
170 FETCH                     371.920000   48.3%   1,166  0.318971  0.000000  4.190000
171 SQL*Net message from client 7.000000    0.9%   1,166  0.006003  0.000000  0.450000
172 latch free                  1.830000    0.2%      62  0.029516  0.010000  0.400000
173 SQL*Net message to client   0.000000    0.0%   1,165  0.000000  0.000000  0.000000
174 -----------------------   ----------  ------  ------  --------  --------  --------
175 TOTAL (5)                 770.730000  100.0%  60,772  0.012682  0.000000  4.190000
```

We should thus expect the 389.98-second *db file sequential read* time to fall to roughly half a second, and the 371.92-second *fetch* time to fall also to roughly half a second. The *latch free* time will probably go away, too. With *mrskew* it would be easy to group by the latch type, which is $p2, to see if the latch acquisition activity is all on behalf of the fetch. However, since (a) it accounts for so little total time, and (b) there's nothing besides fetching that *could* be making latch acquisition calls, the *latch free* time will evaporate, too. The total savings for this statement should, then, be ~389.48 + 371.42 ≈ 760.9 s.

Combining the ~760-second anticipated savings for the *select* statement and the ~1,290-second anticipated savings for the update, the new index should reduce the response time of the ~2,500-second task by ~2,050 to ~450 s.

CONCLUSION

This is a good example of an application that spends the dominant proportion of its duration doing real work: making calls like *exec*, *db file sequential read*, and *fetch*. These are of course legitimate operations for a database application to do, but in this case, the application was doing far more work than was really required for production of the program's output. The skew assessment drill-down got to the root of the problem in just a few steps:

- Which call types were taking the most time?
- Which SQL statements contributed the most to those call types?
- How much result did those statements produce?

- How much work did those statements execute to produce those results?
- Is that amount of work reasonable?

Perhaps the most remarkable aspect of profiling and skew analysis is the accuracy with which you can predict the outcome of a proposed remedy. It gives you the confidence you need and the justifications your colleagues will require to authorize moving forward with the remedies you'll suggest.

EXERCISES

9. How would you find out which latch types were the cause of the *latch free* call duration in this profile?

BOOK ORDER, WITH CONNECTION POOLING

Connection pooling. The mere mention of it inspires fear and dread into the hearts of many Oracle performance analysts. With connection pooling comes an application whose users' tasks can be incredibly difficult to identify on the database server, because each task can scatter dbcalls and syscalls across several processes on the database server. Aggregating these calls into a coherent picture of a user's task is impossible with most monitoring software, but with just a little bit of simple instrumentation, the Method R Tools solve everything. This section shows how.

>   Task name: Book Order
>   Response time: ~50 seconds
>   Trace file size: 10 files, 129 MB total
> Trace file line count: 10 files, 2,327,677 lines total
>
> Typical *mrskew* execution duration: 45 seconds

In this example, several users executing the business task named "oe book" are complaining that their tasks are consuming as much as 50 seconds apiece. Tracing has been enabled for the entire application for a minute or two, during a period when users were experiencing the problem. Here are the trace files:

```
 1  $ ls -al
 2  total 265144
 3  drwx------@ 12 carymillsap  staff       408 Sep 19 17:00 .
 4  drwxr-xr-x   8 carymillsap  staff       272 Sep 17 10:26 ..
 5  -rw-r-----    1 carymillsap  staff  11521997 Sep 16 19:15 V11107_ora_27272.trc
 6  -rw-r-----@  1 carymillsap  staff  21514552 Sep 16 19:15 V11107_ora_27274.trc
 7  -rw-r-----@  1 carymillsap  staff  14331620 Sep 16 19:15 V11107_ora_27276.trc
 8  -rw-r-----@  1 carymillsap  staff  11200383 Sep 16 19:15 V11107_ora_27278.trc
 9  -rw-r-----@  1 carymillsap  staff  11916804 Sep 16 19:15 V11107_ora_27280.trc
10  -rw-r-----@  1 carymillsap  staff  11413236 Sep 16 19:15 V11107_ora_27282.trc
11  -rw-r-----@  1 carymillsap  staff  14924711 Sep 16 19:15 V11107_ora_27284.trc
12  -rw-r-----@  1 carymillsap  staff  11928663 Sep 16 19:15 V11107_ora_27286.trc
13  -rw-r-----@  1 carymillsap  staff  14417278 Sep 16 19:15 V11107_ora_27288.trc
14  -rw-r-----@  1 carymillsap  staff  12568258 Sep 16 19:15 V11107_ora_27290.trc
```

There are ten trace files into which trace data has been accumulated. A quick *mrls* command ensures that they're all from the appropriate time period:

```
15  $ mrls --sort=file
16       R  ORA                    START                           END FILE
17   93.305 11.1 2011-09-16T19:13:47.164-0500 2011-09-16T19:15:20.469-0500 V11107_ora_27272.trc
18  117.673 11.1 2011-09-16T19:13:47.228-0500 2011-09-16T19:15:44.901-0500 V11107_ora_27274.trc
19  101.010 11.1 2011-09-16T19:13:47.194-0500 2011-09-16T19:15:28.204-0500 V11107_ora_27276.trc
20   90.575 11.1 2011-09-16T19:13:47.233-0500 2011-09-16T19:15:17.808-0500 V11107_ora_27278.trc
21   93.103 11.1 2011-09-16T19:13:47.253-0500 2011-09-16T19:15:20.355-0500 V11107_ora_27280.trc
22   91.891 11.1 2011-09-16T19:13:47.383-0500 2011-09-16T19:15:19.274-0500 V11107_ora_27282.trc
23  102.912 11.1 2011-09-16T19:13:47.347-0500 2011-09-16T19:15:30.259-0500 V11107_ora_27284.trc
24   93.341 11.1 2011-09-16T19:13:47.327-0500 2011-09-16T19:15:20.669-0500 V11107_ora_27286.trc
25  101.621 11.1 2011-09-16T19:13:47.451-0500 2011-09-16T19:15:29.073-0500 V11107_ora_27288.trc
26   94.826 11.1 2011-09-16T19:13:47.322-0500 2011-09-16T19:15:22.148-0500 V11107_ora_27290.trc
```

Chapter 5. Cases in Oracle Trace Data Analysis

All the start times for the files are approximately the same, and all the file end times are within a few seconds of each other. It's the set of files I had expected. So, let's cut right to the chase. Let's have a look at the "oe book" task executions:

```
27 $ mrskew *.trc --where='$mod eq "oe" and $act eq "book"' --group='"$mod $act $client_id"' --gl='MOD ACT CLIENT'
28 MOD ACT CLIENT                                                        DURATION       %     CALLS      MEAN       MIN       MAX
29 ---------------------------------------------------------------      ---------   -----   -------   --------  --------  --------
30 oe book 10.17.22.12  XPHELPS    eec4c72f-b685-4b5b-8447-688b8aecbc6f  49.699960  21.4%    74,351   0.000668  0.000000  0.220486
31 oe book 10.17.22.76  VSAUNDERS  ab9fdc58-6c09-4fe2-b253-8b2c191e4671  48.977182  21.1%   108,760   0.000450  0.000000  0.154742
32 oe book 10.17.23.174 PDRAKE     ab8e9d2c-8ba6-4c5f-8673-13a3c958af7a  47.520700  20.4%    49,059   0.000969  0.000000  0.439000
33 oe book 10.17.24.138 VMICHAEL   ced4bdee-f0d8-44cd-a878-f0b938802bc0  43.597261  18.8%    43,983   0.000991  0.000000  0.189084
34 oe book 10.17.22.112 ZMCDONALD  4515c784-028f-4964-9e37-0b283b4ca304  11.584065   5.0%    11,247   0.001030  0.000000  0.171841
35 oe book 10.17.24.80  NRICE      06937ebf-7cd3-4422-9ea7-dc32c3262353   7.863002   3.4%     9,774   0.000804  0.000000  0.124693
36 oe book 10.17.24.107 WBATTLE    2f05d335-f8c6-4724-ab00-edb09a9cdbe4   4.560992   2.0%     5,211   0.000875  0.000000  0.148082
37 oe book 10.17.22.174 RCLEMENTS  e104ee85-6be1-40b2-a413-7f5c5fd9e045   4.096453   1.8%     6,058   0.000676  0.000000  0.079804
38 oe book 10.17.23.146 JGRAVES    1f023512-f2fa-4caa-bc91-f1fb93b690c1   2.699335   1.2%     2,012   0.001342  0.000000  0.084005
39 oe book 10.17.23.249 TGOODWIN   f27ecae9-ca6b-4822-ae4c-e8facb74adba   2.600538   1.1%     3,375   0.000771  0.000000  0.084006
40 16 others                                                              9.233707   4.0%    10,279   0.000898  0.000000  0.338693
41                                                                      ---------   -----   -------   --------  --------  --------
42 TOTAL (26)                                                           232.433195 100.0%   324,109   0.000717  0.000000  0.439000
```

...And there's the answer. during the observation interval, four users had "oe book" response times of nearly 50 seconds. Xavier Phelps, Vern Saunders, Paula Drake, and Vi Michael. Let's drill into Xavier's execution, using the universally unique id (UUID) of his execution as a *where* clause filter. I'll use the Perl "=~" regular expression match operator, which allows me to specify just the UUID part of Xavier's client id:

```
43 $ mrskew *.trc --where='$client_id =~ /eec4c72f-b685-4b5b-8447-688b8aecbc6f/'
44 CALL-NAME                    DURATION      %    CALLS      MEAN       MIN       MAX
45 --------------------------  ---------  -----   ------   --------  --------  --------
46 SQL*Net message from client 40.507440  81.5%   18,585   0.002180  0.000000  0.220486
47 EXEC                         6.684420  13.4%   18,585   0.000360  0.000000  0.128008
48 FETCH                        2.388145   4.8%   18,583   0.000129  0.000000  0.120008
49 SQL*Net message to client    0.094487   0.2%   18,585   0.000005  0.000000  0.018525
50 cursor: pin S wait on X      0.025463   0.1%        4   0.006366  0.000000  0.011166
51 cursor: pin S                0.000005   0.0%        5   0.000001  0.000000  0.000005
52 PARSE                        0.000000   0.0%        2   0.000000  0.000000  0.000000
53 pooled connection free       0.000000   0.0%        1   0.000000  0.000000  0.000000
54 XCTEND                       0.000000   0.0%        1   0.000000  0.000000  0.000000
55 --------------------------  ---------  -----   ------   --------  --------  --------
56 TOTAL (9)                   49.699960 100.0%   74,351   0.000668  0.000000  0.220486
```

The dominant response time contributor is 18,585 calls to *SQL*Net message from client*. Are these durations part of Xavier's response time? Or are they ignorable "idle" events? The answer depends upon how the application is instrumented. If the instrumentation is sloppy (identifying code path as "oe book" that's not really code path for which a user is awaiting "oe book" results), then you wouldn't be able to trust the profile you see here.

However, the instrumentation in this application never calls code path "oe book" unless it is code path for which a user is awaiting "oe book" results. Thus, you can trust the profile. Indeed, 18,585 short-duration *SQL*Net message from client* calls is what Xavier is spending 81.5% of his 49.7 s waiting for. This number of calls—18,585—is approximately the same as both the *exec* call and *fetch* call counts.

Here is the histogram showing all the *SQL*Net message from client* call durations for Xavier's task:

```
57 $ mrskew *.trc --where='$client_id =~ /eec4c72f-b685-4b5b-8447-688b8aecbc6f/' --name='SQL\*Net message from client' --rc=p10
58     RANGE {min ≤ e < max}     DURATION     %     CALLS      MEAN       MIN       MAX
59 ---------------------------  ---------  -----   ------   --------  --------  --------
60  1.     0.000000    0.000001  0.000000   0.0%        3   0.000000  0.000000  0.000000
61  2.     0.000001    0.000010
62  3.     0.000010    0.000100
63  4.     0.000100    0.001000  0.000358   0.0%        5   0.000072  0.000041  0.000092
64  5.     0.001000    0.010000  8.391000  20.7%   13,947   0.000602  0.000104  0.000999
65  6.     0.010000    0.100000  9.307749  23.0%    3,822   0.002435  0.001000  0.009955
66  7.     0.100000    1.000000 20.877546  51.5%      793   0.026327  0.010001  0.099419
67  8.     1.000000   10.000000  1.930787   4.8%       15   0.128719  0.103157  0.220486
68  9.    10.000000  100.000000
69 10.   100.000000 1,000.000000
70 11. 1,000.000000         +∞
71 ---------------------------  ---------  -----   ------   --------  --------  --------
72              TOTAL (11)      40.507440 100.0%   18,585   0.002180  0.000000  0.220486
```

The only legitimate reason for doing a lot of network I/O is to process a lot of data. So let's see how many rows each dbcall returns:

```
73  $ mrskew *.trc --where='$client_id =~ /eec4c72f-b685-4b5b-8447-688b8aecbc6f/' --name=dbcall --select='$row' --sl=ROWS --pre=0
74  CALL-NAME      ROWS      %   CALLS  MEAN  MIN  MAX
75  ---------    ------  ------  ------  ----  ---  ---
76  FETCH        18,378  100.0%  18,583     1    0    1
77  EXEC              2    0.0%  18,585     0    0    1
78  PARSE             0    0.0%       2     0    0    0
79  XCTEND            0    0.0%       1     0    0    0
80  ---------    ------  ------  ------  ----  ---  ---
81  TOTAL (4)    18,380  100.0%  37,171     0    0    1
```

That's just 1 row per call on average, and in fact, *never* more than 1 row per call. It's time to look at the trace file. First, where should we look?

```
82  $ mrskew *.trc --where='$client_id =~ /eec4c72f-b685-4b5b-8447-688b8aecbc6f/' \
83  > --name='SQL\*Net message from client' --group='"$file $line"' --gl='FILE LINE'
84  FILE LINE                    DURATION      %   CALLS      MEAN       MIN       MAX
85  -------------------------    --------  -----  ------  --------  --------  --------
86  V11107_ora_27284.trc 146783  0.220486   0.5%       1  0.220486  0.220486  0.220486
87  V11107_ora_27284.trc 82770   0.181826   0.4%       1  0.181826  0.181826  0.181826
88  V11107_ora_27284.trc 121473  0.164216   0.4%       1  0.164216  0.164216  0.164216
89  V11107_ora_27284.trc 102868  0.128376   0.3%       1  0.128376  0.128376  0.128376
90  V11107_ora_27284.trc 120701  0.126663   0.3%       1  0.126663  0.126663  0.126663
91  V11107_ora_27284.trc 246050  0.120756   0.3%       1  0.120756  0.120756  0.120756
92  V11107_ora_27284.trc 74221   0.119724   0.3%       1  0.119724  0.119724  0.119724
93  V11107_ora_27284.trc 120861  0.119231   0.3%       1  0.119231  0.119231  0.119231
94  V11107_ora_27284.trc 181952  0.109707   0.3%       1  0.109707  0.109707  0.109707
95  V11107_ora_27284.trc 192950  0.109635   0.3%       1  0.109635  0.109635  0.109635
96  18,575 others               39.106820  96.5%  18,575  0.002105  0.000000  0.108649
97  -------------------------   ---------  -----  ------  --------  --------  --------
98  TOTAL (18,585)              40.507440 100.0%  18,585  0.002180  0.000000  0.220486
```

The worst offending *SQL*Net message from client* call is on line 146,783 of the trace file *V11107_ora_27284.trc*, so let's look at the trace data surrounding that line:

```
99   $ nl -ba V11107_ora_27284.trc | head -146793 | tail -16
100  146778 EXEC #4:c=0,e=127,p=0,cr=0,cu=0,mis=0,r=0,dep=0,og=1,plh=3475835415,tim=1316218505289745
101  146779 WAIT #4: nam='SQL*Net message to client' ela= 3 driver id=1952673792 #bytes=1 p3=0 obj#=-1 tim=1316218505308723
102  146780 FETCH #4:c=0,e=66,p=0,cr=3,cu=0,mis=0,r=1,dep=0,og=1,plh=3475835415,tim=1316218505308767
103  146781
104  146782 *** 2011-09-16 19:15:05.530
105  146783 WAIT #4: nam='SQL*Net message from client' ela= 220486 driver id=1952673792 #bytes=1 p3=0 obj#=-1 tim=1316218505529322
106  146784 BINDS #4:
107  146785  Bind#0
108  146786   oacdty=02 mxl=22(22) mxlc=00 mal=00 scl=00 pre=00
109  146787   oacflg=03 fl2=1000000 frm=01 csi=178 siz=24 off=0
110  146788   kxsbbbfp=00322ae4  bln=22  avl=02  flg=05
111  146789   value=48
112  146790 EXEC #4:c=0,e=0,p=0,cr=0,cu=0,mis=0,r=0,dep=0,og=1,plh=3475835415,tim=1316218505530402
113  146791 WAIT #4: nam='SQL*Net message to client' ela= 4 driver id=1952673792 #bytes=1 p3=0 obj#=-1 tim=1316218505569850
114  146792 FETCH #4:c=0,e=119,p=0,cr=3,cu=0,mis=0,r=1,dep=0,og=1,plh=3475835415,tim=1316218505569944
115  146793 WAIT #4: nam='SQL*Net message from client' ela= 29006 driver id=1952673792 #bytes=1 p3=0 obj#=-1 tim=1316218505599051
```

And what is the definition of cursor #4 at for these calls?

```
116  $ head -146783 V11107_ora_27284.trc | grep -n -A1 "PARSING IN CURSOR #4" | tail -2
117  69940:PARSING IN CURSOR #4 len=35 dep=0 uid=81 oct=3 lid=81 tim=1316218463952836 hv=4246579568 ad='28fee054' sqlid='6m3a3v3yjvabh'
118  69941-select * from oe_book where id = :1
```

Time to look at the application code with the question, "Why does '`select * from oe_book where id = :1`' process only one row at a time?" It probably shouldn't. Your goal is for the "oe_book" program to use array processing with both the *exec* and *fetch* dbcalls to bring the *SQL*Net message from client* call count as close to 1 as possible.

How much time will you save if you can eliminate all but one *SQL*Net message from client* call? The answer is in the top line of this profile:

```
119  $ mrskew *.trc --where='$client_id =~ /eec4c72f-b685-4b5b-8447-688b8aecbc6f/'
120  CALL-NAME                   DURATION      %   CALLS      MEAN       MIN       MAX
121  -------------------------   --------  -----  ------  --------  --------  --------
122  SQL*Net message from client 40.507440  81.5%  18,585  0.002180  0.000000  0.220486
123  EXEC                         6.684420  13.4%  18,585  0.000360  0.000000  0.128008
124  FETCH                        2.388145   4.8%  18,583  0.000129  0.000000  0.120008
125  SQL*Net message to client    0.094487   0.2%  18,585  0.000005  0.000000  0.018525
126  cursor: pin S wait on X      0.025463   0.1%       4  0.006366  0.000000  0.011166
127  cursor: pin S                0.000005   0.0%       5  0.000001  0.000000  0.000005
128  PARSE                        0.000000   0.0%       2  0.000000  0.000000  0.000000
129  pooled connection free       0.000000   0.0%       1  0.000000  0.000000  0.000000
130  XCTEND                       0.000000   0.0%       1  0.000000  0.000000  0.000000
131  -------------------------   --------  -----  ------  --------  --------  --------
132  TOTAL (9)                   49.699960 100.0%  74,351  0.000668  0.000000  0.220486
```

If you eliminate all but one of the 18,585 calls, you'll leave .220 seconds of *SQL*Net message from client* time, in the worst possible case (that's if you're unlucky

Chapter 5. Cases in Oracle Trace Data Analysis

enough to eliminate all but the one call with the worst latency). In addition, reducing the number of *exec* and *fetch* calls will reduce the time associated with making those calls as well. This program is a case of an application program that processes its data one row at a time. Performance is not too bad for people who need to process only a few rows, but for Xavier and a few others, who are processing tens of thousands of rows per order, the network I/O overhead of this application design error creates a miserable performance experience.

A fantastic thing about trace data is that with just a little bit of application instrumentation, you have access to per-call timing data about any execution of any task that you've instrumented. In our connection pooling case, all it took was to set each session's client identifier—using either *dbms_session.set_identifier* or the Oracle user session handle attributes described in chapter 3—to contain just three elements:

- The user's IP address;
- The user's login id;
- And a UUID (universally unique identifier) that identifies each execution of a task.

With just this little bit of information in the trace file, you can drill into any task execution you want. That is extraordinary diagnostic power. Here are a few more *mrskew* queries to whet your appetite. First, here's a query that shows all task execution response times in a trace file directory, in descending order of response time:

```
133 $ mrskew *.trc --group='"$mod/$act/$client_id"' --gl=MOD/ACT/CLIENT
134 MOD/ACT/CLIENT                                                       DURATION       %     CALLS      MEAN       MIN       MAX
135 ------------------------------------------------------------------  ---------   -----   -------  --------  --------  --------
136 oe/book/10.17.22.12   XPHELPS  eec4c72f-b685-4b5b-8447-688b8aecbc6f   49.699960   6.7%    74,351  0.000668  0.000000  0.220486
137 oe/book/10.17.22.76   VSAUNDERS ab9fdc58-6c09-4fe2-b253-8b2c191e4671  48.977182   6.6%   108,760  0.000450  0.000000  0.154742
138 oe/book/10.17.23.174  PDRAKE   ab8e9d2c-8ba6-4c5f-8673-13a3c958af7a   47.520700   6.4%    49,059  0.000969  0.000000  0.439000
139 oe/book/10.17.24.138  VMICHAEL ced4bdee-f0d8-44cd-a878-f0b938802bc0   43.597261   5.9%    43,983  0.000991  0.000000  0.189084
140 pa/mtch/10.17.22.115  MSTANLEY 5c01b8e5-e0d3-44c2-ada8-c8b1ed17abee   23.714088   3.2%    21,701  0.001093  0.000000  0.151083
141 pa/reco/10.17.22.249  TIRWIN   2161468f-5504-419a-8226-f5ee0ad39b73   22.946626   3.1%    23,882  0.000961  0.000000  0.132008
142 pa/mtch/10.17.21.167  ESANDERS e463a90b-32a8-49fc-81e8-0c2559269e1e   22.607869   3.0%    24,175  0.000935  0.000000  0.128223
143 oe/pick/10.17.22.98   DHALEY   8a41c465-e00f-43b2-afcd-ba4edd7df899   21.967559   3.0%    22,522  0.000975  0.000000  0.159246
144 oe/ship/10.17.21.239  UDECKER  052b3d18-e992-46a2-8ae3-87427c78598e   20.312153   2.7%    19,922  0.001020  0.000000  0.137756
145 oe/ship/10.17.21.14   LDILLARD 2270f4b4-1c46-4ad7-ac6a-2ed1fc13c283   20.024742   2.7%    19,818  0.001010  0.000000  0.138701
146 158 others                                                           420.181628  56.7%   522,022  0.000805  0.000000  0.517000
147 ------------------------------------------------------------------  ---------   -----   -------  --------  --------  --------
148 TOTAL (168)                                                          741.549768 100.0%   930,195  0.000797  0.000000  0.517000
```

Here is a query that shows response time grouped by only module and action:

```
149 $ mrskew *.trc --group='"$mod/$act"' --gl=MOD/ACT
150 MOD/ACT     DURATION       %     CALLS      MEAN       MIN       MAX
151 --------  ----------   -----   -------  --------  --------  --------
152 oe/book   232.433195   31.3%   324,109  0.000717  0.000000  0.439000
153 pa/mtch   159.855674   21.6%   190,551  0.000839  0.000000  0.293000
154 oe/ship   113.720698   15.3%   129,670  0.000877  0.000000  0.394000
155 pa/corr    94.278553   12.7%   130,234  0.000724  0.000000  0.301000
156 pa/reco    74.152792   10.0%    83,006  0.000893  0.000000  0.413000
157 oe/pick    67.108856    9.0%    72,625  0.000924  0.000000  0.517000
158 --------  ----------   -----   -------  --------  --------  --------
159 TOTAL (6) 741.549768  100.0%   930,195  0.000797  0.000000  0.517000
```

From this report, you can find the inspiration to ask questions like, "Is it appropriate for 31.3% of our database server workload to be 'oe book' processing?"

Finally, here is a *mrskew* query that shows total response time in a trace file directory, grouped by the name of the user who waited for it. From this query, you can tell who's using the most capacity (and doing the most work) on the system.

```
160 $ mrskew *.trc --group='(split(" ", $client_id))[1]' --gl=USERNAME
161 USERNAME     DURATION       %     CALLS      MEAN       MIN       MAX
162 ---------  ----------   -----   -------  --------  --------  --------
163 XPHELPS     49.699960    6.7%    74,351  0.000668  0.000000  0.220486
164 VSAUNDERS   48.977182    6.6%   108,760  0.000450  0.000000  0.154742
165 PDRAKE      47.520700    6.4%    49,059  0.000969  0.000000  0.439000
166 VMICHAEL    43.597261    5.9%    43,983  0.000991  0.000000  0.189084
167 MSTANLEY    23.714088    3.2%    21,701  0.001093  0.000000  0.151083
168 TIRWIN      22.946626    3.1%    23,882  0.000961  0.000000  0.132008
169 ESANDERS    22.607869    3.0%    24,175  0.000935  0.000000  0.128223
170 DHALEY      21.967559    3.0%    22,522  0.000975  0.000000  0.159246
171 UDECKER     20.312153    2.7%    19,922  0.001020  0.000000  0.137756
172 LDILLARD    20.024742    2.7%    19,818  0.001010  0.000000  0.138701
173 152 others 420.181628   56.7%   522,022  0.000805  0.000000  0.517000
174 ---------  ----------   -----   -------  --------  --------  --------
175 TOTAL (162) 741.549768 100.0%   930,195  0.000797  0.000000  0.517000
```

Conclusion

People are justifiably nervous about applications that use Oracle connection pooling, because it complicates the conceptual model of how a business task engages Oracle processes to get work done. But if the application uses standard Oracle instrumentation to identify its code path by assigning a service name, module name, action name, and client identifier, then there are plenty of hooks in the trace data by which to create useful profiles.

Exercises

10. Is there a pattern of poor performance for users at certain geographical locations? Using the *client_id* instrumentation provided in this example, how would you write a *mrskew* query that groups by IP address?

11. What *mrskew* query would show how much activity the user at IP address 10.17.24.138 did between 7:15 P.M. and 7:16 P.M. on 2011-09-16?

Oracle Exadata

How does Oracle Exadata change the way we analyze performance? In this example, you'll see that the steps for analyzing a trace file on Oracle Database 11.2 for Exadata are the same as you've already seen.

Task name: Query running on Oracle Exadata
Response time: ~2.5 seconds
Trace file size: 303 KB
Trace file line count: 3,107
Typical *mrskew* execution duration: <1 second

First thing you should look at is the overall response time for the file:

```
1  $ mrls exa_13899.trc
2       R   ORA                    START                        END FILE
3  51.433  11.2  2011-02-24T19:29:23.881+0000  2011-02-24T19:30:15.314+0000  exa_13899.trc
```

Since the user experience was a response time of ~2.5 s, you can see that we have a familiar problem. This is what a trace file looks like when someone uses Oracle *sqlplus* to trace some code path, but with tracing turned on too early or turned off too late. For curiosity's sake, let's group the time by Oracle module and action name:

```
4  $ mrskew exa_13899.trc --group='"$module / $action"'
5  '"$module / $action"'   DURATION       %    CALLS      MEAN       MIN        MAX
6  ---------------------  ----------  ------   -----   --------  --------  ---------
7  SQL*Plus /              51.457042  100.0%   2,570   0.020022  0.000000  30.447430
8  ---------------------  ----------  ------   -----   --------  --------  ---------
9  TOTAL (1)               51.457042  100.0%   2,570   0.020022  0.000000  30.447430
```

Sure enough, the trace file was created by a *sqlplus* session.

Chapter 5. Cases in Oracle Trace Data Analysis

At this point, you should expect for the profile to contain mostly *SQL*Net message from client* call time. Let's see:

```
10  $ mrskew exa_13899.trc
11  CALL-NAME                        DURATION       %   CALLS       MEAN       MIN       MAX
12  ------------------------------  ---------  ------  ------  ---------  --------  --------
13  SQL*Net message from client     48.924887   95.1%       3  16.308296  0.000209  30.447430
14  cell smart table scan            1.111117    2.2%   2,419   0.000459  0.000001   0.031672
15  FETCH                            1.036843    2.0%       2   0.518421  0.000000   1.036843
16  cell single block physical read  0.272435    0.5%      53   0.005140  0.000561   0.009779
17  cell multiblock physical read    0.062236    0.1%      13   0.004787  0.001750   0.009409
18  PARSE                            0.041994    0.1%       1   0.041994  0.041994   0.041994
19  gc cr grant 2-way                0.003095    0.0%      21   0.000147  0.000077   0.000234
20  gc cr multi block request        0.001626    0.0%       5   0.000325  0.000245   0.000390
21  reliable message                 0.001114    0.0%       1   0.001114  0.001114   0.001114
22  row cache lock                   0.000590    0.0%       2   0.000295  0.000138   0.000452
23  10 others                        0.001105    0.0%      50   0.000022  0.000000   0.000386
24  ------------------------------  ---------  ------  ------  ---------  --------  --------
25  TOTAL (20)                      51.457042  100.0%   2,570   0.020022  0.000000  30.447430
```

Yes. Let's see the skew by call for *SQL*Net message from client* calls:

```
26  $ mrskew exa_13899.trc --name='SQL\*Net message from client' --group='$line' --gl='LINE#'
27     LINE#   DURATION       %  CALLS       MEAN        MIN        MAX
28  --------  ---------  ------  -----  ---------  ---------  ---------
29        27  30.447430   62.2%      1  30.447430  30.447430  30.447430
30     2984  18.477248   37.8%      1  18.477248  18.477248  18.477248
31     2979   0.000209    0.0%      1   0.000209   0.000209   0.000209
32  --------  ---------  ------  -----  ---------  ---------  ---------
33  TOTAL (3) 48.924887  100.0%      3  16.308296   0.000209  30.447430
```

As expected, two calls that dominate the response time don't belong there. One on line 27 is near the top of the file, and the other on line 2,984 is near the end of the 3,107-line file. So let's get rid of them:

```
34  $ mrcallrm exa_13899.trc --lines=27,2984 >fixed.trc
```

Now we can profile the fixed file, and we should see our expected ~2.5-second response time:

```
35  $ mrskew fixed.trc
36  CALL-NAME                        DURATION       %  CALLS      MEAN       MIN       MAX
37  ------------------------------  ---------  ------  -----  --------  --------  --------
38  cell smart table scan            1.111117   43.9%  2,419  0.000459  0.000001  0.031672
39  FETCH                            1.036843   40.9%      2  0.518421  0.000000  1.036843
40  cell single block physical read  0.272435   10.8%     53  0.005140  0.000561  0.009779
41  cell multiblock physical read    0.062236    2.5%     13  0.004787  0.001750  0.009409
42  PARSE                            0.041994    1.7%      1  0.041994  0.041994  0.041994
43  gc cr grant 2-way                0.003095    0.1%     21  0.000147  0.000077  0.000234
44  gc cr multi block request        0.001626    0.1%      5  0.000325  0.000245  0.000390
45  reliable message                 0.001114    0.0%      1  0.001114  0.001114  0.001114
46  row cache lock                   0.000590    0.0%      2  0.000295  0.000138  0.000452
47  log file sync                    0.000386    0.0%      1  0.000386  0.000386  0.000386
48  10 others                        0.000928    0.0%     52  0.000018  0.000000  0.000214
49  ------------------------------  ---------  ------  -----  --------  --------  --------
50  TOTAL (20)                       2.532364  100.0%  2,570  0.000985  0.000000  1.036843
```

Indeed, we now have a properly time-scoped trace file that explains our 2.532-second response time (and, importantly, *only* our 2.532-second response time). The duration was dominated by *cell smart table scan* and *fetch* calls. Let's see what SQL motivated all the work.

```
51  $ mrskew fixed.trc --group='substr($sql,0,80)'
52  'substr($sql,0,80)'                                                   DURATION       %  CALLS      MEAN       MIN       MAX
53  -------------------------------------------------------------------  ---------  ------  -----  --------  --------  --------
54  select count(*) from accesslog_uncompressed                           2.191518   86.5%  2,435  0.000900  0.000000  1.036843
55  SELECT /* OPT_DYN_SAMP */ /*+ ALL_ROWS IGNORE_WHERE_CLAUSE NO_PARALLE  0.329672   13.0%    117  0.002818  0.000002  0.009779
56  #8 fixed.trc                                                          0.010379    0.4%      3  0.003460  0.000452  0.009366
57  select grantee#,privilege#,nvl(col#,0),max(mod(nvl(option$,0),2))from  0.000407    0.0%      4  0.000102  0.000002  0.000214
58  #0                                                                    0.000386    0.0%      2  0.000193  0.000000  0.000386
59  #11 fixed.trc                                                         0.000002    0.0%      3  0.000001  0.000000  0.000002
60  #2 fixed.trc                                                          0.000000    0.0%      1  0.000000  0.000000  0.000000
61  #9 fixed.trc                                                          0.000000    0.0%      1  0.000000  0.000000  0.000000
62  #5 fixed.trc                                                          0.000000    0.0%      1  0.000000  0.000000  0.000000
63  #1 fixed.trc                                                          0.000000    0.0%      1  0.000000  0.000000  0.000000
64  2 others                                                              0.000000    0.0%      2  0.000000  0.000000  0.000000
65  -------------------------------------------------------------------  ---------  ------  -----  --------  --------  --------
66  TOTAL (12)                                                            2.532364  100.0%  2,570  0.000985  0.000000  1.036843
```

So a single SQL statement, a "`select count(*)`", motivated 86.5% of the task's response time. This kind of statement is, of course, where Oracle Exadata really shines. The new *cell smart table scan* code path, which eliminates most of the unnecessary work that non-Exadata databases would have done.

Here is an overview of skew in *cell smart table scan* call durations:

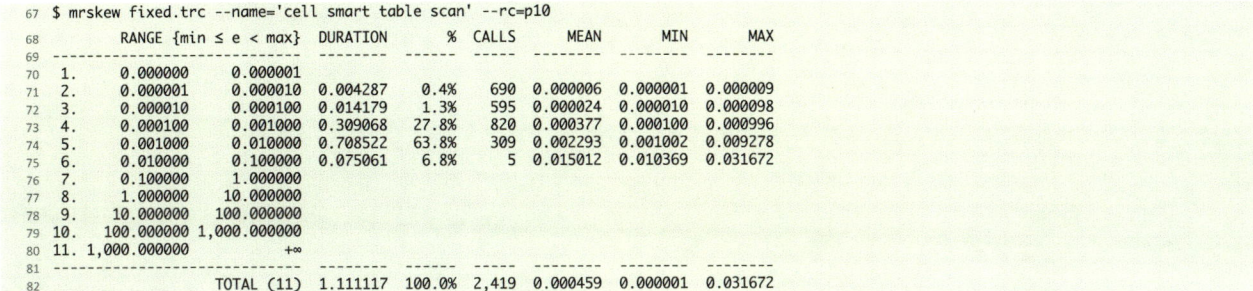

CONCLUSION

Trace files generated by Oracle Exadata are just like trace files generated by Oracle versions since 7.0.12. There are, of course, little differences in trace file formats from one version to the next. The biggest jumps were in version 9.0, 10.2, and 11.2. However, trace files on Oracle Exadata systems are very similar to trace files the Oracle Database was generating over a decade ago on version 7 systems. There are loads of new call names, like *cell smart table scan* and *cell single block physical read*, but the way the trace data works and the way you should analyze it has remained constant for many years.

EXERCISES

12. Once a student asked me, "Why would you ever need to look at a trace file generated on an Oracle Exadata system?" Why would you?

Reference Tables

UNITS OF DURATION

The following units of duration are used extensively throughout this book.

Abbreviation	Unit	Duration (seconds)
h	hour	3,600
m	minute	60
s	second	1
cs	centisecond	.01
ms	millisecond	.001
µs	microsecond	.000 001
	Oracle microsecond	.000 001 024
ns	nanosecond	.000 000 001

These are units commonly used in Oracle Database performance work.

PERFORMANCE INSTRUMENTATION

The following tables suggest the data that you could persist so you can analyze the response time and throughput behavior of specific end-user experiences.

TASK

Attribute Name	Data Type	Description
id	unique id	Key that distinguishes each task from all others
name	string	Optional user-friendly name for the task
service	string	Hierarchical service name (e.g., OCI_ATTR_SERVICE)
module	string	Hierarchical module name (e.g., OCI_ATTR_MODULE)
action	string	Hierarchical action name (e.g., OCI_ATTR_ACTION)

A *task* is a business unit of work. Its attributes are used primarily for identification, so that you can target your traces and other measurements.

Reference Tables

EXPERIENCE

Attribute Name	Data Type	Description
id	unique id	Key that distinguishes each experience from all others
task-id	id	Foreign key id of the task that has been executed
user	string	Identity of the user who executed the task
ip	string	IP address of the user who executed the task
begin	date-time	Time in microseconds at which task execution began
end	date-time	Time in microseconds at which task execution ended
error	error-code	Error code thrown by the execution of the task
work	count	Count of units of work performed by the execution of the task

An *experience* corresponds to a single execution of a *task*. Its attributes give the who/what/when/where information that you'll need to compute response time percentiles, dig into skew in performance among users and locations, and determine the efficiency of the code paths that comprise your system.

Glossary

Amdahl's law. A mathematical model used to find the maximum expected improvement to an overall system when only part of the system is improved (Wikipedia).

axiom. A premise or starting point of reasoning. Also called a *postulate*. As classically conceived, an axiom is a premise so evident as to be accepted as true without controversy (Wikipedia).

bind variable. A *placeholder*.

bottleneck. The resource that dominates the response time for a given task execution.

coherency delay. The duration that a task spends communicating and coordinating access to a shared resource.

connection pooling. An application architecture in which a large number M of users share access to a database through a smaller pool of N permanently maintained connections, where $N < M$. The goal of connection pooling is to reduce connect/disconnect workload on the database by reusing permanent connections. Connection pooling can create additional performance diagnostic difficulty because in a connection pooling configuration, a single user experience no longer maps 1-to-1 to a single Oracle kernel process. In a connection pooling configuration, a single Oracle kernel process may service a tremendously large number of different users (Kyte 2004).

database call. A subroutine in the Oracle database kernel.

DB call, dbcall. A *database call*.

deterministic arrivals. Arrivals into a system whose timing can be predicted with certainty.

efficiency. The inverse of how much of a task execution's total service time can be eliminated without adding capacity, and without sacrificing required business function.

end-to-end tracing. A system of functions with Oracle Database that allows an application developer or database administrator to identify (and thus trace) an individual user experience through every aspect of its Oracle Database processing.

Exadata. The Oracle Exadata Database Machine is a database appliance, designed for extreme high performance, with support for both transactional and analytical database systems.

experience. The collection of observable results of a single execution of a task.

extended SQL trace. An Oracle Database feature that allows you to print to a trace file a sequential record of every database and operating system call a given user experience inspires within the Oracle Database kernel.

fixed view. An Oracle pseudo table whose name begins with a prefix like v$ or gv$, which provide SQL access to instance information stored in shared memory. Also called *dynamic performance view* (Millsap & Holt 2003).

GUID. A globally unique identifier. The term GUID typically refers to various implementations (specifically, the Oracle PL/SQL implementation) of the Open Software Foundation universally unique identifier (UUID) standard (Wikipedia).

interactive response time law. If N is the number of users on a system, X is system throughput, and Z is think time, then response time $R = (N / X) - Z$ (Jain 1991, 563).

JDBC. The Oracle Java Database Connectivity API.

knee. The utilization value in an M/M/m queueing system at which response time divided by throughput is at its minimum (Vernon 2001).

LIO. An Oracle logical I/O, an operation in which the Oracle kernel obtains and processes the content of an Oracle block from the Oracle database buffer cache. The code path for an Oracle LIO includes instructions to determine whether the desired block exists in the buffer cache, to update internal data structures such as a buffer cache hash chain and an LRU chain, to pin the block, and to decompose, decrypt, type convert, and filter the content of the retrieved block. (Millsap & Holt 2003).

load. Competition for a resource induced by concurrent task executions.

ltrace. A Linux debugging utility that shows a record of calls that a userland application makes to dynamically linked shared libraries.

M/M/m. A mathematical model used to predict response times, queue lengths, and other features of a system having m homogeneous, parallel, independent service channels, where arrivals are determined by a Poisson process, job service times have an exponential distribution, there is no restriction on queue length, and the queueing discipline is first come, first served (Jain 1991, 527–534).

Method R Profiler. A utility used to format SQL trace output into human readable form. The Profiler is distinc-

Glossary

tive in its ability to explain the exact response time for a properly traced end-user experience.

Method R Tools. A collection of utilities for querying and manipulating Oracle trace files. Often used in conjunction with Method R Profiler.

Method R Trace. An extension for Oracle SQL Developer that simplifies creating and retrieving Oracle extended SQL trace files for specific end-user experiences.

mrcallrm. A Method R Tools utility used to remove database or system calls from an Oracle trace file.

mrls. A Method R Tools utility that works much like the Unix *ls* command for listing attributes of Oracle trace files.

mrskew. A Method R Tools utility used to answer questions about performance within sets of Oracle trace files.

mrtim. A Method R Tools utility used to convert Oracle *tim* values to human readable format and back.

mrtimfix. A Method R Tools utility used to fix timing errors in Oracle trace files, especially those created by bugs present in Oracle Database versions prior to 11.2.

OCI. The Oracle Call Interface, a comprehensive, high performance, native C language interface to Oracle Database.

operating system call. A subroutine in the operating system kernel. Also called a *system call* or a *syscall*.

optimize. To maximize the economic value of some target. Compare *tune* (Millsap & Holt 2003)

Oracle kernel. The code that executes the features of Oracle Database.

Oracle SQL Developer. A free integrated development environment that simplifies the development and management of Oracle Database systems.

OS call. An *operating system call*.

PARSING IN CURSOR. A section in Oracle trace data that reveals the mapping of a cursor id to its SQL text.

percentile specification. A specification of performance expectations of the form, "Task *t* will respond in less than or equal to *r* units of time in at least proportion *p* of executions."

placeholder. A token such as "?" or ":sys_b0" used in a SQL statement to represent a value that will be bound in at statement execution time. For example, "select ename from emp where empno = :eno". Also called a *bind variable*.

postulate. An *axiom*.

preemptive multitasking. A term used to distinguish a multitasking operating system that permits preemption of tasks, from a *cooperative multitasking* system wherein processes or tasks must be explicitly programmed to yield when they do not need system resources (Wikipedia).

profile. A tabular decomposition of response time, typically listed in descending order of component response time contribution.

queueing delay. The duration that a request spends enqueued at a given resource, awaiting its opportunity to consume that resource.

random arrivals. Arrivals into a system whose timing cannot be predicted with certainty.

resource. A service provider, such as a device or a subroutine call, whose participation in an execution's response time can be measured.

response time. The duration of an experience. The term *response time* is also used to refer to the random variable R representing the average of such durations.

risk. Uncertainty about future benefits or costs. We quantify that uncertainty using probability distributions (Bodie et al. 1989, 112).

sequence diagram. A type of graph specified in the Unified Modeling Language (UML), used to show the interactions between objects in the sequential order that those interactions occur.

service channel. A resource that shares a single queue with other such resources.

service level agreement (SLA). An agreement between an information supplier and an information consumer that defines expected application performance and availability levels.

service time. The duration that a request spends consuming a given resource, measured in time per execution (e.g., seconds per click). The term *service time* is also used to refer to the random variable S representing the average of such durations.

skew. A non-uniformity in a list of values.

sqlplus. An Oracle Database utility that provides a basic command line interface for SQL and PL/SQL access to the database, commonly used by users, administrators, and programmers.

strace. A Linux utility that shows a record of system calls executed by programs on Linux systems, used for diagnostic, instructional, and debugging purposes.

surrogate measure. A measure that isn't what you need, but that is easy to obtain and seems related to what you need.

syscall. An *operating system call*.

system. To an information provider, a *system* is typically regarded as a collection of processes, files, and shared memory segments that comprise an application. To an information consumer, a *system* is an entity that implements business tasks. The mismatch between these two perceptions often results in "optimizations" executed by information providers that affect the performance of important business tasks either negligibly or negatively (Millsap & Holt 2003).

task. A business unit of work, such as a click, a report, or a batch job.

think time. The duration between request arrivals into a system. The term *think time* is also used to refer to the random variable Z representing the average of such durations. In general, *think time* is any time consumed in an architectural tier that rests in a level closer to the end-user in the technology stack than the one you're analyzing (Millsap & Holt 2003).

throughput. The count of task executions that complete within a specified time interval.

timed event. In Oracle Database instrumentation, an event that corresponds to either a database call or one or more operating system calls.

time scope. An attribute defined by the begin and end time of either an experience or a trace file. In a performance diagnosis project, you want the time scope of your trace file to exactly match the time scope of the experience you want to diagnose.

Tow-Millsap law. "No human ever wants to see more than ten rows."

tkprof. An Oracle Database utility used to format SQL trace output into human readable format. The *tkprof* executable is located in the *$ORACLE_HOME/bin* directory.

trace file. A file emitted by Oracle Database, typically named with a *.trc* suffix, which contains output governed by the pseudo-error debugging events described in the file *$ORACLE_HOME/rdbms/mesg/oraus.msg*.

trace file identifier. A string provided to Oracle Database through an *alter session* command that will appear in a trace file name, used to facilitate finding a given trace file.

tune. To attempt to improve some target. Compare *optimize* (Millsap & Holt 2003).

unaccounted-for time. Any portion of an experience's duration that is not explained by your diagnostic data.

universal scalability law (USL). A mathematical model used to predict throughput without requiring detailed internal system measurements the way that typical queueing models do (Gunther 1993).

utilization. Resource usage divided by resource capacity for a specified time interval.

UUID. A universally unique identifier, standardized by the Open Software Foundation. Anyone can create a UUID and use it to identify something with reasonable confidence that the same identifier will never be unintentionally created by anyone to identify something else (Wikipedia). See also *GUID*.

wait event. In Oracle Database instrumentation, a timed event that corresponds to one or more operating system calls.

waste. Anything that can be eliminated with no loss of utility. In the context of computer system workload, *waste* is any workload that can be eliminated with no loss of functional value to the business (Millsap & Holt 2003).

Bibliography

Bodie, Zvi, Alan J. Marcus, Alex Kane. 1995. *Investments*, Homewood IL: Irwin.

Boehm, Barry W. 1981. *Software Engineering Economics*, Englewood Cliffs NJ: P T R Prentice Hall.

Garvin, David A. 1993. "Building a learning organization" in *Harvard Business Review*, Jul. 1993.

General Electric Company. "What Is Six Sigma? The roadmap to customer impact" at *http://www.ge.com/sixsigma/SixSigma.pdf*.

Goldratt, Eliyahu M., and Jeff Cox. 1992. *The Goal: a process of ongoing improvement*. Great Barrington MA: North River Press.

Gunther, Neil J. 1993. "Universal law of computational scalability" at *http://en.wikipedia.org/wiki/Neil_J._Gunther#Universal_Law_of_Computational_Scalability*.

Gunther, Neil J. 2000. *The Practical Performance Analyst*. Lincoln NE: iUniverse.

Gunther, Neil J. 2007. *Guerrilla Capacity Planning*. Berlin: Springer.

Gunther, Neil J. 2008. "Support materials for Dr. Gunther's CMG presentations" at *http://www.perfdynamics.com/cmg.html*.

Gunther, Neil J. 2009. "Mind your knees and queues" at *http://www.cmg.org/measureit/issues/mit62/m_62_15.html*.

Gunther, Neil J. 2013. "How to quantify scalability" at *http://www.perfdynamics.com/Manifesto/USLscalability.html*.

Hoogland, Frits. 2012. "Getting to know Oracle wait events in Linux" at *http://fritshoogland.wordpress.com/2012/04/26/getting-to-know-oracle-wait-events-in-linux/*.

Jain, Raj. 1991. *The Art of Computer Systems Performance Analysis: techniques for experimental design, measurement, simulation, and modeling*. New York: John Wiley & Sons.

Knuth, Donald E. 1974. "Structured programming with Go To statements" in ACM Journal *Computing Surveys*, Vol. 6, No. 4, Dec. 1974.

Kyte, Thomas. 2004. "Kayode — Thanks for the question regarding 'connection pooling', version 8.0.5 at *http://asktom.oracle.com/pls/asktom/f?p=100:11:0::::P11_QUESTION_ID:22140261281764*.

Kyte, Thomas. 2009. "A couple of links and an advert..." at *http://tkyte.blogspot.com/2009/02/couple-of-links-and-advert.html*.

Lilja, David J. 2000. *Measuring Computer Performance: a practitioner's guide*. Cambridge UK: Cambridge University Press.

Menascé, Daniel A., and Virgilio A. F. Almeida. 1998. *Capacity Planning for Web Performance: metrics, models, and methods*. New York: Prentice Hall.

Menascé, Daniel A., and Virgilio A. F. Almeida. 2001. *Capacity Planning for Web Services: metrics, models, and methods*. New York: Prentice Hall.

Menascé, Daniel A., Lawrence W. Dowdy, and Virgilio A. F. Almeida. 2004. *Performance by Design: computer capacity planning by example*. New York: Prentice Hall.

Bibliography

Menascé, Daniel A., Virgilio A. F. Almeida, and Lawrence W. Dowdy. 1994. *Capacity Planning and Performance Modeling: from mainframes to client-server systems*. New York: Prentice Hall.

Method R Corporation. 2008. "Instrumentation library for Oracle (ILO)" at *http://method-r.com/software/ilo*.

Method R Corporation. "Method R Tools" at *http://method-r.com/software/mrtools*.

Millsap, Cary, and Jeff Holt. 2003. *Optimizing Oracle Performance: a practitioner's guide to optimizing response time*. Sebastopol CA: O'Reilly.

Millsap, Cary. 2009. "Dang it people, they're syscalls, not 'waits'…" at *http://carymillsap.blogspot.com/2009/02/dang-it-people-theyre-syscalls-not.html*.

Millsap, Cary. 2009: "My whole system is slow. Now what?" at *http://carymillsap.blogspot.com/2009/12/my-whole-system-is-slow-now-what.html*.

Millsap, Cary. 2009: "On the importance of diagnosing before resolving" at *http://carymillsap.blogspot.com/2009/09/on-importance-of-diagnosing-before.html*.

Millsap, Cary. 2009: "Performance optimization with Global Entry. Or not?" at *http://carymillsap.blogspot.com/2009/11/performance-optimization-with-global.html*.

Millsap, Cary. 2011. "An axiomatic approach to algebra and other aspects of life" at *http://carymillsap.blogspot.com/2011/01/axiomatic-approach-to-algebra-and-other.html*.

Morle, James. 2012. "Who stole gettimeofday() system calls from Oracle strace() sessions?" at *http://www.scaleabilities.co.uk/2012/12/18/who-stole-gettimeofday-from-oracle-straces/*.

Nørgaard, Mogens, Dave Ensor, Tim Gorman, Kyle Hailey, Anjo Kolk, Jonathan Lewis, Connor McDonald, Cary Millsap, James Morle, David Ruthven, and Gaja Krishna Vaidyanatha. 2004. *Oracle Insights: Tales of the Oak Table*. Berkeley CA: Apress.

Oracle Corporation. 2011. "Oracle Call Interface Programmer's Guide 11*g* Release 2," at *http://docs.oracle.com/cd/E14072_01/appdev.112/e10646/title.htm*.

Smith, Connie U., and Lloyd G. Williams. 2001. *Performance Solutions: a practical guide to creating responsive, scalable software*. Boston: Addison-Wesley Professional.

Tow, Dan. 2003. *SQL Tuning: generating optimal execution plans*. Sebastopol CA: O'Reilly.

Vernon, Mary K. 2001. "CS 547: Computer system modeling fundamentals" at *http://www.cs.wisc.edu/~vernon/cs547/01/assighments/s5.pdf*.

Wikipedia. "Clarke's three laws" at *http://en.wikipedia.org/wiki/Clarke%27s_three_laws*.

Wikipedia. "Radium" at *http://en.wikipedia.org/wiki/Radium*.

Index

Symbols

\ 80
=~ 102
% (modulus operator) 35
.rc file 81
* (regular expression operator) 80

A

action 104, 105
ADDM (Oracle Automatic Database Diagnostic Manager) 50
airport ticket counter 17
Amdahl, Gene M. 11
Amdahl's law 11
array size 33, 34
   determining the optimal value of 35, 89
   too large 88
arrivals
   deterministic 19
   random 19
ASH (Oracle Active Session History) 48
auditors 36
auto-commit 50
AWR (Oracle Automatic Workload Repository) 50
axiomatic approach 1

B

background_dump_dest 53
begin time
   calculating 60, *61*
BEQ protocol adapter 95
"best practices" 41, 43
bind variable. *See* placeholder
Boehm, Barry W. 55
bottleneck **10**
buffer busy waits 18, 67
bug
   affecting Oracle trace data 63
   as possible cause of unaccounted-for duration 61
   SQL*Net message to/from client accounting 75

C

c 29, 32, 34, **58**, *60*

accuracy to only within ±10,000 μs 58
capacity 104
capacity planning 3, 21
cell single block physical read 107
cell smart table scan 106, 107
centiseconds 93
C language 27
Clarke, Arthur C. 41
Clarke's fourth law 41
client_id 51, 105
clock_gettime 73
close 57, 58
CMG (Computer Measurement Group) 23
coffee break
   perils of taking while tracing 77
coherency delay 17, **18**, 20, 23
collateral benefit 15
commit 40, 41, 57
connection pool
   tracing with 54, 101
CPU service, unreported call(s) 78
cr **58**
cu **58**
cursor
   handle id 31, 58, 59
cursor_sharing 38

D

data store
   developers' opinion of a database as 27
db file scattered read 67, 73
db file sequential read 13, 68, 90, 98, 99, 100
dbms_application_info
   set_action 52
   set_module 52
dbms_monitor 49, 54
   client_id_trace_enable 51, 53
   database_trace_enable 49, 50, 53
   serv_mod_act_trace_disable 51
   serv_mod_act_trace_enable 51, 53
   session_trace_disable 78
   session_trace_enable 49, 50, 53, 71, 78
dbms_session
   set_identifier 52, 104
debug 43

Index

debug logging 2, 47
debug option 79
dep **59**, 60
deterministic **16**
diminishing returns 33
direct path read 68
documentation
 limitations of 70
dtruss 70

E

e 29, 32, 34, 38, **58**, *60*
efficiency **15**, 29, 42
ela 30, 32, 38, **59**, *60*
end time 60, *61*
end-to-end tracing 51
enqueue 18, 68
Erlang, Agner Krarup 17
"estimating task start time..." mrls message 89
Exadata 105
EXEC 29, 41, 58, 68, 99, 100, 103
execute 31, 37
executeUpdate 40
experience 79, 81
extended SQL trace 29, 42, 47, 51, 67
 advantages of 42
 historical milestones 51

F

feedback 29, 42
fetch 33, 68, 87
FETCH 29, 57, 58, 86, 100, 102, 103, 106
FogBugz 24

G

Garvin, David A. 25
General Electric Company 5
getrusage 29
gettimeofday 73
 missing calls in strace 73
global cache lock 99
The Goal 15
goal state
 why not knowing is inefficient 11
Goldratt, Eliyahu M. 15
grep 71, 92
guess
 guessing vs. knowing 10, 29, 35, 41, 86, 100
Gunther, Neil J. 3, 18, 20

H

Harkey, James R. 1, 2
head 71, 80, 81, 92
hello world 56, 63
highway 16, 17
Holt, Jeffrey L. 17, 29, 58, 63, 85
Hoogland, Frits 73
hot stove 29
hyperbola 18

I

"idle" event 79, 83, 95
ILO (Method R Instrumentation Library for Oracle) 42, 52, 83
IPC protocol adapter 95

J

Jain, Raj 3
JDBC (Oracle Java Database Connectivity API) 30, 33, 34, 39, 86, 88

K

knee **19**
Knuth, Donald E. 25, 41
Kyte, Thomas 25

L

latch 18, 68, 95, 100, 101
Linux 73
LIO 58
load **15**, 19, 22
LOBARRTMPFRE 58
LOBREAD 58
log file sync 18, 37, 40, 41, 57, 69
log writer 37
ls 101
lseek 72
lsof 48, 71, 74, 75
ltrace 73

M

Måløv, Denmark 14
man (Unix utility) 71
measurement intrusion effect 25, 53, 54
Menascé, Daniel A. 3
Method R Profiler 32, 63, 78, 82, 84
Method R Tools 77
Method R Trace 55, 83
microsecond

Index

1,024 ns instead of 1,000 ns in Oracle 62, 84
Microsoft Windows 59
microstate accounting 58
mis **58**
M/M/m queueing model **17**, 18, 19, 20
module 104, 105
Morle, James 73
mrcallrm 81, 82, 83, 106
mrls 77, 82, 84, 88, 89, 94, 96, 101, 105
mrskew 32, 63, 77, 78, 80, 81, 85, 86, 88, 90, 92, 93, 95, 104, 105
mrtim 62
mrtimfix 63, 84
multiplexed architectures
    tracing 54
multitasking 17

N

nam **59**
next (JDBC method) 33, 86
Nørgaard, Mogens L. 29

O

obj# **60**
OCI_ATTR_ACTION 52
OCI_ATTR_CLIENT_IDENTIFIER 52
OCI_ATTR_MODULE 52
OCI_ATTR_SERVICE 52
OCI (Oracle Call Interface) 30, 56
    OCIAttrGet 56
    OCIAttrSet 52
    OCIBindArrayOfStruct 56
    OCIBindByName 56
    OCIBindByPos 56
    OCIBindDynamic 56
    OCIBindObject 56
    OCIDefineArrayOfStruct 56
    OCIDefineByPos 56
    OCIDefineDynamic 56
    OCIDefineObject 56
    OCIParamGet 56
    OCIStmtExecute 31, 56
    OCIStmtFetch 31, 56
    OCIStmtFetch2 56
    OCIStmtPrepare 31, 56
    OCIStmtPrepare2 56
    OCITransCommit 37
OE History Delete 89
OEM (Oracle Enterprise Manager) 50, 53
og **59**
OPI (Oracle Program Interface) 31, 40
Oracle E-Business Suite 89, 94, 96
Oracle kernel process 48

Oracle Payroll 94
Oracle Purchasing 96
Oracle SQL Developer 50, 83

P

p **58**
parallelism **21**, 22
parent-child call relationship
    db and sys calls 60
parse 31, 69
PARSE 29, 57, 58
PARSING IN CURSOR 31, 58, 59
percentile specification 4, 5, 21
performance
    as a feature 24
    instrumentation 24, 42, 43, 56, 69, 70
    knowing whether yours is as good as it should be 28, 36, 89
    modeling 17
    modeling vs. testing 23
    predicting 11, 12, 13, 24, 28, 33, 42, 86, 88, 91, 96, 99, 100, 103
    testing 23
performance problem
    array fetch size too small 15
    chatty Java program 14, 28, 32, 38
    commercial applications 15
    network configuration mistake 95
    preemption, paging, swapping 61
    returning rows that nobody wants 36, 89
    row-by-row processing 83, 86, 103
    row lock holder goes to lunch 18
    SAN (storage area network) misbehaving 91
    slow insert 36
    SQL with excessive database buffer cache activity 15, 98
    sweater that made author hot 14
    time scope of trace file doesn't match experience 62, 77, 79
    too much load 19
    unshareable dynamic SQL 15
    whole system is slow 6, 14
Perl 27
placeholder 31, 37, 40, 49, 57
plh **59**
PL/SQL 42, 49, 50, 52, 83
pread 59, 73, 74
preemptive multitasking 17
premature optimization 41
PreparedStatement 40
problem diagnosis
    good and bad problem statements 6
    need for knowing current and goal states 6, 11
Pro*C 50

Index

process id
  finding from sqlplus 70
Process Monitor 70
profanity
  author's shame at expressing himself using 24
profile 9, 11, 29, 32, 34, 38, 39, 47, 61, 78, 79, 84, 85, 86, 90, 94, 96, 97, 99, 102, 103, 104, 106
  by experience 102
  defining characteristics of 9
proving 1, 2, 42
ps 48
PX (Oracle Parallel Execution) 48
PYUGEN 94

Q

queueing delay **16**, 17, 23

R

r 31, **59**
radium 29
random **16**
read 71, 74, 91, 92
  asynchronous 73
read system call 31
requirement
  legitimacy of 36, 42
response time **3**, 17, 24, 33, *61*
  mean latency information is not enough 91
restaurant 16
risk 14

S

SAN (storage area network) 90
scalability 40
scale 28, 43
scanmax 90
scope 14
sctrace 70
sequence diagram **7**, 8, 9, 17, 22, 28, 79
service channel 3, **17**
service time **16**, 17
session 48
setAutoCommit 41
setDefaultExecuteBatch 40
setEndToEndMetrics 52
setFetchSize 34, 88
setInt 40
Six Sigma 5
skew **13**, 92, 98, 106, 107
Smith, Connie U. 3
Solaris 58

SORT 58
SourceForge 52
sqlid 92, 97
SQL*Net 31, 89
  packet size 14
SQL*Net message from client 57, 62, 69, 74, 76, 78, 81, 82, 83, 86, 89, 95, 96, 102, 103, 106
  perils of ignoring 32, 74, 79, 82
  [think time] 80
SQL*Net message to client 31, 35, 57, 75, 76
SQL*Net more data to client 35, 69, 89
sqlplus 49, 50, 55, 70, 77
SQL trace
  difference from extended SQL trace 49
statistics_level 54
strace 47, 48, 59, 67, 70, 74, 75
  attaching to Oracle kernel 71
  limitations of 73
straceNT 70
substr 93
surrogate measure 21, 24
sweater 14
sys.aud$ 57
sys_context 50

T

tail 81, 82, 87
task **2**
TCP protocol adapter 95
testing
  futility of 23, 24
  necessity of 23
thermonuclear
  database tracing option 50
think time **3**, 80
throughput **3**, 24
tim **59**, **60**, 61, 62, 81, 83
times 29
time scope 75, 77, 83
timeslicing 16. *See also* preemptive multitasking
tkprof 63
tnsnames.ora 95
Tow, Dan 36
Tow-Millsap law 36
trace data
  activating and deactivating 49, 55
  end-to-end tracing 51
  first rule of using 79
tracefile_identifier 53
traceoff.sql 55
traceon.sql 55
trcanalzr 63
trigger 50

    after logon 50
truss 70
tuning
    as a perjorative 42
tusc 70
type I and type II statistical error 24

U

UML (Unified Modeling Language) 7
unaccounted-for 69
    negative 34
unaccounted-for between dbcalls *62*, 78, 84, 85, 89
unaccounted-for within dbcalls *61*, 78, 84
UNMAP 58
user_dump_dest 53
USL (Universal Scalability Law) 18
utilization **15**, 21
    temporary spikes in 19
utilization ceiling 19, 20, 21
    procedure for computing *20*
UUID (universally unique id) 102, 104

V

v$ fixed views 48
    v$event_name 91
    v$session 48
    v$session_event 54
    v$session_wait 54
    v$sesstat 54
    v$sqlstat 50
variance 5
Vernon, Mary K. 19

W

wait
    as Oracle synonym for "syscall" 59
WAIT 30, 58
waste 15. *See also* efficiency
Williams, Lloyd G. 3
write 72, 76

X

XCTEND 40

Made in the USA
Charleston, SC
21 September 2013